Getting Started in

Garden Railroading

**Build the railroad
of your dreams...
in your own backyard**

Allan W. Miller

Published by

krause
publications

700 East State Street • Iola, WI 54990-0001
715/445-2214 • FAX: 715/445-4087   www.krause.com

Please call or write us for our free catalog. To place an order or to receive our catalog, call 800-258-0929 or use our regular business telephone at 715-445-2214.

Library of Congress Catalog Number: 00-111291

ISBN: 0-87349-232-3

Printed in the United States of America

With flags proudly flying, a classic 4-4-0 "American" class locomotive works the line on Charles Bednarik's Rancocas, Red Hawk, and Rutland garden railroad—the "Triple-R Route." America grew up on trains, and today thousands of garden railroaders share Charles' passion for keeping that heritage alive. The Large Scale locomotive, in 1:20.3 scale, is made by Bachmann.
Photo courtesy of Charles Bednarik

 # Acknowledgments

Sincere thanks go to the following individuals, firms, and organizations for their generous assistance and gracious support of this project.

Content review:
Charles Bednarik, Dwight Ennis, Linda Fox, Steve Galovics, Ken Johnson, Tony McAndrew, Jon D. Miller, and Dan Veiga.

Manufacturers:
Lewis Polk, at Aristo-Craft; Rob Smentek, at Bachmann Industries; Dale Suiters, at Hartland Locomotive Works; Ron Gibson and Dave Buffington, at LGB of America; Fred Gates, Jeff Stimson, and Brenda Julin, at Märklin, Inc.; and Charles Ro, Sr., Charles Ro, Jr., and Rita, at USA Trains.

Photo contributors:
Charles Bednarik, Gary Buchanan, Larry Buerer, Teya Caple-Woods, Ken Fillar, Linda and Bill Fox, Steve Galovics, Richard Golding, Ray Jakabcin, Ken Johnson, Scott Johnson, Mike and Pat Ledley, Bob Maisey, Richard Marty, David Meashey, Dennis R. Paulson, Tiny Pearce, Tom Ruddell, Mike Sheridan, Gus Sitas, David Snow, Scott Suleski, Del and Linda Tapparo, Peter Thornton, Robert Utley, Ronald Wenger, Dean Whipple, and David Winter.

Content contributors:
Participants of the always-interesting discussion forums at www.MyLargescale.com (hosted by Shad Pulley), www.LargescaleCentral.com (hosted by Bob McCown), and www.Aristocraft.com (hosted by Lewis Polk) provided a wealth of tips, techniques, and useful information.

The collective membership of the Tidewater Big Train Operators club, in Southeastern Virginia, assisted in a great many ways, as did the staff of Star Hobby, in Annapolis, Maryland.

Illustrator: Dennis Auth

Cover photo: The noon express passes a freight depot on the Capleville & Sugkat Valley garden railroad in Southeastern Virginia. The layout was created by Teya Caple-Woods, and details of its construction are featured in Chapter 9 of this book.

Back cover photo: A high-stepping Pacific locomotive, modeled in Large Scale, rumbles along the mainline on the Rancocas, Red Hook, and Rutland garden railroad constructed by Charles Bednarik.
Other photos of the "Triple-R Route" are featured throughout this book.

A beautifully detailed and weathered Forney locomotive exits a tunnel on Scott Johnson's garden railroad. The 1:22.5 scale model is by LGB, and the finishing touches were applied by Scott.
Photo courtesy of Scott Johnson.

Contents

Garden railroading is truly a hobby for the entire family. Twelve-year-old Ryan Bednarik prepares his train for a run on the family's Rancocas, Red Hawk, and Rutland garden railroad (the Triple-R Route). You'll find additional photos of the Bednarik family layout featured throughout this book.
Photo courtesy of Charles Bednarik

Getting Started in Garden Railroading

WELCOME TO THE WORLD OF GARDEN RAILROADING!

Welcome to the fastest-growing and most family-oriented segment of the model railroading hobby: Garden railroading!

If you have an interest in trains and railroading in general, love to do things in the great outdoors with family and friends, and are seeking a creative pastime that will provide a welcome respite from the stresses, strains, and constraints of everyday life, this book might just be your one-way ticket to a lifetime of new experiences, relaxation, and constructive fun.

There's no doubt about it: "Model railroading *is* fun!" That simple slogan, inspired and promulgated by the late Al Kalmbach, founder of *Model Railroader* magazine nearly seventy years ago, is as true today as it was back then. In fact, thanks to the wealth of new products that are currently available—and thanks to some new modeling scales and improved mechanisms and techniques that have evolved over the years—it's probably safe to say that the "fun" aspect of model railroading has extended its reach far beyond Mr. Kalmbach's fondest hopes and expectations. Model railroading in general is a creative, diverse, and pleasurable leisure activity that cultivates individual talents in design, carpentry, electrical work, artistry, scenery construction, detailing, operations, and any number of other areas. There is no other hobby quite like it when it comes to variety and unlimited creative potential.

Model railroading in the garden is even *more* fun! This more recent adaptation of the original slogan is one that nearly all practicing garden railway enthusiasts would be quick to agree with. Combine all of the ingredients of conventional indoor model railroading with the stimulating and often challenging environment of an outdoor setting—the very same one in which the real railroads operate—and you have the necessary ingredients for a satisfying lifelong hobby pursuit that will appeal to you, your family, and to all who eventually partake of your handiwork.

In general, garden railroading is most closely associated with what are today known as "Large Scale" trains, a designation customarily applied to sizable model trains made to operate on #1 gauge track, which measures 45mm (about 1-3/4") between the running rails. This does not preclude modelers in other model railroading scales—say O scale, S scale, or HO scale, for example—from becoming active garden railroaders if they choose to construct their layouts and run their trains outdoors (a great deal of garden railroading in O scale takes place in Great Britain, for example), but in most cases it's not nearly as practical or convenient to erect and maintain smaller-scale electric train layouts in

an exposed environment. Most Large Scale trains are intentionally built by their manufacturers for rugged and reliable outdoor operation, whereas the vast majority of trains in the smaller scales are not designed with anything even approaching this "weatherproofed" feature. Perhaps most importantly, the #1 gauge track commonly used in garden railroading is sturdy and durable enough to withstand long periods of exposure to the elements and even the abuse of foot traffic. Trackwork in other scales simply doesn't hold up well to this sort of treatment. Suffice it to say that the somewhat generic term "Large Scale," is used throughout this book to describe model trains of several scales, or sizes, that all operate on 45mm gauge track.

The truth be known, there are a good many garden railroaders who have selected Large Scale trains as a second modeling scale. These folks may still have an operating Z, HO, N, S, or O scale layout somewhere inside their homes, but they have also discovered that there are some unique and enticing features in garden railroading that allow them to further expand both their knowledge and their overall enjoyment of the hobby.

An attractive and interesting garden railroad doesn't necessarily require a whole lot of space. Ken Fillar's railroad was built on a deck area adjacent to his home. A large fountain at one end provides a striking visual attraction.
Photo courtesy of Ken Fillar

Garden railroading involves much more than just the trains! Two young railroaders-to-be are spotted checking out action in the fish pond as the "Grizzly Flats Special" approaches Sweetwater on Richard Golding's Kaskaskia Valley Railway.
Photo courtesy of Richard Golding

A view of the rest of Ken Fillar's layout, as seen when viewing it from near the fountain end.
Photo courtesy of Ken Fillar

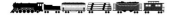

And, there are certainly more than a few garden railroaders around who have abandoned the smaller scales and indoor model railroading completely, and who now devote exclusive attention to running their trains in a real-world environment. Large Scale trains are very forgiving, in the sense that they are large enough to be easily seen and handled, and, for the most part, they require a minimum amount of maintenance. These features make them particularly attractive to both older members of the model railroading fraternity, as well as to youngsters who simply enjoy playing with trains. Garden railroading is indeed a hobby that transcends gender and generations!

• **The evolution of trains in the garden**

Although many model railroaders seem to view garden railroading as something of a recent innovation dating back some twenty-five years or so, the truth is that the outdoor operation of miniature trains ranks among the oldest forms of model railroading. That being the case, it's appropriate for us to take a brief look back at how the hobby has evolved over the years before we turn our attention to the nuts-and-bolts of garden railroading techniques.

The roots of garden railroading actually extend all the way back to the last quarter of the nineteenth century, when steam power itself was still the focus of considerable experimentation and improvement. Locomotive builders of the time frequently relied on scale models of their latest creations, operating outdoors, to test new ideas relating to the more efficient generation and use of steam. In Germany and Great

Britain, in particular, this activity even attracted the attention of a few well-to-do barons and lords, who erected what were perhaps the earliest miniature outdoor railroads on the grounds of their lush and expansive estates.

But it wasn't until the German firm, Märklin, introduced the first commercially-available line of model trains in the late 1880s that model railroading in general, and garden railroading in particular, got the shot in the arm needed to assure its perpetuation and long-term success.

Märklin's first trains were substantial in size, comprising what the manufacturer called Gauge 1, Gauge 2, and Gauge 3. The even larger #2 and #3 gauges disappeared within a relatively short time, but #1 gauge, with track measuring 45mm between the rails, established something of a *de facto* standard for garden railroads that survives to this day.

But even though the Germans are quite properly credited for creating model trains large and rugged enough to operate outdoors on the earliest garden railroads, it was the British who, in the early years of the twentieth century, most fervently advocated the intriguing combination of model railroading and landscape gardening, and who ultimately coined the term "garden railway." Ever the avid gardeners—perhaps "landscape artists" might be a more appropriate term—the British discovered early-on that miniature trains running amongst the flora and fauna complemented the overall effect, and added a distinctive touch that assisted in leading the viewer's eyes from one scene or feature to the next.

Details make the difference! This town scene on Scott Johnson's garden railroad depicts the early morning passing of a local freight. The town's residents are not yet up-and-about, but they will be soon, having been awakened by the bark and rumbling of the 2-6-0 Mogul and its consist. *Photo courtesy of Scott Johnson*

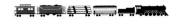

Garden railroading can well be a year-round activity, as this snow-plowing scene on Tiny Pearce's Desert Springs and Rattle Gap Railroad clearly shows. A plow train clears the mainline so the day's operations can get under way. Neither rain, nor snow, nor gloom of night need interfere with running Large Scale trains outdoors.
Photo courtesy of Tiny Pearce.

During this same period, enthusiasts in the United States who enjoyed large model trains were being led down a somewhat different and divergent path. The Lionel Corporation, the nation's premier manufacturer of electric toy trains, had also devoted early attention to large, all-metal models very similar in size to those designed for the European #1 gauge track. However, in an effort to corner the lion's share of the domestic market, Lionel deviated from the European standard by designing its trains to run on Lionel's unique three-rail track system, measuring about 2-1/8" between the outside running rails. Lionel elected to designate its trains and the track system upon which they operated as "Standard Gauge," in something of a self-serving effort to confirm this line as a "standard." The net result was that Lionel rather effectively, albeit perhaps unintentionally, stemmed interest in garden railroading in the United States throughout the period leading up to World War II, and even for some years beyond.

To be sure, a few enterprising American modelers had dabbled in garden railroading as early as the 1930s, but it really wasn't until 1968 that yet another German firm, Ernst Paul Lehmann Patentwerk, established a foothold for garden railroading in the U.S. with the introduction of its colorful, durable, and highly reliable "LGB" line of 1:22.5 scale model trains. These trains were purposefully designed to be run either outdoors or indoors on the firm's own two-rail, #1 gauge track. LGB trains—the letters stand for "Lehmann Gross Bahn," which loosely translates to "Lehmann Big Train"—enjoyed rapid acceptance and success in the U.S. market, even though the earliest releases were based almost solely on European narrow gauge prototypes. Over the years, LGB's lineup, which came to be misnamed as "G" gauge, has greatly expanded, and it now includes credible models of a number of U.S.-style locomotives, cars, and accessories, most of which represent narrow gauge prototypes.

As the popularity of the LGB product line grew in the 1970s and beyond, hobbyists became increasingly aware of the advantages of railroading in the great outdoors, especially since average-size homes in most regions of the country were often not particularly well-suited to accommodate even a modest-size LGB layout. A back or side yard, however, afforded the space needed to enjoy a special kind of model railroading that closely replicated the conditions in which real railroads operate.

As growing numbers of enthusiasts built and/or expanded their outdoor rail lines, they naturally relied on the readily available LGB track components, so it wasn't long before the vast majority of garden railroads throughout the nation were strongly rooted to this 45mm track system. When competing manufacturers finally decided to enter this growing market by providing models that represented the other types of real-life railroading more commonly seen in this country, including modern-day standard gauge railroading, they elected to stick with the already-in-place and widely accepted 45mm track gauge. After all, how many enthusiasts could be expected to tear up and replace an entire garden railway full of permanently implanted track?

But producing models in several different scales, all of which could conveniently operate on #1 gauge track, has led to a somewhat confusing situation that is rather unique to garden railroading. For one thing, the various scales can hardly all be referred to as "G scale" because, first, there really is no such recognized scale, and second, that designation, even if it was appropriate, could not be accurately applied to more than one modeling scale. The solution, to date, has been to group all of the various scales that operate on #1 gauge track under an umbrella term: Large Scale.

Today, the term "Large Scale" generally encompasses trains made in 1:13.7, 1:20.3, 1:22.5, 1:24, 1:29, and 1:32 scales, and you'll find that term used throughout this book unless a particular scale is being discussed. We'll examine this business of scale and gauge in more detail a bit later in this book in a chapter devoted to

Trapped by the snow! Scott Suleski didn't fare quite as well as Tiny Pearce in bucking new-fallen snow on his Suleski Transportation. Inc. railroad—at least not until the plow train showed up. The crew is left standing in the cold, awaiting help. Winter fun, garden railroad style!
Photo courtesy of Scott Suleski

Garden railroading affords real-life realism because it *is* real! This scene on Scott Johnson's layout captures the essence of what railroading in the great outdoors is all about, as the industrial switcher, an LGB product, attends to one of its many daily runs. *Photo courtesy of Scott Johnson*

railroading, and even live steam operations are once again becoming a fixture on a growing number of garden layouts. Designated as "small-scale live steam" to distinguish this segment of the hobby from the larger ride-aboard trains and the full size prototype steam locomotives, this niche has re-emerged primarily because a greater volume of small scale live steam equipment is now being produced in ready-to-run form at affordable prices. For those truly interested in doing things the way the real railroads did, live steam is an area well worth considering.

Garden railroading, spearheaded by an active and ever-growing marketplace for Large Scale trains, has matured to the point where what was once a small and rather fragmented segment of the hobby has assumed a significant status with an equally significant following. Garden railroading is about as close as you can get in the model railroading hobby to experiencing all of the things—good and bad—that real-life railroads face on a day-to-day basis. Building your own garden railroad certainly requires some time and effort, but the reward is in the thrill you'll experience as you watch your creation come to life in an environment that replicates, as closely as possible, the real world of railroading. Moreover, all who see your railroad are sure to savor the experience with a smile on their face, and therein lies what is perhaps the greatest pleasure and reward of this fascinating hobby!

that topic. But for now, suffice it to say that there are, indeed, at least six scales of trains currently being made for operation on #1 gauge (45mm) track, and that this particular topic warrants your careful study and consideration before you purchase your first Large Scale train set, if possible.

In recent years, there has been something of a resurgence of interest in the very early days of garden

• *Inspiring thoughts*

Garden railroading today is certainly a hobby that enjoys international appeal. There are garden railroads and Large Scale model train enthusiasts in just about every part of the world, and this widespread fraternity of folks who share a common interest has been brought much closer together in recent years via the medium of the World Wide Web and the instantaneous and open form of cyberspace communication it promotes. In concluding this introduction to the hobby, I thought it appropriate to include an insightful and inspiring observation that a woman in Australia recently posted on the MyLargescale.com forum, one of several Internet sites devoted exclusively to Large Scale trains and garden railroading. The words of Wendy Robinson pretty well sum up what this hobby is all about—and really should be all about:

"As the wife of an avid model railroader, I'd like to put in my two bob's worth (as we say down under).

"My first experience with model railroading was with an N gauge layout set up on the dining room table where we ate our daily meals. That was twenty-two years ago. Since then we have had several layouts of varying sizes and gauges, two of which still exist in the family room upstairs—or to give it

the correct name: the train room.

"The latest addition is the Gauge 1 layout in our back garden. I must admit that my 'other half' doesn't smoke, and seldom has a drink, so trains were his only vice until they were combined with my garden. Now we both enjoy our garden railway, even though it still has a long way to go before it is finished, if such a thing is ever possible.

"The best thing about the trains is the mateship they have inspired between my husband and our son! Trains are high on the gift lists in our house, and I think I get as much enjoyment from every new acquisition as do the males in my life. I hope they never feel the need to hide a new purchase from me, as I hear some do.

"I think trains are probably in my blood, as my grandfather was a loco driver in Britain many years ago. As the old saying goes: 'if you can't beat em, join em.' Or, perhaps the one that says that 'the family that plays together, stays together' is more apt. Anyway, I've had my say now, so here's wishing Happy Garden Railroading to all of our fellow railroaders!"

—*Wendy Robinson, wife of Ralph, from Down Under*

Wendy's family has obviously experienced some of the magic associated with garden railroading. More than just a hobby, garden railroading is truly an interactive activity that helps to bond family members and instill a sense of sharing and caring that is not often seen in more solitary leisure pursuits. Garden railroading is also addictive, and once you get started, you'll find the attraction becomes even more compelling. It's all just a matter of taking that first step! Our hope is that you will be inspired to join in the fun. If so, welcome aboard, and enjoy your journey!

The station at Winter Valley, on David Winter's indoor *and* outdoor Large Scale railroad, provides a striking feature on the shelf-type Interior Division, which also serves as a train staging area, as well as a workbench. The locomotive is a USA Trains model that David custom-painted and lettered for his self-conceived Winter Valley Regional Railway theme.
Photo courtesy of David Winter

The view from above Cajon Pass, as a K-28 locomotive in Large Scale struggles around the curve on Charles Bednarik's nicely landscaped Rancocas, Red Hawk & Rutland garden railroad. An imposing sight in any scale, but brought closer to life by larger models performing in concert with the real-world environment.
Photo courtesy of Charles Bednarik

Chapter 1
FREQUENTLY ASKED QUESTIONS
FAQs about garden railroading

Q: *Exactly what is a garden railroad?*

A: In general terms, a garden railroad is any model railroad that is constructed in a natural environment that includes living plants and/or other natural objects or features. The model trains themselves could be in any scale, from Z Scale at the smallest end of the model railroading spectrum to anything short of the full-size prototype at the large end, but, in general, most garden railroads are constructed for "Large Scale" trains that are purposefully designed for either indoor or outdoor operations. Likewise, the "garden" could be indoors or (far more commonly), outdoors, where the trains blend in with a natural landscaping. Most often, the garden is constructed after the railroad, but sometimes the reverse is true.

Q: *I see the term "Large Scale" being used here. What does "Large Scale" mean?*

A: "Large Scale" is the proper term applied to any model trains designed to operate on #1 gauge track, which measures 45mm between the top inside edges of the rails (the railheads). Most garden railroads, in the United States at least, are constructed with this #1 gauge track. Since a fair number of scale models of different sizes are made to operate on this same track, the collective group is usually referred to as "Large Scale." In general, this includes models in the following most common scales: 1:13.7, 1:20.3, 1:22.5, 1:24, 1:29, and 1:32. Most Large Scale trains are designed for indoor and outdoor operation—the primary distinguishing features being that their motor blocks and other electrical or operating components are weather resistant and sealed to protect them from exposure to the elements, and the entire model is generally made from thicker, UV-resistant plastic.

Q: *So, how does Large Scale differ from the "G scale" and "G gauge" trains I hear some folks talking about?*

A: The truth be known, there really is no such thing as "G scale" or "G gauge" in model railroading, although printed advertisements and the packaging labels still used by some manufacturers might lead you to believe otherwise. The term "G scale/gauge" is actually something of an innovation most closely associated with a German model train manufacturer, E. P. Lehmann Patentwerks. The Lehmann firm was primarily responsible for popularizing Large Scale trains and garden railroading in this country beginning in 1968, when they introduced their LGB line of electric trains. Some say the "G" in LGB—"Gross," or "Grand" in English—is the root of the so-called "G gauge" designation. Others contend that the "G" stands for "Garden." Whatever the case, in the formative years of garden railroading in the United States, the trains were popularly referred to as G gauge and/or G scale, and this rather confusing and misleading label has carried through even to the present day. You're far better off saying that the trains running in your garden are such-and-such a scale, operating on #1 gauge track—for example, 1:29 scale on #1 gauge track.

Q: *With so many different scales of trains all being made to operate on the same track, how can I decide which one to choose?*

A: That can be a difficult choice, but it's easier to select a suitable scale if you know in advance the type of railroading that most appeals to you. For example, if you are leaning toward modeling contemporary American railroading, you might want to consider 1:29 scale, since most of the more modern diesel locomotives and cars are currently being made in that scale. If you're partial to modeling early American narrow gauge railroads, you might choose 1:20.3 scale, since there are some fine narrow gauge models being made in that scale. If European narrow gauge models strike your fancy, the 1:22.5 scale trains made by LGB might be the way to go. And, for that matter, 1:24 scale is visually very close to the 1:22.5 scale, and 1:32 scale is not terribly far removed from 1:29 scale. Some garden railroaders even model in two scales—one for contemporary mainline operations, and another for narrow gauge—and there are some who simply run what they like, regardless of scale. The scale and gauge chapter in this book provides the details you'll need to make an informed decision.

Q: *If different manufacturers make locomotives and cars in different scales, do I have to pick one manufacturer or scale and stick with that? If I don't, won't I have a problem operating the different locomotives and cars together in the same train?*

A: Good question! Fortunately, the answer generally is "no." With some rare exceptions, you won't have any real problem with compatibility of equipment. Although manufacturers do tend to specialize by offering just one or two scales in their respective lines, the trucks, wheelsets, and couplers on their locomotives and cars do, in most cases, conform well enough so different scales will operate properly when used together. Different makes of couplers may not mate together automatically, but you can couple and uncouple most rolling stock by hand, if need be. Do keep in mind that things may not look quite right when you mix, for example, some 1:22.5 narrow gauge cars with 1:29 standard gauge cars in the same train, but from the standpoint of operation, as long as both are equipped with couplers that will mate together, everything will roll smoothly along the rails.

Q: *Won't trains operated outdoors require a lot of maintenance?*

A: Not really! In fact, most Large Scale equipment often requires less maintenance than trains that are intended for indoor operation. The motor units of most Large Scale locomotives are encased and sealed to protect them from the elements, and thus require very little attention. Any regular maintenance procedures that are required are usually easy to perform, and they take very little time if done on a regular basis of about every fifty hours or so. Because they are designed to be weatherproof, some locomotives and cars can even be rinsed with water and then wiped dry to keep their exterior surfaces clean and bright.

Q: *Where is the best place to build a garden railroad?*

A: There really is no single *best* place. Once you have determined how large (or small) your layout might be—and starting out relatively small is almost always recommended—you should take a close look at your existing real estate and see where things might work to best advantage. A fenced-in back or side yard may well be the most obvious choice, since those locations generally afford some privacy and a measure of security. To the extent possible, you'll want to protect your railroad from possible vandalism and/or prowling critters, and you'll also want to consider the privacy needs of your neighbors, especially if you plan to operate sound-equipped trains, or want to run your trains at night. The only real limits are the total amount of space you have available for your railroad, and your own imagination.

Q: *This book is about garden railroading, and I live in an apartment. I guess that leaves me out of the fun, huh?*

A: Not so! As suggested earlier, condo or apartment dwellers might even consider a modest indoor garden railway, if space permits. I live in a small two-bedroom apartment, which I share with my Australian Shepherd pooch. The spare bedroom is a home office, so I really have very little space for an operating railway of any type, let alone a garden railway. Nevertheless, I do have a very small indoor garden railroad—the Whiskey Hollow Shortline—which is constructed atop a surplus whiskey cask. Small as it is, this little layout has provided me hours of enjoyment in its construction. The layout even includes a working waterfall, along with live plants and shrubs, so it does qualify as a true "garden" railroad. Whenever I'm inclined to run much larger and longer trains, I can enjoy a pleasant operating session at the home of one of my fellow garden railway club members, or assist in the construction and operation of one of our club's frequent public displays. If your apartment or town home has a deck of some sort, that area may also accommodate your garden layout.

Q: *How much will it cost me to build a garden railroad?*

A: That's kind of a tough question to answer, since the total cost of a garden railroad is pretty much dependent on the amount of work needed to adapt the existing terrain; the overall size and complexity of the layout; the power source you select; and even the type of trains you prefer to run. A very compact garden railway, consisting of one basic train set running on a fairly simple, but expanded, oval of track that has been set up on relatively level ground could possibly cost as little as $500 or so, including power source and appropriate track and landscaping items. Larger and more complex layouts can, of course, eventually run well into the thousands of dollars. That's another reason we recommend starting out with something modest, then letting it grow as your interests develop and resources allow.

Q: *How much space will I need for my railroad?*

A: Assuming that you will want, if at all possible, four-foot radius (eight-foot diameter) curves as a minimum on your railroad, and further assuming that you don't want the train to simply chase itself by running around in a complete circle, it should be entirely possible to construct a fun-to-operate garden railroad in a space approximately thirty feet long by about ten feet wide. This would allow for a couple of passing or stub-end sidings, and the possibility of operating two or more trains at the same time. That 300-square-foot area will also afford you ample opportunities to develop some creative landscaping and add a number of bridges, structures, and other accessories. If space is really tight, you can even go with two-foot radius curves (four-foot diameter), but be aware that this may severely limit any future use of longer locomotives and cars.

Q: *How long will it take me to build a complete garden railroad?*

A: It has often been said that a model railroad—whether indoors or outdoors—is never truly completed. There are always new details to be added, and existing elements that can be changed. However, a small garden railroad can be constructed in a few evenings, or over a weekend, if it doesn't involve a whole lot of major reconfiguration of the existing landscape. This assumes that your initial goal is to get the track down and a train or two up and running—landscaping and other scenic elements can be added over time. The majority of garden railroads tend to evolve over a considerably longer period of time, measured in months or even years of leisure-time work. One garden railroad prominently featured in this book was constructed over the course of three years, measured from the time the first shovel of dirt was turned to the date of the "golden spike" ceremony. Nevertheless, the woman who built and owns this railroad does not consider it to be "complete" in any sense of the word, and she is constantly adding to the layout and making improvements.

Q: *What's the single most important step in building a garden railroad?*

A: No question about it: Creating solid and reliable trackwork! That means trackwork that is erected

on a firm surface that is as level as possible (or that has very gentle and well planned upgrades and down-grades); that is electrically sound and secure at each rail joint; that affords proper drainage so it does not shift with the changing seasons or elements; and that can be easily kept clean and clear of any obstacles. These are the very same challenges the real railroads face!

Q: *Which brands of Large Scale trains are the best ones to start with?*

A: As with anything else, "best" is really what suits your own needs and interests. Many garden rail-roaders prefer LGB trains because of their long-standing reputation for rugged and reliable performance, but today there are numerous other brands that are equally well made. Your best bet is to visit a local Large Scale train dealer; talk with some garden railroaders in a local club (these are active in most parts of the country); read-up on what's available (see the References appendix in this book); and, if possible, check out a few of the on-line Internet forums to see what hobbyists are saying about particular products. The URLs (web site addresses) for the most popular Large Scale and garden railroading forums are also listed in an appendix of this book.

Q: *Should I try to model narrow gauge railroads or standard gauge railroads?*

A: That's strictly a matter of personal preference. If you're a nostalgia buff, or have a fondness for log-ging or mining operations in particular, perhaps steam operations on narrow gauge railroads might appeal to you. Some folks prefer to model what they see in real life—meaning the trains they might view each day as they drive about in their cars. However, it's worth not-ing that models of contemporary standard gauge loco-motives and rolling stock, such as SD40-2 locomotives and 89-foot container cars, can be very large and long because their prototypes are also very large and long. If reliable operation and realistic appearance is a goal for you, you'll need to plan for some very large-radius curves to handle this modern-day equipment.

Q: *What will I need to get started in garden rail-roading? Should I begin with a complete "starter set," or should I just purchase each component individually?*

A: You'll need a place to put your garden railroad, a train to operate on your railroad, track for that train to run upon, and some sort of power supply to provide electricity to the locomotive's motor. A Large Scale starter set generally consists of a locomotive, a couple of cars, enough track sections to form a complete circle, and a small power pack. That's really enough to get you started in a very modest way, but just watching

trains go around in a small circle is probably not going to satisfy you for long. At minimum, you'll likely want to purchase additional straight and curved track sec-tions, and probably a more "robust" power pack to handle the greater requirements of a larger outdoor lay-out. The advantage of a starter set is that the full set price is generally lower then the cost of the individual components sold separately.

The advantage of purchasing individual components instead of a starter set is that you'll end up with a com-plete train that meets your individual tastes, prefer-ences, and needs. You'll pay a bit more for this, but you'll likely be more satisfied in the long run.

Q: *Is it difficult to maintain the permanent fea-tures on a garden railroad?*

A: Not really! Like anything else, it just takes a bit of time and patience. If you have planned things prop-erly, and have constructed firm and reliable trackwork, the rest is pretty easy. The track and its supporting bal-last will need to be cleaned and touched-up regularly, especially if you're using the track to conduct electricity to your trains, but that's a simple enough task, as you will see later in this book. Structures, bridges, and the like will need to be repainted or repaired from time to time, especially if they remain outdoors year-round. And, of course, you'll need to spend some time clip-ping, pruning, and shaping your landscape items, but that's the fun of the gardening aspect of garden rail-roading.

Q: *Can I leave my trains outdoors, or will I need to take my trains and buildings indoors after I've fin-ished operating my railroad for the day?*

A: Well, it's probably a good idea to take the trains themselves indoors, and store them in the house or garage when you're not actually using them. After all, these items represent a major investment on your rail-road, and they deserve to be treated with some care. And, of course, you don't want to openly invite dam-age or theft! Many garden railroaders leave their struc-tures and other such accessories outdoors for the full operating season, or even year-round. If properly con-structed, and provided with a bit of maintenance from time-to-time, these objects are durable enough to be left exposed to the elements.

Q: *Where can I learn more about garden railroad-ing techniques?*

A: The appendices in this book will provide you with a up-to-date list of the best sources of supplies and information. In addition to names and addresses of all of the major manufacturers and after-market suppliers,

we have also provided printed and video reference sources, a list of garden railroading periodicals, names and addresses of clubs and associations, and even Web sites of particular interest to garden railroaders. If you can't find what you're looking for in those lists, you probably won't find it anywhere!

Q: *Is it best to model my garden railroad after a real railroad, or should I just "freelance" the layout?*

A: Again, that's entirely up to you! There is no "best" way to approach this. Some modelers delight in researching a particular prototype railroad and its operations in a particular geographic location and time, and they then set out to re-create a segment of that operation. Others delight in simply developing their own freelanced rail line. Some even go a giant step further and develop totally fanciful garden railroads with imaginative and outlandish locomotives and rolling stock of all types. One railroad I recently heard of is based on the imaginary world created by J. R. R. Tolkien's *The Lord of the Rings* trilogy of books. The only truly important thing is that you have fun doing what-

ever you choose to do. Having fun is the ONLY requirement for success in garden railroading!

Q: *Are there any national or international organizations for garden railroaders?*

A: At the present time, there are no formal national or international organizations specifically targeted to the interests of garden railroaders. However, there are a good number of local and regional clubs (more than 100) that comprise a loose network of garden railway societies in the U.S., and this group holds a national convention each year in a different part of the country. There are also manufacturer-sponsored collector clubs for LGB and Aristo-Craft trains. Also, Large Scale operators in general are currently working to develop an International Society of Large Scale Model Railroaders, of which garden railroading will be an important part. There are also Large Scale train shows held on both the East Coast and West Coast each year. These organizations and events are listed in the appendix sections of this book.

A prototype narrow gauge Mack Railbus, designed for operation on a three-foot track gauge. Many garden railroad enthusiasts elect to model nineteenth and early twentieth century U.S. narrow gauge, while others prefer more contemporary standard gauge operations, which often feature larger steam locomotives and modern diesels.
Photo courtesy of Richard Golding

Chapter 2
ALL ABOUT GARDEN RAILROAD SCALES AND GAUGES

Two terms that tend to confuse newcomers to the hobby of garden railroading in particular, and which spark controversy amongst more than a few experienced hobbyists, are "gauge" and "scale." Basically, the problem arises from the fact that Large Scale trains of several scales (sizes) are all made to operate on the same track gauge (width), i.e. 45mm. Let's see what we can do to clarify things by first defining each term in more detail, and then reviewing how each of these terms is applied in both real-life railroading and model railroading in the garden.

Gauge" defined:
"Gauge" in real railroading and model railroading—whether indoors or outdoors—refers *solely* to the distance between the top inside edges of the two running rails of railroad track. It has absolutely nothing to do with the physical dimensions (size) of the trains that operate upon that track, nor with the size of the rail itself.

"Scale" defined:
"Scale" refers solely to the proportional size of a model itself (including track), when it is compared with a real-life example of the identical object. It has nothing to do with the width between the running rails of track. Scale may be expressed as a proportion, or as a fraction. For example, HO scale may appear in print as a proportion of 1:87, or as the fraction 1/87, meaning that the model itself is one eighty-seventh the size of its prototype. An HO scale locomotive operating on HO gauge track is, for all intents and purposes, a correct 1/87-size modeled representation of what would, in the real world, be a full-size locomotive operating on standard gauge track.

• Prototype railroad gauges

Track gauge is a precise measurement, in feet and inches (or in meters, in the case of European and some other overseas rail lines), that, according to the above definition, is determined by measuring the distance between each running rail. In the United States, this measurement starts and ends at a point 5/8-inch below the inside top edge of each railhead, to allow for the rail's slight curvature at the top. In the most general sense, there are two track gauges in real-life railroading in the United States: standard gauge and narrow gauge, with standard gauge being, by far, the more common gauge used today.

Standard gauge American railroads—the trains you may see blocking your way as you drive to or from work each day—measure exactly four feet, eight-and-one-half inches (4' 8-1/2") between the running rails. Don't try this experiment at home—just take our word for it—but if you were to take a tape measure down to your local rail line, and affix one end to the top inside edge of one running rail, 5/8-inches from the top, then extend the tape until it touches the inside top of the other running rail 5/8-inches from the top, you would confirm a rail-to-rail measurement of exactly four feet, eight-and-one-half inches!

Why four feet, eight-and-one-half inches, you may reasonably inquire? Well, prior to the building of the first transcontinental railroad across the United States, individual railroads pretty much used whatever track gauge was most convenient and affordable in their respective situations. Track gauges of the time ranged anywhere from two feet to seven feet wide, and more. Naturally, this made the interchange of rolling stock from one railroad to another virtually impossible, in most cases. Since two independent railroads were charged with construction of that first transcontinental line, some sort of "standard" had to be set. After much dickering in Washington, a measure of four feet, eight-and-one-half inches was finally chosen. Reportedly, this measure is related to the width of wheel ruts made by chariots in the days of the Roman Empire, and it later carried through to early hand- and horse-drawn rail lines in England and elsewhere. Whatever the true explanation behind this somewhat odd measure, the fact remains that, today, all major railroads in the United States operate with this "standard" track gauge.

Narrow gauge is perhaps a bit more complicated, but the term is generally applied to any railroad that operates on rails spaced *less* than 4' 8-1/2" apart. One of the most common narrow gauge measurements in the U.S. is three-foot gauge, wherein the railheads are spaced three feet apart. There are, however, other narrow gauges, such as 42-inch gauge. You won't find many narrow gauge railroads still operating in the United States these days, but in the nineteenth century, and even into the early years of the twentieth century, narrow gauge rail lines—normally associated with logging and mining operations—were quite prevalent. A number of overseas rail lines still operate on narrow gauge track, although not necessarily to a 3' gauge. In fact, many, if not most, European and other overseas narrow gauge rail lines operate on meter gauge (39.37") track. And, as was alluded to earlier, in real-life early American railroading there were even a few systems that operated on what is known as wide gauge track — track with railheads placed further apart than standard gauge. In some cases, wide gauge track measured in excess of seven feet between the railheads.

Comparison of popular model railroad track gauges. From bottom to top: N gauge, HO gauge, O gauge (Lionel three-rail), Marklin #1 gauge track with Code 250 rail, and LGB #1 gauge track with the larger and more common Code 332 rail.

• Model railroad gauges

In model railroading, as in real-life railroading, gauge refers solely to the distance between the running rails of the track. There are six popular model railroad track gauges in the United States, each of which, depending on what scale is being modeled (more on that later), can represent either standard gauge track or narrow gauge track for a specific scale of model trains that operates over them.

Bear in mind that these model railroad track gauges are somewhat standardized, meaning that they remain the same regardless of how large or how small a locomotive or car is placed on them, as long as the wheels of the car rest properly on the railheads. In terms of the actual, measurable distance between the two running rails, the most popular, commercially available model railroad track gauges in the U.S. are:

Z gauge track= 6.5 mm between the running rails

N gauge track= 9 mm between the running rails

HO gauge track= 16.5 mm between the running rails

S gauge track= 22 mm (7/8 inch) between the running rails *

O gauge track= 32 mm (1-1/4 inches) between the running rails *

#1 gauge track ("G" gauge)= 45 mm (approx. 1-3/4 inches) between the running rails

* In the case of "S" and "O" gauges, a measurement in inches is more commonly used since these gauges were established in the United States.

The vast majority of garden railroads—in the United States, at least—are constructed with a 45mm track gauge (also known as #1 gauge, from its European roots), which simply means that a measurement taken from the top inside edge of one railhead to the top inside edge of the opposite railhead is exactly 45mm. The original #1 gauge was created by the German firm, Märklin, a pioneer in the development of the model railroading hobby worldwide. Years later, this track gauge came to be somewhat generically and incorrectly known as "G gauge," primarily because the first mass-market electric trains intended for indoor and/or outdoor operation were introduced in this country by another German firm, E. P. Lehmann Patentwerk, under the trademark name of **LGB**, or **L**ehmann **G**ross-**B**ahn (which roughly translates to Lehmann Big Train). At the time, Lehmann referred to their product line as "G gauge." In fact, despite LGB's influence in the marketplace, there really are no "G gauge" or "G scale" trains, even though you'll see some Large Scale manufacturers label their advertisements and packaging in that way. The proper designation for Large Scale items carries both a track gauge and a scale designation: Gauge 1, 1:29 scale, for example.

LGB track, regardless of what you choose to call it, became rather quickly accepted as the *de facto* standard for most garden railroads because it was readily available, ruggedly constructed, very durable, and offered in a wide variety of individual components. Today, LGB-type track provides the supporting rail network for many thousands of model trains winding through countless homes and gardens throughout the U.S. and the world.

All that would be well and good if it weren't for one fairly significant discrepancy: Lehmann's LGB trains, and the track system upon which they operate, were originally designed to closely represent European-style narrow gauge railroad equipment, the prototype

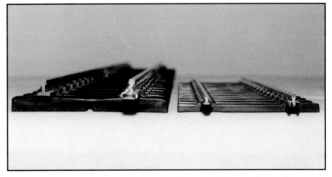

An LGB track section (left), alongside a Märklin track section. Both of these tracks are correct #1 gauge (45mm), so the measurement between the railheads is identical. However, the Märklin #1 gauge track has a lower and more correct-to-prototype rail profile, as well as a lower tie height. All Large Scale trains will operate fine on the LGB track, or similar track made by other manufacturers, but only locomotives and cars with scale-size wheel flanges can operate properly on the truer-to-scale Märklin track (or similar low-profile track).

19

of which operates on narrow gauge trackwork that is measured in meters. Indeed, the earliest LGB model trains all represented European-style locomotives and rolling stock, and the 1:22.5 scale proportion of these items was chosen because that scale properly matched an existing 45mm model track gauge—the #1 gauge developed by Märklin—that could be used to represent European narrow gauge trains operating on European narrow gauge railways.

None of that mattered much to American model railroaders in the formative years of garden railroading in this country. Hobbyists delighted in the large, colorful, durable, and very reliable LGB trains, and they marveled at trains that could be operated outdoors, seemingly impervious to rain, sleet, snow, or any other elements that Ma Nature could subject them to.

As the popularity of the LGB line grew, people naturally built and/or expanded their outdoor rail lines using the readily available LGB track, or matching track provided by competing manufacturers. It wasn't long before the vast majority of garden railroads throughout the nation were deeply rooted—quite literally, in fact—to this 45mm track gauge. So, when a growing number of competing firms elected to offer locomotive and rolling stock models that more closely represented the type of real-life railroading more commonly seen in this country today, they chose to stick with the well-established 45mm track gauge. After all, how many enthusiasts could be expected to tear up and replace an entire garden railway full of permanently implanted track?

And this, quite naturally, leads us to a discussion of "scale"—the major area of confusion and some consternation in garden railroading, in particular.

• Prototype railroad scales

This is an easy one! All full-size prototypes upon which a model of any size is based are in a ratio of 1:1. That is, they measure twelve inches to the foot, if that is the measuring system you elect to use. For that matter, your own body is in a scale of 1:1, and any scaled-down model made of you would be proportionally smaller in all dimensions!

• Model railroad scales

Model railroad scales designate proportionally smaller (usually) reproductions of a full-size prototype. The scale chosen is indicated as either a fraction or a proportion. Thus, a particular model designated as being in a scale of 1:32—if it is indeed made precisely to scale—is 1/32 the size of its real-life counterpart in all respects. This concept shouldn't be too hard to understand if you keep in mind that the smaller the number in the denominator (the bottom number in a fraction) the larger the model will physically be. By that reasoning, a 1:32 scale model is physically larger than, say, a 1:87 scale model of the same object. And, that same 1:32 model would be proportionally smaller than a 1:24 model of the same thing. Clear enough?

Comparison of standard gauge locomotives in the popular model railroad scales. From left to right: N scale (1:160), HO scale (1:87), O scale (1:48), and Large Scale (1:29 scale depicted here).

The following are the most popular, commercially available model train scales that conform to the various track gauges listed above:

Z scale= 1:220 (or 1/220)

N scale= 1:160 (or 1/160)

HO scale= 1:87 (or 1/87)

S scale= 1:64 (or 1/64)

O scale= 1:48 (or 1/48)

Large Scale=1:13.7, 1:20.3, 1:22.5, 1:24, 1:29, and 1:32 scales

•1:32 is the correct proportion for modeling American standard gauge trains on 45mm gauge track, assuming that the 45mm model track measurement represents "real" track spaced 4' 8-1/2" apart. Somewhat surprisingly, relatively few of the major manufacturers have chosen 1:32 for their product lines. Märklin, Model Die Casting, and some high-end custom builders currently offer models in this scale, with M.T.H. Electric Trains soon to join that group.

•1:29 is the scale selected by, among others, Aristo-Craft and USA Trains to represent American standard gauge railroad models operating on a 45mm track gauge, assuming that the 45mm model track measurement represents "real" track spaced 4' 8-1/2" apart. Both firms apparently chose this scale as something of an "acceptable medium" between the more accurate 1:32 scale for standard gauge models on #1 Gauge track and the already-plentiful examples of 1:22.5 scale models made by LGB. That said, 1:32 would still be the more accurate scale for modeling "mainline" American railroads on a 45mm track gauge.

•1:24 is the scale used by Hartland, some Bachmann items, and select products in the Aristo-Craft line, among others, to represent American narrow gauge locomotives and rolling stock operating on 42" narrow gauge prototype track—six inches wider than the more customary 36" American narrow gauge measurement. Generally, however, the modeling community has tended to gravitate toward 1:20.3 scale models as the more representative scale for most American narrow gauge modeling.

Comparison of two popular Large Scale locomotives, made in different scales. The locomotive in the foreground is a Bachmann Shay, in 1:20.3 scale. Behind it is a 1:29 scale SD40-2 diesel locomotive from USA Trains. In the real world of railroading, the Shay would be considerably smaller in size when compared with a modern large diesel, such as the SD40-2. Both models depicted here operate on 45mm #1 gauge track.
Photo by Teya Caple-Woods

Comparison of Large Scale figures in various scales. From left to right: Märklin 1:32 scale; Lionel 1:24 scale; Preiser 1:22.5 scale; and Bachmann 1:20.3 scale (approximate). Obviously scale *does* make a difference, even though all of these figures are considered to be "Large Scale" items.

•1:22.5 is a correct scale for representing European one-meter gauge trains operating on a 45mm track gauge, assuming that the 45mm model track measurement represents European one-meter gauge trackwork. LGB trains popularized this scale worldwide, and this firm's products continue to enjoy a widespread and devoted following.

•1:20.3 is the correct scale for modeling American three-foot narrow gauge trains operating on a 45mm track gauge, assuming that the 45mm model track measurement represents "real" track spaced 3' apart. Bachmann's "Spectrum Line" led the way in affordable ready-to-run 1:20.3 scale model railroading, although Accucraft, Trail Creek Models, and several others have also embraced this scale.

•1:13.7 (also known as 7/8 scale) is the correct scale for modeling American two-foot narrow gauge trains on a 45mm track gauge, assuming that the 45mm model track measurement represents "real" track spaced 2' apart. Most locomotives and rolling stock in this scale are either custom-built or "kitbashed" using components adapted from other scales.

Whereas real-life railroads have nearly always matched their locomotives and rolling stock to the track gauge being employed—small locomotives and cars operating on narrow gauge track, and large locomotives and cars operating on standard gauge track—the model makers have made everything suitable for operation on the same 45mm gauge track. So what was, and still basically is, both cost effective and convenient for

the manufacturers has led to some understandable confusion within the Large Scale modeling community. This leads us to the dilemma that nearly all Large Scale model railroaders—the vast majority of whom are garden railroaders—face at one time or another: Which scale to choose?

If American narrow gauge model railroading is what interests you, and assuming that you are planning to stick with the common and readily-available 45mm track gauge, you might well consider 1:20.3 as your scale of preference. Bachmann's Shay, Climax, 2-6-0, and 4-4-0 locomotives have been widely and warmly accepted, and more products from that manufacturer and others are on the way. All that's really lacking at the present time is a suitable rolling stock assortment to accompany the superb motive power. But we can reasonably expect that one or more of the leading manufacturers will correct that oversight at some point.

On the other hand, if contemporary mainline model railroading suits your fancy, and again assuming that a 45mm track gauge is what you plan to use to represent American standard gauge track, either 1:32 scale or 1:29 scale might be right for you. Those two scales are actually close enough, in terms of their general proportions, so a bit of mixing-and-matching will satisfy all but the most avid scale fanatics, who are often referred to as "rivet counters." Just keep in mind that, today at least, far more 1:29 scale motive power and rolling stock is available in the marketplace. This may well change at some point in the future, and the vocal 1:32 scale enthusiasts may indeed find more manufacturer support, but for the present time the impetus seems to be with the slightly-larger 1:29 models.

At this point, you may well be asking yourself:

What difference does it make if I choose just one scale or choose several different scales to run on my railroad? They all run on 45mm gauge track, don't they? Indeed they do! However, if you choose to mix your scales up a bit, you will likely be confronted with something of a visual disparity. That disparity is easy enough to see, and perhaps better understood, if you take the time to compare a few model locomotives or cars in several of the Large Scales side-by-side, and compare these with photos and dimensions of the real-life prototypes.

Real-life narrow gauge locomotives and rolling stock are (or were) quite diminutive in size, especially when compared with the dimensions of a modern-day diesel locomotive, but a correctly proportioned narrow gauge Shay steam locomotive in 1:20.3 scale will seemingly dwarf a correctly modeled modern-day SD40-2 diesel in 1:29 scale, assuming that both have been built to scale and constructed to operate on 45mm track. In reality, the situation should be just the opposite—the Shay, a relatively tiny logging locomotive from years past, should be greatly overshadowed by the contemporary diesel behemoth. Simply stated: If you choose to mix-and-match Large Scale trains of various scales, things may tend to look a bit awkward and kind of "funny." Nevertheless, this is not an insurmountable problem, and there are some viable solutions that might be considered.

Solution #1: As suggested earlier, select one particular modeling scale that most appeals to you, and stick with it. If mainline standard gauge is what intrigues you, plan your railroad empire for 1:29 scale or 1:32 scale operations. If American narrow gauge captures your fancy, you might select 1:20.3, where you can still use some of the 1:22.5 models without too much worry about a visible discrepancy. Some even prefer 1:24, since many dollhouse accessories, die-cast automobiles, and other accessories are readily available to closely match that particular scale.

Solution #2: If you have a fondness for both narrow gauge *and* standard gauge operations, alternate from time to time between exclusively narrow gauge operating sessions and exclusively contemporary railroad operating sessions. The only real problem with this will be that buildings, other structures, and the little people and animal figures that populate your layout may appear too large or too small, depending on which scale you are running. You'll want to see if you can

strike a happy medium with these accessories—say 1:24 scale, for instance.

Solution #3: Stick with one specific manufacturer's line of locomotives and rolling stock, assuming that the manufacturer in question has more or less "specialized" in one particular scale. The only problem with this solution is that many of the leading manufacturers have, from time to time, "dabbled" with a few items made to another scale, so you'll want to check to make sure that the catalog description or actual packaging is labeled for your preferred scale.

Solution #4: Just operate anything you like, regardless of scale appearance, and enjoy your garden railroad. It's *your* railroad, and you can do anything that pleases you!

Although the track *gauge* generally stays the same in most Large Scale model railroading—that is, #1 gauge track, measuring 45mm between the rails—it's important to keep in mind that track, like everything else on and around a model railroad, also has a scale of its own. LGB and LGB-compatible track, for example, has rails that are considerably larger than they would be if they were truly to scale. This is something of an acceptable compromise though, since track that's intended for use outdoors needs to be heavy and rugged enough to withstand the abuse that it will receive by being walked on or subjected to the elements. Track will be covered in more detail in the track-work chapter of this book.

Garden railroading with Large Scale trains is about as close as you can get to experiencing the variety of conditions—good and bad—that real-life railroads face on a day-to-day basis. Your family, friends, and neighbors won't give a hoot about scale and/or gauge inconsistencies. They'll simply delight at seeing your handiwork, and they'll be enthralled by observing model trains running amidst real-life landscaping. And therein lies the true pleasure!

Here's the bottom line regarding scale and gauge in garden railroading: Don't allow yourself to become overly concerned over which of the various Large Scales is the "right" one. If *you* like it and it adds fun to your life, go for it! Purchase, operate, and have fun with whatever most appeals to you! Relax, enjoy yourself, and have a ball! After all, that's what this hobby—or any hobby for that matter—is all about.

Period structures establish a unifying theme on Charles Bednarik's "Triple-R Route" garden railroad, which is featured throughout this book. The "Midnight Special" glides into the station at the end of the run. Steam exhaust was added electronically to the photograph by twelve-year-old son Ryan, whose talents obviously extend beyond model railroading!
Photo courtesy of Charles Bednarik

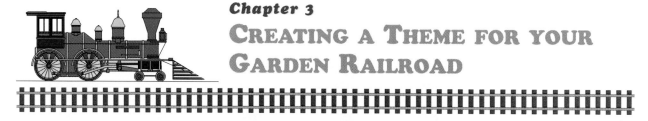

Chapter 3
CREATING A THEME FOR YOUR GARDEN RAILROAD

A great way to enhance your enjoyment of model railroading—whether in the garden or elsewhere—is to focus on developing a theme for your rail empire. Themes help to tie everything together, and give the railroad a sense of history and purpose. Working with a specific theme also tends to instill a bit of financial discipline in terms of the resources you devote to the hobby.

The theme you select could be tied to a time or event in history, a geographic location, a particular prototype railroad, a specific industry or commodity serviced by the railroad, a childhood memory, a place you used to live, or just about anything else. It could even be a freelanced or fantasy theme—something created in your own imagination rather than something that actually exists.

Scott Suleski's garden railroad employs a variety of custom-painted locomotives and rolling stock to establish a unifying theme. Here, an Aristo-Craft U-25 diesel threads its load through a barren winter landscape along the Suleski Transportation, Inc. mainline.
Photo courtesy of Scott Suleski

A distinct advantage in choosing an appropriate theme for your railroad, *before* you begin actual planning or construction, is that the theme itself can help you determine the proper modeling scale and equipment for your enterprise, and it can even assist you in conceptualizing your layout's ultimate configuration. Dan Veiga, the owner of a hobby shop that primarily caters to the needs of Large Scale and garden railway enthusiasts, always tells his customers that a model railroad, be it located outdoors or indoors, should be constructed with two principles in mind: continuity and purpose. Continuity means selecting equipment—locomotives, cars, and accessories—that conform to a given era, location, or type of railroading activity. Purpose, in this context, means giving the railroad a reason for being, whether that involves commuter service for passengers, transporting some select type of commodity, or serving a particular industry. If continuity and purpose are both considered *before* you invest in any major purchases, you'll save yourself some money, and be well on your way to developing a unified theme for your railroad.

Remember that Large Scale—the combined group of model trains made to operate outdoors—is actually made up of a number of individual modeling scales, all of which will operate on 45mm #1 Gauge track. Certain of these scales are more closely related to specific types of railroading, or eras in railroad history, and you may want to selectively zero-in on a scale most closely related to your own interests. For example, if you select an American narrow gauge railroading theme, then you

It's difficult to distinguish this scene on Scott Johnson's garden railroad from a prototype railroad scene that might have been snapped by the camera in the closing years of the nineteenth century. Everything seems to "fit" properly, even down to the attire of the miniature workmen. Continuity and purpose are two key features of a visually convincing model railroad: Continuity in terms of the era modeled, and purpose in regard to the railroad having a reason for being. This photograph demonstrates both features.
Photo courtesy of Scott Johnson

may want to stick with 1:20.3 or 1:24 as your preferred modeled scale, because most American narrow gauge equipment is manufactured in one or the other of those scales. Likewise, if European narrow gauge (meter gauge) appeals to you, then 1:22.5 might be the best scale for you in terms of equipment availability since LGB, the preeminent name in European-type Large Scale models, offers the largest product assortment—both trains and related accessories—in that category.

If mainline operations and more contemporary railroading are what you find yourself most attracted to, you will likely want to explore the assortment of offerings in 1:29 scale and/or 1:32 scale, since these two scales tend to dominate the range of equipment prevalent throughout the latter half of twentieth century. For all but the very finicky, those two scales are close enough in proportion so most equipment looks just fine operating in a mix-and-match manner.

The theme you select also impacts the form your layout should take. If narrow gauge equipment is your choice, you will be able to get by with somewhat tighter curves and steeper inclines than if you elect to operate modern diesel-electric locomotives and long intermodal cars or streamline passenger cars. Even the structures and other accessories you place along your right-of-way are, or should be, closely related to the theme you select. It's not very likely that you'll see many SD-45 diesel locomotives roaring through towns made up of "Old West" structures, unless there's a theme park tourist attraction alongside your railroad.

Last, but certainly not least, a theme definitely helps to instill some financial discipline to your hobby pursuits. By focusing on a specific era, a particular scale, a special type of motive power and rolling stock, and perhaps even a single railroad, you'll be better able to resist the temptation that many hobbyists feel when a wealth of new items are released by the various manufacturers. Although the benefit of this frugal approach may not be readily apparent in the initial stages of your involvement in the hobby, it will definitely serve you well as your equipment inventory expands.

Selecting a theme

Perhaps you already have a theme in mind for your proposed railroad. If you do know what you would like to model, go for it! But first, it does pay to do a bit of homework and see if there is really enough available in the way of locomotives, rolling stock, structures, and other accessories to support your chosen theme. If not, you may have to resort to some custom painting, "kitbashing" (creating a new item out of two or more commercially available items or kits), or "scratchbuilding" (creating a new item out of raw materials), to provide you with what you want and need. Some folks really enjoy custom painting and detailing, scratchbuilding, and kitbashing, but others find it too time consuming, or feel they lack the level of skill needed to do a credible job, and these folks would rather devote their energy and hours to running the railroad. Determining what resources are available, in advance of forging

ahead with finalizing a theme and starting actual construction of your railroad, will save you time, money, and frustration in the long run.

If you don't already have a particular theme in mind for your rail empire, don't be overly concerned. A great many garden railroads are started without any sort of pre-planned concept, and the theme tends to evolve over time as the hobbyist's knowledge, experience, and personal interests develop. It's often better to get on with it and to start your railroading activity now than to sit idly by for months on end—what's known as armchair model railroading—waiting for a theme to pop into your head.

However, if you are interested in giving a bit of a "kick start" to this theme-development process, your thoughtful responses to the following questions will help to get you headed in the right direction:

• Do you have a favorite railroad that you've always admired and wanted to model?

• Are you primarily interested in American, Canadian, European, or some other type of railroading?

• Of the four general eras in railroading history--nineteenth century, early twentieth century, mid-twentieth century, or contemporary—which do you find the most interesting and personally appealing?

• Which geographic region of the country (or world) would you most like to represent with your garden railroad?

• Do you prefer narrow gauge railroads, standard gauge railroads, or a combination of the two types?

• Do your personal interests in prototype railroading lean toward steam-powered locomotives, diesel-electric power, or electric-outline (trolley and overhead catenary) power?

If you can provide ready answers to most or all of these initial questions, you're already well on your way to identifying your special railroading interests and selecting an appropriate modeling theme that will bring you many hours of railroading fun, and significantly increase both your real and model railroading knowledge in the process!

Actually, if you can answer just the very first question—the one relating to a favorite railroad that you would like to model—you already have the makings of a nicely focused theme! All you need do then is select an era from that particular railroad's history, and identify a favorite geographic location that you might like to represent from along the prototype railroad's line. It's also a good idea to consult a few published references to learn as much as you can about the prototype road and how it operated. You may even want to consider joining that railroad's historical society, since there's at least one around for nearly all of the major railroads, and most well-known narrow gauge lines. You'll soon

find all the relevant information you need to determine the type of equipment most appropriate for the particular time and place you want to represent, and published photographs of the railroad in its real-life environment will even help you determine the proper structures and trackside items to use.

But sometimes developing a theme isn't quite that easy. Say, for example, that you don't really have a "favorite" railroad, but you do know that you are primarily interested in American narrow gauge railroading in the early years of the twentieth century (which, by default, implies steam-powered locomotives), and you know you favor the scenery and topography of the Pacific Northwest, even though you currently live in Ohio. If that's the case, your next step should be to research the general topic of American narrow gauge railroading in some depth through visits to your local library or book store, or, if you're connected to cyberspace, through resources available on the Internet.

Continuing with the above example, you'll likely find that many, if not most, narrow gauge railroads operating in the Pacific Northwest during the early part of the twentieth century were primarily logging or mining lines. They frequently employed Shay, Climax, and Heisler geared locomotives, which were able to effectively negotiate hastily laid and often-uneven track, along with sharp curves. The rolling stock used on these railroads depended on the line's specific type of operation, of course, but would likely have consisted of log cars or log disconnects (separate wheelsets placed under longer log loads), ore cars, short wood-side hoppers, wood-side boxcars, two-axle bobber-type cabooses, and even a wood-side passenger car or two.

Having completed some basic research and exploration, you're now better prepared to answer a few additional questions, each of which will help to further identify and focus your interests:

• Do you prefer branchline railroading activities and operations, or is mainline railroading what you would most like to emulate?

• Which appeals to you the most: Passenger operations, freight service, or some combination of the two?

• If freight service is your preference, what particular commodities and/or industries do you find most appealing?

Again, if American narrow gauge railroading in the Pacific Northwest during the early years of the twentieth century is what fascinates you, the answers to most of these questions will fall logically into place. For example, you would probably be focusing on branchline operations that are primarily freight-oriented—the usual commodities being logs, lumber, ore, and the like. You could still justify some passenger operations, of course, since lumberjacks, miners, other workers, and even company officials would require transportation to and from the work sites.

However, if mainline modeling in the Pacific Northwest or elsewhere during that same time period is what captures your attention, you will likely find that your equipment needs will be somewhat different. Diesel locomotives will be out of the question, of course, since they weren't even developed until after the first decades of the twentieth century. Nevertheless, the standard gauge mainline railroads of the period generally used larger and heavier steam power to perform freight and passenger hauling tasks, and the cars they moved were also longer and heavier. So, you'll likely want to secure a few catalogs from the major manufacturers and see what's currently being offered in 1:29 scale and/or 1:32 scale.

If the period from about 1920 through the 1950s captures your imagination—the days when massive steam power ruled the mainline rails—you'll find somewhat fewer offerings in Large Scale, at least at this date. This is because larger steam locomotives also require wider curves on which to operate, and for a good number of years the major manufacturers of Large Scale trains chose to produce equipment that would be capable of negotiating the tight four-foot diameter curved track sections that were commonly supplied with most Large Scale starter sets. However, this line of thinking is changing now, and increasing numbers of locomotives—both steam and diesel—are being designed to operate on, at minimum, eight-foot and ten-foot diameter curves. If you want to run some of these large steamers on your layout, you'll need to be sure to plan for suitably large curves to handle the equipment. Generally speaking though, the choices in large steam power for Large Scale are still somewhat limited when compared with the available models of smaller steam locomotives, such as those used in steam's early years, and more recent examples intended for yard switching duties and light road service.

Fans of the late 1940s and early 1950s—the steam-to-diesel transition era—are well-served by a good number of appropriate Large Scale models, particularly in regard to early diesel units. ALCO, General Motors (EMD), and General Electric (GE) diesel-electric locomotives are well represented in product lines offered by nearly all major manufacturers. The only real problem, as noted earlier, might be in finding a suitable variety of steam locomotives to represent the transition, particularly larger steamers.

The point is, there truly is something out there to meet just about any interest, and if something you would like to have is not yet available, chances are the it will be at some time in the not-too-distant future. And, if you find that a particular item is being made, but not in your favorite road name, this provides an excellent opportunity for you to develop some skills in repainting and lettering items for your favorite railroad.

Remember, though, that your garden layout will most likely consist of more than just the trains. Model railroaders tend to give inordinate amounts of attention to locomotives and rolling stock because, as has been noted before, these items most often tend to be the stars of the show. Nevertheless, the "stage" upon which

Whimsical and fun items—and even complete layouts developed on a fanciful theme—seem to be more prevalent in garden railroading than in other model railroading scale. Perhaps it's because a good number of garden railroaders don't take things too seriously, and just enjoy having fun! Jeannie Buerer is apparently one of those folks, as this trainload of birdhouses on her railroad amply illustrates.
Photo courtesy of Larry Beurer

these featured characters perform is equally important if you're going to give a convincing performance. That means providing an appropriate environment that conforms to the era you are representing, and that, in turn, is directly related to the type of commodities your railroad would commonly handle.

Say, for example, that you have definitely decided to model a narrow gauge logging line from around the turn of the century. You have purchased—or, if you're lucky, have been given—a Shay geared locomotive to operate on your railroad, and you've acquired a few logging cars, a boxcar or two, and a small bobber-type caboose. You might even have picked up a Mack Railbus to handle a bit of commuter traffic along the line. What's next?

Well, for one thing, you'll want to examine a few Large Scale catalogs to see what is available in the form of structures and other accessories that might conform to, or be modified to conform to, your chosen theme. This could include trestles, bridges, tunnel portals, buildings, trackside structures of all types, signals, trucks and automobiles, and even scale-size animal and people figures appropriate to the theme and era you are modeling. These accessories are what truly give a sense of scale to your garden layout, so you'll want to choose carefully to make sure that the items themselves do not dwarf the trains, or the other way around. Bridges, tunnel portals, and other similar items won't pose any real scale-related problems, since all will be pretty much made to conform to the 45mm track gauge in terms of their general dimensions. Structures, vehicles, and figures, however, may need to be selected a bit more carefully.

For example, a six-foot tall human figure rendered in 1:20.3 scale would measure about 3-1/2 inches tall. That same six-foot figure rendered in 1:29 scale should be just 2-1/2 inches tall. Put another way, the 3-1/2 inch tall 1:20.3 figure, if placed on an otherwise 1:29 scale layout, would represent a person over 8-1/2 feet tall—a genuine basketball star, to be sure! Nevertheless,

Another whimsical scene. This diminutive mining train is doing double duty on Ken Johnson's indoor garden railroad. A small hopper at the far end of the train bears a load of crushed white rock, while the ore car in the foreground carries the raw materials that will soon see a similar fate.
Photo courtesy of Ken Johnson

A well-executed and convincing theme ties everything together on a garden railroad, almost fooling the viewer into believing that the real world has been somehow reduced to miniature size. Charles Bednarik shows how this is achieved in this and many other scenes that might be viewed along the "Triple-R Route."
Photo courtesy of Charles Bednarik

figures of somewhat different scales can be used on your layout if overly tall ones are placed further back in the scene, and are not place too near similar figures of other scales.

Human figures, in particular, need to be chosen with some care for yet another reason. You'll want to make sure that the attire of your miniature population approximates the era you are modeling. With some exceptions, frilly dresses and top hats will look strangely out of place on a layout that features 1990s railroading. In many cases, careful use of a modeling knife and a new set of painted-on clothes will enable you to transform many of the commercially available plastic figures into credible models for the specific time and place you wish to represent.

A good many of the structures made for Large Scale railroading, in both built-up and kit form, are made to 1:22.5 scale or 1:24 scale simply because those two scales were really the most popular in the early days of the hobby. Since that time, 1:20.3 scale has emerged as a significant narrow gauge modeling scale, and 1:29 scale has developed into the scale-of-choice for a good many standard gauge modelers. A structure made to 1:24 scale may look good enough on a layout equipped with 1:20.3 scale and 1:22.5 scale locomotives and rolling stock, but some of them may be a bit too imposing in a 1:29 scale or 1:32 scale standard gauge setting. Actually, it's the structure's features that will look most out of place—doors and windows that appear too large, and

that sort of thing. This will be especially true if the structure is placed very close to the track.

With these considerations in mind, always remember that, in concept and execution, your railroad can really be *anything* you want it to be. You may decide to construct a railroad based solely on your imagination and individual creativity, with its own fanciful name, reason for being, geographic location, custom-designed paint scheme, and customized lettering and logos. There's absolutely nothing wrong with that approach. What ranks as one of the most spectacular and inspirational model railroads of all time—the Gorre & Daphetid Railroad, constructed in HO scale by the late John Allen—provided a splendid example of what can be accomplished when imagination is combined with creativity, a sense of humor, and a good amount of loving labor. (Kalmbach Publishing Co. offers a complete book about Allen and his railroad.) Some model railroaders carry theme development to the extreme, as John Allen did, by concocting detailed historical accounts of the fictitious railroad's founding and history, and even, on occasion, developing creative and fanciful stories about the daily activities of "folks" who work on the railroad or who live and labor along the line. It's *your* railroad, so don't be bound by convention or what others tell you to do. Approach theme development, or any other aspect of building your garden rail empire, in whatever way *you* want to!

Two Large Scale locomotives labor on the "Triple-R Route" garden railroad created by Charles Bednarik and his family. In the foreground a 1:20.3 scale Bachmann Shay narrow gauge locomotive waits for orders, and at the rear an LGB Mallet, a 1:22.5 scale model of another narrow gauge prototype, works a string of lumber cars.
Photo courtesy of Charles Bednarik

Chapter 4
LARGE SCALE LOCOMOTIVES

Trains are, of course, the lead performers on your model railroading stage. Trackwork is certainly very important, and accessories, structures, and creative landscaping surely contribute to the overall effect, but the train itself is truly what steals the show. So it comes as no surprise that Large Scale model railroaders, like most of their comrades in the other modeling scales, tend to devote inordinate amounts of time and money to researching, evaluating, purchasing, caring for, displaying, and operating their locomotives and rolling stock.

Today's garden railroader is fortunate, indeed, because a growing number of Large Scale equipment manufacturers and suppliers are devoting considerable resources to providing an ever-expanding line of beautifully constructed and very durable locomotives and cars intended to meet the seemingly insatiable appetite of hobbyists in the garden railroading niche. No matter what type of model railroading you prefer, and regardless of the era that your railroad represents, you'll likely find some form of motive power and rolling stock appropriate to your interests and needs.

Since personal preferences do play such an important role in determining what you might operate on your garden railroad, this chapter provides an overview of the ever-growing range of locomotives available for your consideration. Rolling stock items are covered in the subsequent chapter. Select offerings of nearly all of the major Large Scale manufacturers are represented in both chapters, but the list is by no means comprehensive. You should certainly plan to spend time reviewing each manufacturer's current catalog and Internet web site, and reading the various hobby magazines, to learn more about the full array of items available for your railroad's equipment roster.

• The evolution of prototype locomotives

It's probably a good idea to briefly review the history of prototype locomotive development before moving into a discussion of their Large Scale model railroad counterparts. This will help to place things in proper perspective, particularly for the benefit of those readers who have not yet decided on a specific era or theme to model on their railroad.

Just as steam power spurred the industrial revolution in general, so, too, did it inspire the creation and development of a transportation system known as the railroad. From the mid-1800s until the early 1930s, prototype railroad locomotives were driven almost exclusively by steam. As the technology for harnessing steam energy to create usable and efficient horsepower continued to evolve, steam locomotives became larger and more powerful, and the relatively light engines of the nineteenth century gradually gave way to imposing giants of the rails that could handle mile-long strings of cars. To be sure, electrically powered locomotives, trolleys, and interurban cars, along with a few gasoline-powered railcars and such, also plied the rails starting as early as the late 1800s, but by and large the real workhorses on railroads through the first thirty years of the twentieth century were chuffing and puffing steam-powered locomotives constructed in a wide variety of sizes and configurations.

Indeed, so varied were these steam locomotive configurations that it is difficult to even keep track of them all. Some types were given nicknames, of sorts, by their builders or the railroad that bought them, but sometimes the same basic locomotive was bestowed with several different names. Fortunately, a Dutch citizen named Frederick M. Whyte developed a classification system for U.S. steam locomotives that greatly simplifies things, and it remains in use even to this day.

Hot on the heels of steam locomotives were those powered by electricity. As early as the 1880s, electric power was used on trolley systems in burgeoning metropolitan areas, and shortly thereafter electric-outline locomotives, powered by overhead catenary wires,

It can be fairly said that LGB's 2-6-0 Mogul locomotive was a driving force behind the real growth of garden railroading in the United States. This locomotive has been offered in a variety of paint schemes and road names over the years, and is today available in an unlettered version for those who wish to adorn the locomotive and tender with their own railroad's graphics.
Photo courtesy of Ernst Paul Lehmann Patentwerk

• Whyte Classification System for steam locomotives

The classification system devised by Frederick M. Whyte describes locomotives by their wheel arrangement. The first number designates the total number of leading or pilot wheels; the second number, or sets of numbers, designates the total number of powered driving wheels; and the last number designates the total number of trailing wheels. A "T" after the number set indicates a tank locomotive.

With the exception of the 6-8-6 wheel arrangement, steam turbine locomotives are described using the same classification system that is applied to diesel-electric locomotives, with non-powered axles designated by numbers and powered axles designated by letters.

The following list includes a number of the more prevalent and popular steam locomotives that were used in U.S. railroading, some of which have been made available as Large Scale models:

wheel arrangement:	common name (where applicable):	wheel arrangement:	common name (where applicable):
0-4-0	Four-coupled	4-4-2	Atlantic (also Chautauqua and Milwaukee)
0-4-0T			
0-4-2T		4-4-4	Reading (also Jubilee and Lady Baltimore)
0-4-4T	Forney four-coupled		
0-4-6T	Forney four-coupled	4-4-4-4	Baltimore & Ohio (also Duplex)
0-6-0	Six-coupled	4-6-0	Ten Wheeler
0-6-4T	Forney six-coupled	4-6-2	Pacific
0-6-6-T	Forney six-coupled	4-6-4	Hudson (also Milwaukee, Baltic, and Shore Line)
0-8-0	Eight-coupled		
0-8-8-0	Angus	4-6-6-2	Cab Forward
0-10-0	Ten-coupled	4-6-6-4	Challenger
0-10-2	Union	4-8-0	Twelve-wheeler
2-2-0	Planet	4-8-2	Mountain (also Mohawk and New Haven)
2-2-2	Single		
2-4-2	Columbian	4-8-4	Northern (also Confederation, Dixie, Golden State, Greenbrier, Montana, Niagara, Pocono, Potomac, Wyoming, Generals, and Governors)
2-6-0	Mogul		
2-6-2	Prairie		
2-6-4	Adriatic		
2-6-6-2T			
2-6-6-2			
2-6-6-6	Allegheny (also Blue Ridge)	4-8-8-2	Cab Forward
2-8-0	Consolidation	4-8-8-4	Big Boy
2-8-2	Mikado	4-10-0	Mastodon
2-8-4T	Berkshire Tank	4-10-2	Southern Pacific (also Overland)
2-8-4	Berkshire (also Kanawa and Lima)		
		4-12-2	Union Pacific
2-8-8-2	Cab Forward (also Chesapeake)	6-2-0	Crampton
2-8-8-4	Yellowstone	6-4-4-6	Pennsylvania
2-8-8-8-2	Triplex	6-8-6	Turbine
2-8-8-8-4	Triplex	2+C+C+2	UP steam turbine
2-10-0	Decapod	2-C1+2-C1+B	C&O steam turbine
2-10-2	Santa Fe (also Central and Decapod)	C+C+C+C	Jawn Henry (steam turbine)
		2- or 3- or 4-truck	Shay (geared locomotive)
2-10-4	Texas (also Colorado and Selkirk)	2- or 3-truck	Willamette (geared locomotive)
		2- or 3-truck	Heisler (geared locomotive)
4-4-0	American (also Eight-wheeler)	2- or 3-truck	Climax (geared locomotive)

made their appearance on several of the nation's major rail lines—an appearance mandated, in part, by the need to reduce smoke pollution in long tunnels and urban areas. By the late 1920s, several major rail lines on both coasts were relying heavily on electric power, generally fed to the locomotives through overhead lines, to supplement steam-driven locomotives in many areas, if not to fully replace them.

In the 1930s, small diesel-powered locomotives entered the scene. In truth, they were, and still are,

diesel-electric locomotives, since diesel fuel is burned to generate electric power, which is what actually drives the powered traction motors on the axles of these locomotives. Functioning mostly as yard engines assigned to light switching duties in their formative years, the diesel-electric engine was not yet seen as a formidable threat to the established supremacy of steam power.

All this began to change in the 1940s, as diesel-electrics, like the steam locomotives before them, became larger, heavier, faster, and more powerful. In

the age of "streamlining" steam locomotives to make them more attractive to the public and to draw attention to speedy and reliable passenger service, railroad executives soon found that diesel-electric locomotives could be manufactured to provide an even more sleek appearance, and these colorful new units increasingly saw duty at the head end of some of the nation's crack passenger trains.

By the early 1950s, diesel-electric power had fully come of age. As passenger service on the nation's railroads faded—largely the result of the influence of the automobile and the airplane—diesel-electric units were assigned to more and more freight-hauling duties. Once railroad officials recognized that diesels could be operated more efficiently and more cost effectively than the steamers, the days of the steam locomotive were numbered. By the late 1950s, steam had virtually disappeared from this nation's railroads, save for a few isolated instances where they continued to labor for a few more years on smaller shortlines and in some railyard areas.

Today diesel-electrics rule the rails, although electric-outline locomotives still see limited use in passenger service along some select Eastern corridors, and on transit systems in a number of major cities. Today's diesel-electric locomotives may lack the clean lines and sleek appearance of some of their mid-twentieth century predecessors, but the concern of railroads today is raw power and easy maintenance, and contemporary diesel-electrics best meet those criteria. Times have certainly changed, and these days about the only place you can enjoy the thrill of viewing, or even riding behind, a full-size functioning steam locomotive is on a museum or tourist line, where the heritage of steam is still being lovingly preserved.

• Large Scale locomotive models

A distinguishing feature of many, if not most, Large Scale model locomotives is, of course, their rather unique suitability for outdoor use in virtually all types of weather conditions. In fact, it's this unique "bullet-proofed" feature that separates garden railroad equip-

ment from the rest of the Large Scale fraternity, and from other modeling scales as well, because even though not all Large Scale model locomotives are built to tolerate the extremes of outdoor operation in all climates and weather conditions, those most often selected by garden railroaders do, indeed, exhibit this distinctive versatility.

Perhaps the single most important feature of any model locomotive designed for regular outdoor operation is its enclosed and tightly sealed motor block and related drive-gear mechanism, and the extra measure of protection given to any electrical or electronic components. The encapsulated drive mechanisms of most Large Scale locomotives are called "bricks" by garden railroad enthusiasts, first because they somewhat resemble a brick in their sealed, water-tight configuration, and second, because they are just about as solid and rugged as a real brick. Yet another advantage of these "bricks" is the relative ease with which they can be assembled, disassembled, serviced, or replaced.

Another feature you'll find on many locomotives designed for outdoor use relates to the means by which electric current passing through the track is delivered to the locomotive's motor. In almost all instances, all of the driving wheels, and perhaps even some non-driving wheels, on Large Scale locomotives are wired to transfer electrical current from the railhead to the internal motor. Some locomotives are even equipped with sliding pickup "shoes" that glide along the rails to provide an extra measure of conductivity (and to help keep the track clean), although larger steam and diesel locomotives, because they have so many wheels in contact with the rails, do not really require this extra assist. The locomotive bodies of most trains designed for outdoor use are commonly made of metal or of special ultra-violet-resistant plastics, with the latter material being far more prevalent due to its considerably lower cost. Even though a great many model locomotives and cars in other scales are also made of plastic, those intended to be exposed to the elements are generally constructed with thicker components, and feature molded-in colors or fade-resistant paint and detailing to impart a lasting durability that models in most other scales simply don't have.

When all is said and done, Large Scale locomotives rank among the most durable, long-lasting, and trouble-free in all of model railroading. And, of course, they are just plain BIG!

• Large Scale steam locomotives

Although steam locomotives may have disappeared from the tracks of most of the world's real railways, they have by no means been forgotten in the hearts and minds of model railroaders—especially garden railroaders! Today, literally thousands of miniature steamers chuff their way through countless back yard landscapes around the world. Our fascination with steam locomotives seems to transcend the time in which the real thing operated, as memories of billowing clouds of

The Aristo-Craft "Rogers" is a rugged and affordable little workhorse suitable for indoor or outdoor operation. This near-1:24 scale locomotive was initially offered as a tank-type 0-4-0T, but now comes equipped with a tender.
Photo courtesy of Aristo-Craft

smoke, flashing rods and linkage, and the haunting sound of a steam whistle are kept alive in scaled-down form and, hopefully, passed along to future generations of hobbyists and rail fans.

Large Scale enthusiasts and garden railroaders are blessed with a good and ever-growing assortment of steam power for their rosters. In keeping with our objective of developing appropriate themes for our railroads, it may be most useful to examine what is available in Large Scale steam power based on the periods of American railroading these locomotives most closely relate to.

Throughout the discussion that follows, bear in mind that Large Scale model railroading, of which garden railroading is a significant part, is actually comprised of a number of somewhat diverse modeling scales that all operate on 45mm gauge track. Although you can certainly mix-and-match scales and equipment to your heart's content (it's your railroad, after all), you may want to select locomotives and rolling stock that more closely match your prototype railroading interests, and to the era you choose to represent.

If, for example, you are primarily interested in modeling narrow gauge railroads, you'll most likely want to seek out locomotives and rolling stock that are made to 1:20.3, 1:22.5, or 1:24 scale, since the vast majority of narrow gauge models fall into one of those categories. If standard gauge modeling is the way you want to go, you'll likely want to focus on the 1:29 and 1:32 scale models, since those two scales are most often used by the major manufacturers in producing trains based on standard gauge prototypes.

• Narrow gauge locomotives in Large Scale

Let's begin by examining what's currently available for those modelers interested in narrow gauge railroading. If American narrow gauge railroading in the late nineteenth and early twentieth century appeals to you, you'll have no trouble locating a good representation of steam power, including a wide assortment of the ever-popular 4-4-0 Americans and 2-6-0 Moguls, and the always-intriguing Shay and Climax geared narrow gauge locomotives used by so many mining and logging lines.

Aristo-Craft's 2-6-0 Mogul, at 1:24 scale, is part of the firm's "Classics" line, which is manufactured with upgraded molds and mechanisms from a line formerly offered by Delton.
Photo courtesy of Aristo-Craft

Aristo-Craft's popular "Classics" line of 2-8-0 Consolidation locomotives are made to 1:24 scale. Although these models are painted and lettered for a number of both narrow gauge and standard gauge railroads, the "Classics" line itself is most closely associated with narrow gauge rail lines. Aristo's line of standard gauge model steam locomotives, described below, are made to 1:29 scale. Interestingly, the Aristo 2-4-2T Rogers locomotive is designated as 1:29 scale by the manufacturer, but the proportions of the model, which comes equipped with a tender, are probably more accurate for a 1:24 narrow gauge locomotive. The "Classics" line of 1:24 scale models also includes a Railbus, based on an early twentieth century gasoline-powered vehicle made by Mack. This model will fit well in both narrow gauge and early-period standard gauge garden railroad settings.

The Aristo-Craft Railbus, in 1:24 scale, is an appropriate addition to any rail line that represents the time when forms of power other than steam began to ply the nation's rails.
Photo courtesy of Aristo-Craft

Accucraft currently imports a variety of narrow gauge models in 1:20.3 scale, including a variety of 2-8-0 steamers, a 4-4-0 American, a 2-6-0 Mogul, a 2-8-2 K27 class "Mudhen" steamer, a Rio Grande Southern gas-powered "Galloping Goose" railcar in three versions, and a Whitcomb 0-4-0 gas-mechanical industrial switcher. All of the Accucraft models are crafted of brass. Accucraft also offers a variety of affordable live-steam locomotives in the same 1:20.3 scale.

Bachmann's Shay locomotive, a part of the firm's "Spectrum" line, is a finely detailed 1:20.3 scale model of a type of geared narrow gauge locomotive that saw service on early logging and mining railroads.
Photo courtesy of Bachmann Industries

Bachmann's Spectrum line of Shay, Climax, 4-4-0 American, and 2-6-0 Mogul locomotives are all 1:20.3

scale models of narrow gauge equipment, despite the fact that some of items may be painted and lettered for railroads that only operated on standard gauge. Bachmann's more affordable line of "Big Haulers" trains, including a 2-4-2 Columbia, a 4-6-0 ten-wheeler, and an 0-4-0T Porter are generally made to something approximating 1:22.5 scale, although Bachmann simply designates them as "Large Scale."

The Bachmann Climax geared locomotive, in 1:20.3 scale, provides yet another example of the superb level of detail attainable on Large Scale models.
Photo courtesy of Bachmann Industries

Hartland's 0-4-0, 0-4-0T, 2-4-0, 2-4-4T Forney, 0-4-4-0T "Big John" logging locomotive, 4-4-0 American, and Baldwin 2-6-0 narrow gauge locomotives, are all made to 1:24 scale. Hartland also offers two models of gasoline-powered railway workhorses built by Mack Truck in the first quarter of the twentieth century: a four-axle model of the ACX "Doozie" Railbus, and a two-axle center-cab switcher.

LGB's very popular 2-6-0 Mogul, along with their 0-4-4T Forney, also represent American narrow gauge

Bachmann's 4-4-0 American-type locomotive, another recent entry in their 1:20.3 scale "Spectrum" line, represents what was surely the most common of all locomotives to operate on U.S. lines during the latter half of the nineteenth century.
Photo by Ken Patterson, courtesy of Bachmann Industries

locomotives, but are modeled in 1:22.5 scale, as are that firm's impressive 2-6-6-2 and 2-6-6-2T Mallet (articulated) locomotives. The firm's Lehmann line of 0-4-0T Porter locomotives are reported to be very close to 1:20.3 scale. Other American narrow gauge models offered by LGB include renditions of two tiny 0-4-2T steamers that are part of railroading history and lore: the "Chloe," owned by Walt Disney cartoonist Ward Kimball, and the "Olomana," which served in the sugar cane and pineapple fields of Hawaii.

LGB's diminutive "Olomana" locomotive, in 1:22.5 scale, is typical of the motive power used in Hawaii's sugar cane and pineapple industry during the late nineteenth and early twentieth centuries. LGB also offers a number of other small locomotive models based on both American and European prototypes
Photo courtesy of Ernst Paul Lehmann Patentwerk

This impressive narrow gauge Mallet locomotive, in 1:22.5 scale, is one of several offered in the LGB product line.
Photo courtesy of Ernst Paul Lehmann Patentwerk

A number of other manufacturers and suppliers also provide Large Scale models of narrow gauge locomotives. Since supply and availability of these items are sometimes hard to predict, it's best to stay abreast of developments by regularly reading the Large Scale oriented magazines, such as *Garden Railways* and *Finescale Railroader*, and by participating on one or more of the Internet forums devoted to Large Scale railroading—always a terrific source of current product information.

• Standard gauge steam in Large Scale

As we venture into the relatively more recent era of standard gauge steam locomotives, keep in mind that these models, if correctly proportioned for use on 45mm gauge track, will normally be made to 1:29 or 1:32 scale. This is where the "scale/gauge" issue in Large Scale model railroading really becomes somewhat obvious. For example: If you were to place a 1:29 scale Aristo-Craft standard gauge model of their 4-6-2 Pacific alongside a 1:20.3 scale Bachmann Shay (a narrow gauge model), you would immediately notice that the Shay appears to be quite large—far larger than what you would see if real-life locomotives of these two different types and track gauges were placed side by side. In real life, the narrow gauge Shay would be dwarfed by the much-larger Pacific. Again, this relates to the difference in modeled scales, which was covered in some detail in an earlier chapter.

Aristo-Craft's 4-6-2 Pacific locomotive ranks as perhaps the most often-seen large steam power on garden railroads throughout the United States.
Photo courtesy of Aristo-Craft

Standard gauge steam power in Large Scale model railroading is, at present, somewhat more limited than the plentiful narrow gauge offerings, although this situation is rapidly changing as the hobby grows.

Aristo-Craft currently produces 0-4-0 and 0-4-0T switching locomotives, along with the aforementioned 4-6-2 Pacific locomotive—all made to a scale of 1:29. Aristo has also announced plans to manufacture 2-8-2 Mikado, 2-8-8-2 Mallet, and 4-8-4 Northern locomotives, and when these 1:29 scale items are available they're certain to be popular items with Large Scale standard gauge enthusiasts.

Bachmann has announced plans for a 2-8-0 Consolidation, which is slated for release in late 2001 or early 2002.

Märklin's 2-6-0 Mogul locomotive, from the firm's 1:32 scale MAXI line, would look right at home in either a narrow gauge or standard gauge setting. The MAXI line is constructed of metal, finished with durable, baked-on, automotive-quality paint.
Photo courtesy of Märklin, Inc.

A Märklin MAXI line starter set in 1:32 scale, headed by an 0-6-0T locomotive. The MAXI sets feature all-metal construction of both the locomotive and the cars.
Photo courtesy of Märklin, Inc.

Märklin's all-metal MAXI line features several American-prototype standard gauge steam locomotives, all made to 1:32 scale, including a 2-6-0 Mogul dating from around 1900 in several variations, along with a couple of "Americanized" 0-6-0T and 0-4-0T switchers, which are relatively credible U.S. models derived from European designs.

USA Trains reportedly plans to introduce a 4-6-4 Hudson locomotive, in plastic, at an early date, although a final release date had not been established at the time of this book's publication.

And, LGB released a limited edition 1:29 scale 4-6-4 Hudson locomotive, of all-brass construction, late in 2000, and the firm has announced plans to produce a 2-8-2 USRA Mikado, as well. The Hudson locomotive was made for LGB by Aster, of Japan.

M.T.H. Electric Trains, a leading manufacturer in the O scale field, has announced that it will manufacture a 4-6-4 Hudson and 4-6-6-4 Challenger locomotives—both in 1:32 scale—to launch that firm's entry into Large Scale. With M.T.H. Electric Trains venturing into the Large Scale arena, one can reasonably assume that the firm will approach this market with the same fervor that has spawned something of a revolution in O scale in recent years.

LGB's all-brass 4-6-4 Hudson locomotive, in 1:29 scale, was made in limited numbers by Aster, of Japan.
Photo courtesy of Ernst Paul Lehmann Patentwerk

Custom-made, costly, all-brass, limited edition standard gauge steam locomotives in 1:32 scale are also offered from time to time by such firms as Aster, Ro & Company, and a few others. Aster, for example, has previously produced a 2-8-2 Mikado and a 2-6-6-6 Allegheny in 1:32 scale. For its part, Ro & Company has produced a variety of limited-run steam and diesel locomotives in recent years, with new models making their debut on a regular basis.

• Large Scale diesel-electric locomotives

Garden railroaders interested in the steam-to-diesel transition era in the United States have nearly the full assortment of steamers noted above to choose from, plus the added availability of a wealth of early diesel power, ranging from small switchers—a few of which are designed as narrow gauge models—to larger road units, and even a diesel-powered rail car.

Aristo-Craft's ALCO FA diesels, in 1:29 scale, are available in a wide range of paint schemes and roadnames, including the ever-popular Santa Fe "Warbonnet" livery.
Photo courtesy of Aristo-Craft

Early generation diesel-electric locomotives include yard switchers representing several builders, center-cab locomotives, and ALCO, GE, and EMD (GM) road-type units.

Two of the leading manufacturers of affordable Large Scale models of American prototype diesel-electrics are Aristo-Craft and, more recently, USA Trains. Both firms offer a broad and growing assortment of early and more contemporary diesel-electrics, all done in 1:29 scale.

Aristo-Craft's 1:29 scale models of early diesel-electrics include ALCO FA-1s, ALCO RS-3s, GE U25-Bs, EMD E-8s and E-9s (recently announced), and somewhat freelanced models of a "Lil' Critter" two-axle diesel switcher, as well as a four-axle center-cab switcher based on the "Lil' Critter's" design. Aristo-Craft also offers a 1:29 scale RDC-1 Rail Diesel Car, which is essentially a diesel-powered streamlined passenger car. Nearly all of the Aristo-Craft models are available in a variety of roadnames.

The Aristo-Craft U-25B diesel-electric locomotive, like the firm's FA-1 and RS-3 offerings, has been made in a large number of paint schemes and roadnames. The U-25Bs are 1:29 scale models.
Photo courtesy of Aristo-Craft

Aristo-Craft's new Rail Diesel Car (RDC), in 1:29 scale.
Photo courtesy of Aristo-Craft

Aristo-Craft's Lil' Critter diesel locomotive, in 1:29 scale, is a plausible, albeit freelanced, representation of a small ALCO switcher.
Photo courtesy of Aristo-Craft

Aristo-Craft's ALCO RS-3 diesel-electric locomotive, in 1:29 scale.
Photo courtesy of Aristo-Craft

The Aristo-Craft Center Cab diesel switcher, like the Lil' Critter, is a 1:29 scale freelanced representation of what might have been produced in ALCO's plants.
Photo courtesy of Aristo-Craft

This LGB industrial diesel, in 1:22.5 scale, has been made in several roadnames. It is a faithful model of a prototype that operated on the Denver & Rio Grande Western.
Photo courtesy of Ernst Paul Lehmann Patentwerk

LGB's F-7 diesel, shown here in an A-B combination adorned in attractive Canadian Pacific livery, measures close to 1:26 scale.
Photo courtesy of Ernst Paul Lehmann Patentwerk

LGB's American-prototype diesels are all early-generation models, and they include an ALCO DL535E locomotive, which is actually based on a narrow gauge diesel-electric prototype, and standard gauge EMD F-7 diesels, with both "A" (units with cabs) and "B" (units without cabs) types available for the latter. LGB's F-7 diesels are estimated to be about 1:26 scale, apparently a sort of "compromise scale" arrived at so the units would look okay pulling LGB's 1:22.5 scale freight and passenger cars. Another LGB diesel-electric workhorse is their 1:22.5 scale two-axle industrial switcher, based on a narrow gauge prototype that operated on the Denver & Rio Grande Western railroad. This item has been reissued several times in various other roadnames and paint schemes.

Märklin's MAXI line also includes an American F-7 diesel in 1:32 scale. This model is made entirely of metal, and is currently available in both Union Pacific and Santa Fe paint schemes.

Märklin's F-7 diesel, available in both Santa Fe and Union Pacific versions, is part of the firm's MAXI line of all-metal locomotives and cars in 1:32 scale.
Photo courtesy of Märklin, Inc.

USA Trains, a division of the Charles Ro Supply Company, manufacturers several early generation diesel-electrics in 1:29 scale. These models include an EMD NW-2 switcher in "cow-and-calf" combinations; a generic 20-ton switcher; a GE 44-ton center-cab switcher; award-winning models of EMD's GP-7 and GP-9 road diesels; and a gleaming assortment of EMD F-3 diesels, along with their matching "B" units. As was the case with Aristo's models, all of the USA Trains diesels are available in a wide range of paint schemes and popular roadnames.

USA Trains 20-ton diesel switcher, in 1:29 scale. All USA Trains locomotives are available in a wide variety of paint schemes and roadnames.
Photo courtesy of USA Trains

USA Trains popular NW-2 diesel switcher, in 1:29 scale.
Photo courtesy of USA Trains

USA Trains F-3 diesel-electric locomotive, in 1:29 scale.
Photo courtesy of USA Trains

USA Trains award-winning GP-7/9 diesel-electric locomotive models are made in 1:29 scale.
Photo courtesy of USA Trains

Fans of more contemporary North American railroading have access to a growing number of heavy-duty modern road diesels, thanks largely to USA Trains and Aristo-Craft offerings, and their motive power needs can logically and easily be supplemented by any of the earlier hooded diesel locomotives, such as the GP-7 and GP-9, along with the F-3 and F-7 units, and virtually any or all of the earlier diesel switcher models—all of which continue to see some service on today's railroads.

Aristo-Craft was the early leader in producing North American-style diesel electric models for the Large Scale community. Aristo's diesels are all made to 1:29 scale. Several models of their early-generation diesels were previously mentioned, but Aristo-Craft is now making a concerted effort to capture a larger share of the emerging market for contemporary diesel-electric models. Their first announced model in that area is an EMD SD-45 diesel, which will be followed by a GE Dash-9 diesel and an EMD SD-9 locomotive.

For their part, USA Trains, a relative newcomer to the Large Scale scene, has produced a number of U.S.-style diesel-electric locomotives—a total of seven different models, thus far. Current offerings in modern-day motive power include a GP38-2 locomotive, along with the largest of all the mass-produced Large Scale diesels made to date: a six-axle SD40-2 locomotive that measures more than twenty-six inches long. All USA Trains models are made to 1:29 scale.

A contemporary SD40-2 diesel electric locomotive is offered by USA Trains, in 1:29 scale. A variety of roadnames and paint schemes are available.
Photo courtesy of USA Trains

M.T.H. Electric Trains plans to release a modern GE Dash-8 diesel-electric locomotive, in a variety of roadnames, in 1:32 scale. This locomotive will be available in both four-wheel and six-wheel truck versions, depending on the roadname purchased.

At the high end of the range of diesel-electric locomotive models made in Large Scale, St. Charles Station has thus far custom-crafted brass models of more than thirty different diesel and electric locomotives, including GP and SD road units, ALCO RS series locomotives, SW-1 and MP-15 yard switchers, a steeple cab electric, and a wide variety of other motive power. St. Charles Station paints and letters each of their locomotives for whatever roadname the customer prefers.

• Large Scale electric-outline locomotives and trolleys

Another type of motive power that merits some mention are the electric-outline locomotives and trolleys. A real advantage in operating trains off overhead trolley lines or catenary wires is that this provides a viable means for operating two trains independently on the same track—one powered by the overhead wires, and the other powered by track power. Offsetting this convenient advantage, at least as far as outdoor operation is concerned, is the requirement for additional regular maintenance that's needed to keep the overhead wire system rigid, aligned, and functioning properly. And, the network of poles and wires also pose a real obstacle to track cleaning—a significant consideration for an electrically-powered outdoor layout.

Märklin's Steeple Cab electric loco is a part of the firm's MAXI line of 1:32 scale products. Although based on a European prototype, similar electric-type locomotives saw service on a number of U.S. railroads in the early to mid-twentieth century.
Photo courtesy of Märklin, Inc.

At present, only LGB offers an electric-outline locomotive of the type that might be seen operating on North American railroads. This unit heads their contemporary and super-sleek "Amtrak City Express" and Lehmann City Express" train sets, which are actually based on the high-speed Inter-City Express (ICE) trains operating in Germany. The locomotive, which comes complete with matching passenger cars, does not operate off overhead power, but it is equipped with a pantograph. However, models of a number of European electric-outline locomotives are available from both LGB (1:22.5 scale) and Märklin (1:32 scale), including two-axle steeple-cab electrics from both firms that can be rather easily modified to become credible U.S. models. Aside from the aforementioned ICE train model, all of the LGB and Märklin electric-outline locomotives can easily be switched from track power to overhead trolley or catenary power.

LGB also offers European-type 1:22.5 scale trolleys in a variety of paint schemes, and in both open-end and

closed-end versions. As with the locomotive units noted above, these LGB trolleys come factory-equipped for overhead operation. A convenient switch on the trolley allows the operator to easily change over from track power to overhead power without any further modification or fuss.

A typical LGB trolley, accompanied by a service car for working on the overhead lines. LGB's trolleys are made in 1:22.5 scale, and are based on European prototypes.
Photo courtesy of Ernst Paul Lehmann Patentwerk

Bachmann manufactures an American-style trolley in approximately 1:22.5 scale—one with open sides and ends, and another with enclosed sides and ends—although neither of these are configured or wired to operate directly through their trolley poles.

• Whimsical and fanciful locomotives

While it may be true that a majority of model railroaders are devotees of a particular railroad or historical period, that's certainly not always the case. Some hobbyists—and garden railroad enthusiasts in particular, it seems—are inclined to follow a far more whimsical approach in their railroad modeling. Perhaps this is the result of garden railroading being a more laid-back, relaxed, and family oriented pursuit for many hobbyists, or maybe it's just because these big trains bring out more of the "kid" in all of us. Whatever the reason, whimsical and fanciful trains—complete with similarly whimsical and fanciful locomotives and rolling stock—are part and parcel of a good many Large Scale railroads, both indoors and outdoors.

In fact, there is enough of a following for this offbeat form of model railroading that a special organization is devoted to its perpetuation: the Always Whimsical, Not Usually to Scale (A.W.N.U.T.S.) Large Scale group, which even publishes its own magazine (see listing in the References appendix). These folks not only make good use of commercially available items of a whimsical design, they also create their own sometimes bizarre and outlandish versions.

It's probably safe to say that far-and-away the most popular whimsical train items are those associated with the Christmas holidays or with a circus theme. Nearly all of the leading Large Scale manufacturers offer

Christmas- and circus-theme locomotives, rolling stock, and accessories, and some of these items even feature blinking lights and/or play traditional holiday of circus music!

One of Bachmann's Christmas train sets, in 1:24 scale.
Photo courtesy of Bachmann Industries

LGB Christmas train set, in 1:22.5 scale. Over the years, LGB has produced a number of Christmas-theme sets and separate-sale items.
Photo courtesy of Ernst Paul Lehmann Patentwerk

LGB led the way in Christmas-related Large Scale trains, and over the years this firm has produced a number of complete Christmas sets in 1:22.5 scale, most of which are headed by the firm's hallmark "Stainz" 0-4-0T European-style locomotive, or a "westernized" version thereof. A powered Christmas tender is also available for use with the 0-4-0T locomotives. Other powered Christmas-theme units from LGB include a Santa Handcar, a Santa Rail Cycle, a Christmas Trolley, a Christmas Rail Truck, and even a Christmas cable car system, all in 1.22.5 scale. And, of course, LGB provides a good and ever-growing variety of Christmas-theme rolling stock for their locomotives to pull.

Not to be outdone in the area of holiday-theme train items, Aristo-Craft offers a number of Christmas locomotives and powered units in 1:29 scale, including gaily decorated 0-4-0T, Rogers 2-4-2, and ALCO FA-1 locomotives; a Christmas "Lil' Critter" diesel switcher; a Christmas Railbus; and a fanciful wrapped-like-a-Christmas-present "Lil' Eggliner" powered passenger car (truly a whimsical item). All of the aforementioned items are also available in a variety of "regular" roadnames. And, of course, Aristo-Craft also provides a varied assortment of Christmas passenger and freight cars for their locomotives to pull, as well as a nice range of Christmas-decorated accessories, including two passenger stations, a farm house, a water tower, a covered bridge, a waiting platform, and a watch tower.

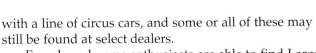

A USA Trains Christmas passenger set, in 1:29 scale. The firm also offers a Christmas freight set, along with other holiday-decorated locomotives and cars.
Photo courtesy of USA Trains

with a line of circus cars, and some or all of these may still be found at select dealers.

Even brand name enthusiasts are able to find Large Scale locomotives and rolling stock that has been painted and decorated for some of the most popular trademarks. Aristo-Craft has a Hershey's "Lil' Critter" switcher and a good assortment of locomotives and cars decorated for the Napa Valley Wine Train; LGB provides an ALCO DL535E in Coca-Cola livery and a Campbell's Soup industrial diesel; and USA Trains manufactures a Pepsi-Cola NW-2 diesel switcher.

Aristo-Craft's intriguing and whimsical 1:29 scale "Eggliner" has a real-life prototype, although the real one didn't actually operate over the rails. The Eggliner is available in a variety of roadnames and special themes.
Photo courtesy of Aristo-Craft

For its part in commemorating the holiday, USA Trains provides a 1:29 scale Christmas 20-Ton diesel switcher, an NW-2 diesel switcher, a Christmas GP-7 road diesel, Christmas Bay Window cabooses, and a series of Christmas-theme refrigerator cars and combines, some of which play seasonal music, that are released on an annual basis.

Bachmann provides holiday enthusiasts with Large Scale "Night Before Christmas" and "Polar Express" train sets, both headed by 4-6-0 steamers, along with a Santa & Elf handcar, and a Christmas trolley.

If a carnival or circus theme appeals to you, Aristo-Craft, LGB, and Bachmann have all provided the means to get performers and animals to the Big Top in style. LGB provides a circus train set, again headed by their popular Stainz 0-4-0 in circus livery, and they also offer additional circus cars and even a circus handcar. Bachmann offers a couple of circus sets, including one headed by an 0-4-0T steamer, and another led by a 4-6-0. To supplement these ready-to-run sets, Bachmann also provides flat cars with circus wagon cage car, and Calliope loads, as well as stock cars with elephants and horses. Aristo-Craft previously offered an 0-4-0T steam locomotive and an FA-1 diesel in circus livery, along

In short, regardless of whether you prefer true-to-prototype motive power for your trains, or want to expand your horizons into the realm of the imaginative, there's probably something already available in Large Scale that will appeal to your interests. And, at the rate the hobby is growing these days, you can be fairly sure that if your favorite locomotive hasn't yet been produced in Large Scale, or if it hasn't been offered in the road name of your choice, it likely will be in the not-too-distant future!

Bachmann's "Ringmaster" circus set, in 1:24 scale.
Photo courtesy of Bachmann Industries

Wood-side coaches await their passengers at Rancocoas Station on Charles Bendarik's garden layout. There's a sharp horseshoe curve through the town at this point, which provides the engine crew with an excellent view along the full length of the train. Be they passenger or freight cars, there's no doubt that rolling stock defines a railroad's reason for being.
Photo courtesy of Charles Bendarik

Chapter 5
LARGE SCALE ROLLING STOCK

A locomotive alone, no matter how powerful and grand it may be, does not constitute a train. In order to achieve that status, the locomotive has to be pulling (or perhaps pushing) one or more cars. And, of course, that's what railroading is all about—the movement of people or goods from point "A" to point "B," with perhaps some intermediate stops along the way!

Today, Large Scale garden railroaders are blessed with a great and ever-expanding variety of rolling stock of every conceivable type, ranging from diminutive two-axle ore cars and ornate wood-type passenger coaches all the way up to sleek smooth-sided streamline passenger cars and modern-day 53' RoadRailers (highway-type trailers fitted with flanged railroad wheelsets). This marks quite a significant change from as recently as a decade ago, when much of the Large Scale rolling stock was based on European prototypes, and when very little was available that represented equipment commonly seen from the mid-point of the twentieth century to the present day.

In discussing the wealth of rolling stock items available to Large Scale railroaders, it's probably easiest to first group items into one or the other of two broad categories: freight cars or passenger cars. Then, for each of these two primary categories, we can associate rolling stock with the general period or era in which it was operated, bearing in mind that there often is a considerable amount of overlap between these periods. For example, much of the rolling stock commonly used around the midpoint of the twentieth century still sees service on many of today's contemporary rail lines. In general, though, most rolling stock can be classified as being late nineteenth and early twentieth century (including narrow gauge equipment), mid-twentieth century, or contemporary.

In reviewing some of the Large Scale rolling stock that's currently on the market, it again helps to keep the designated or estimated scale of these diverse offerings in mind. Although nearly all Large Scale equipment, regardless of scale, will operate properly together because all are made to perform on 45mm-gauge track, certain cars made to one scale may not look quite right when mixed in a train comprised of cars made to some other scale. In general, however, most equipment from a given era in railroading history will look just fine mixed with other equipment from the same general era, and any size or proportion differences won't be all that apparent.

We'll begin with a look at freight cars, since that is the type of rolling stock that seems to attract the attention of most garden railroaders. Keep in mind that the following listings are by no means complete. Although most of the major manufacturers of ready-to-run Large Scale rolling stock are included, there are numerous others—both large and small—that offer Large Scale rolling stock in a variety of different scales, types, and roadnames. Some manufacturers even offer rolling stock in kit form, so you can build, paint, and modify the equipment in a way that more closely conforms to your needs and interests. If you have decided to firmly settle on a particular modeling scale or era, you would be well advised to peruse the magazine ads and/or manufacturer web sites to see what's currently being offered, and to learn more about any planned releases of new items.

Be sure to read the sections titled "rolling stock wheels" and "couplers" at the end of this chapter for important information relating to wheel types and coupler compatibility issues.

• Narrow gauge and early standard gauge freight cars

First, a word about the availability of appropriately scaled narrow gauge items. Nearly all wood-side or outside-braced rolling stock will look fine operating on a narrow gauge layout, although there is still a definite shortage of cars made to 1:20.3 scale—the emerging scale-of-choice for narrow gauge modelers primarily due to the influence that Bachmann has had on that scale's development with its Shay, Climax, 4-4-0, and 2-6-0 Mogul locomotives. At the time of this writing, none of the major manufacturers offer a designated line of 1:20.3 scale rolling stock, although this situation is likely to change at some point. For all practical purposes, cars made to 1:22.5 scale or even 1:24 scale are close enough to appear correct when running behind a 1:20.3 scale Shay, Climax, or similar narrow gauge locomotive, so these scales may be the appropriate ones to consider if your intent is to eventually develop an early-era narrow gauge roster.

Aristo-Craft's 20-foot tank car is close to 1:24 scale, as are the other cars in this series of two-axle old time freight haulers. *Photo courtesy Bachmann Industries*

Aristo-Craft has a series of somewhat freelanced old-timer freight cars consisting of a 20-foot gondola, 20-foot tank car, 20-foot flatcar, 20-foot boxcar, and a wood-side bobber caboose. Although the precise scale of these items isn't specified by the manufacturer, they appear to be closest to 1:24 scale in most respects, since they are built upon the same chassis as that used for Aristo-Craft's 1:24 scale bobber caboose from it's "Classics" series. In that "Classics" series, which is, indeed, identified by the manufacturer as being 1:24 scale, Aristo-Craft offers a wood-side gondola, wood-side coal hopper car, wood-side bobber caboose, wood-side boxcar, wood-side reefer, and a flatcar with cable reel load.

Bachmann doesn't specify a precise scale for its rolling stock, but most items can be assumed to be in 1:22.5 scale since they are generally made to match the 1:22.5 scale locomotives in the firm's "Big Haulers" line. Bachmann's early-era rolling stock assortment includes wood-side refrigerator cars, 20-foot wood-side boxcars, single-dome tank cars, 20-foot wood-side gondolas, skeleton log cars, wood-side ore cars, 20-foot flatcars, side-dump ore cars, and wood-side bobber and center-cab cabooses. At this date, Bachmann has delayed introducing a line of true 1:20.3 scale rolling stock to accompany its fine Shay, Climax, 4-4-0, and other locomotives

in the firm's Large Scale "Spectrum" line. Many hobbyists hope this delay is only temporary, since there does appear to be considerable market demand for these truer-to-scale items.

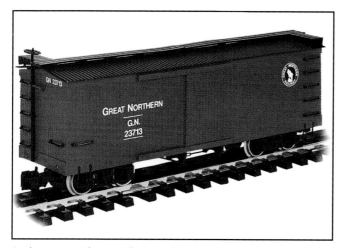

Bachmann's early-era rolling stock, such as this wood-side refrigerator car, are made to about 1:22.5 scale. Bachmann has not yet manufactured 1:20.3 scale cars to match its "Spectrum" series of locomotives in that scale.
Photo courtesy of Bachmann Industries

Hartland Locomotive Works offers 1:24 scale flat/log cars, wood-side boxcars, wood-side gondolas, a wood-side bobber caboose, and a wood-side work caboose, among other items.

The LGB line of early-era freight cars in 1:22.5 scale includes wood-side boxcars, wood-side refrigerator cars, stock cars, low-sided gondolas, flat cars, single-dome tank cars, and wood-side cabooses.

LGB wood-side refrigerator car, in 1:22.5 scale.
Photo courtesy of Ernst Paul Lehmann Patentwerk

For its part, USA Trains commemorates the early days of American railroading with a wide assortment of 1:22.5 scale wood-side boxcars, wood-side refrigerator cars, outside-braced boxcars, and wood-side cabooses in an equally wide variety of roadnames.

A wood-side caboose, in 1:29 scale, from USA Trains.
Photo courtesy of USA Trains

• Mid-twentieth century standard gauge freight cars

Much to the chagrin of some purists in the hobby, 1:29 scale seems to have emerged as the scale-of-choice in Large Scale for modeling U.S. standard gauge railroad equipment on a 45mm track gauge. With the investment that manufacturers such as Aristo-Craft and USA Trains have already put into their respective 1:29 scale product lines, it's not likely that the more correct 1:32 scale for standard gauge will receive much industry support in the near future.

Aristo-Craft's extensive 1:29 scale rolling stock offerings include a 40-foot drop-end gondola, covered gondola, covered hopper, single-dome tank car, triple-dome tank car, long caboose, 40-foot steel boxcar, stock car, steel-side refrigerator car, 40-foot stake flatcar, searchlight car, 40-foot bulkhead flatcar, three-bay 100-ton hopper car, 3-6 bay cylindrical covered hopper, and a wedge snowplow. Aristo-Craft also offers a 1:24 scale track-cleaning car, which consists of a cleaning pad device mounted underneath the firm's "Classics" series bobber-type caboose. Due to its special-service function, the track-cleaning car is appropriate to just about any Large Scale railroad, regardless of era modeled.

A typical Aristo-Craft boxcar, in 1:29 scale.
Photo courtesy of Aristo-Craft

Bachmann's line of early- to mid-twentieth century freight cars includes a gondola, flatcar with trailer, hopper car, and a flatcar with logs—all made in 1:22.5 scale, but nevertheless appropriate to standard gauge operations. Bachmann also offers a series of 1:22.5 scale circus

cars, including flatcars with wagon, calliope, and cage loads, as well as stock cars with horses and elephants. These circus cars are equally appropriate for both early and mid-twentieth century rosters.

LGB freight cars are, for the most part, suitable for use in both narrow gauge and standard gauge operations, depending on the era a given car's construction represents. U.S.-style freight cars available from LGB in 1:22.5 scale include: boxcars, bulk head flat cars, tank cars, hopper cars, low-sided gondolas, high-sided gondolas, stock cars, refrigerator cars, container cars, flat cars, covered hoppers, and cabooses.

A Great Northern steel-side boxcar from LGB, in 1:22.5 scale.
Photo courtesy of Ernst Paul Lehmann Patentwerk

Märklin's MAXI line if 1:32 scale rolling stock includes this colorful State of Maine boxcar.
Photo courtesy of Märklin, Inc.

Märklin offers all-metal U.S. style boxcars, cabooses, and other rolling stock to complement its MAXI line of 1:32 scale trains.

USA Trains supplies a number of 1:29 scale freight cars based on mid-twentieth century prototypes, including a depressed-center flat car, bay window and extended vision cabooses, a 40-foot boxcar and 40-foot refrigerator car, a steel boxcar, a two-tier auto carrier, and a piggyback flat car with trailer—the latter two of which are equally appropriate for a contemporary-era freight consist. USA Trains also offers an extensive "Work Train series" of cars consisting of a derrick car with boom, rail and tie car, kitchen car, engineering car, work train flatcar, bunk car, power and light car, operating 25-ton crane car, work caboose with crane tender, and a rotary snow plow. These work train components are suitable for just about any era, since the real railroads have almost always kept this equipment in use until it was no longer functional.

USA Trains piggyback flat car, in 1:29 scale.
Photo courtesy of USA Trains

USA Trains refrigerator car, in 1:29 scale.
Photo courtesy of USA Trains

USA Trains extended vision caboose, in 1:29 scale.
Photo courtesy of USA Trains

• Contemporary standard gauge freight cars

Until somewhat recently, the leading manufacturers in Large Scale paid scant attention to large and long rolling stock of the type commonly seen on today's major railroads. There were several good reasons for this apparent neglect, including a lack of contemporary locomotive models to pull these modern and somewhat hefty cars, and related concerns over the problems that long, contemporary cars and locomotives might experience in negotiating the tight curves of a typical garden railroad. This is beginning to change though. USA Trains has already released a 1:29 scale SD40-2 locomotive; Aristo-Craft has a 1:29 scale SD-45 diesel-electric

on the way; and M.T.H. Electric Trains has announced a Dash-8 diesel. So, now that some large and powerful motive power is becoming available, the manufacturers are starting to produce cars for these rail giants to pull. The offerings remain rather limited, but this is expected to change in a relatively short period of time.

Keep in mind, too, that many mid-twentieth century freight cars, even though they were originally designed and built a good number of years ago, still see service on today's railroads. That being the case, many of those items are entirely appropriate in a modern freight consist.

Aristo-Craft's planned Triple-Crown RoadRailer car, in 1:29 scale, will be an appropriate addition to contemporary rolling stock rosters.
Photo courtesy of Aristo-Craft

Aristo-Craft's 1:29 scale model of a 53-foot RoadRailer car, which is basically a long-haul highway trailer fitted with a put-'em-on-and-take-'em-off set of railroad trucks, ranks among the more unusual items in the contemporary car fleet. Hard on it's heels is the firm's Kaolin tank car, which boasts a sleek, contemporary look quite unlike the conventional domed tank cars. Another contemporary freight hauler from Aristo-Craft is the 53-foot double-door boxcar. All of these cars are available in unpainted versions, as well as in a number of railroad or brand names.

USA Trains' intermodal container car measures nearly thirty inches in length—currently ranking as the longest of the modern-day freight cars available in Large Scale. Other contemporary freight cars from USA Trains include a 50-foot boxcar, a 50-foot mechanical refrigerator car, a center beam flatcar, a pipe load flatcar, and a generator flatcar.

USA Trains thirty-inch long intermodal container car, in 1:29 scale.
Photo courtesy of USA Trains

• Narrow gauge and early standard gauge passenger cars

The transportation of passengers played an important role in the development of railroading in the United States, particularly in the period leading up to, and through, World War II. Although rail passenger service in this country is pretty much limited to Amtrak and a few commuter lines today, this is not the case on thousands of garden railroads that dot the landscape throughout the nation.

Many garden railroaders have at least one passenger train operating somewhere on their layout. These range from diminutive and ornate old-time wood coaches being hauled by a steam locomotive, to the sleek bullet-nosed Amtrak express trains that ply the rails today. Most popular, it seems, are the early-period passenger trains, and this is where many of the major Large Scale manufacturers have focused their efforts.

Aristo-Craft doesn't actually specify the scale of their Sierra passenger car series (representing a popular prototype from the late 1800s), although the cars are assumed to be 1:24 scale, matching the scale of locomotives in the firm's "Classics" line. The Sierra series includes wood-side coaches, combines, and observation cars, each of which is available in five different roadnames. An undecorated coach is also available for those who prefer to paint and letter a train for their own railroad, or for one not offered in pre-painted form.

Bachmann "South Pacific Coast" wood-side coach, in 1:24 scale.
Photo courtesy of Bachmann Industries

Bachmann offers a series of old-time passenger cars as part of its 1:24 scale "Big Haulers" line of affordable Large Scale trains.

Hartland's 1:24 scale early-era passenger car releases include "Shorty" wood-side coaches and combines, as well as longer wood-side coaches, combines, and mail cars.

LGB—the German family enterprise that popularized Large Scale trains and garden railroading in the United States and elsewhere—provides an extensive array of both European and U.S. narrow gauge passenger equipment in 1:22.5 scale. Although the majority of LGB's passenger cars are based on European prototypes, the U.S. market has not been overlooked. For example, the firm's 3006 series of two-axle wood-side coaches are available painted and lettered for U.S. railroads, even though the cars themselves are distinctly European in design. LGB's longer four-axle 3080-84 series of wood-side coaches, combines, and baggage cars are, in fact, based on actual U.S. narrow gauge prototypes. Cars in both series are offered in a variety of roadnames, ranging from the fictitious and fanciful Lake George & Boulder (LG&B) to the historic Denver & Rio Grande Western. LGB also offers an open sightseeing car for those who might like to incorporate a tourist or rail museum line as part of a more contemporary overall operation.

Typical wood-side passenger car in 1:22.5 scale—a part of the extensive assortment from LGB.
Photo courtesy of Ernst Paul Lehmann Patentwerk

Märklin offers 1:32 scale all-metal passenger coaches as part of the MAXI line of trains designed for operation on #1 gauge track.

USA Trains has an assortment of wood-side Overton passenger cars that do not carry a manufacturer-designated scale, but they are appropriately sized for any turn-of-the-century setting in 1:24 scale, and even 1:29 scale. Cars currently offered in the series include a coach, a combine, and an observation car.

• Mid-twentieth century passenger cars

Aristo-Craft is currently the only manufacturer to offer large, steel-construction twentieth century passenger cars of the type that preceded the streamliner era. Their 1:29 scale line of "heavyweight" coaches, Pullman sleepers, diners, railway post office cars, combines, and observation cars are based on a passenger car design introduced by Bethlehem Shipbuilding Company in the early 1920s. The Aristo-Craft models, which are available in a number of different roadnames, come complete with detailed and lighted interiors. These long cars require eight-foot minimum diameter curves.

A "heavyweight" passenger coach from Aristo-Craft, in 1:29 scale. At present, Aristo-Craft is the only Large Scale manufacturer offering models of these heftier steel-construction cars that preceded the lighter-weight streamlined cars.
Photo courtesy of Aristo-Craft

• Streamliners and contemporary passenger cars

Aristo-Craft offers a striking assortment of both fluted-side and smooth-side streamline passenger cars. Coaches, diners, baggage cars, dome cars, and observation cars are all available in a wide variety of roadnames. Both versions of these 1:29 scale cars feature extruded aluminum bodies, full interior lighting, and other details. The fluted-side streamline cars require five-foot diameter curves, at minimum, for efficient operation, while the smooth-side cars require eight-foot minimum diameter curves.

Streamlined passenger coach, in 1:29 scale, from Aristo-Craft.
Photo courtesy of Aristo-Craft

LGB has produced a series of streamline passenger coach, dome, and observation cars in several popular roadnames as complements to their F-7 diesel-electric locomotives. Since LGB's F-7 locomotives are made to approximately 1:26 scale, it can be reasonably assumed that these cars pretty much conform to that scale, although the manufacturer doesn't specify an exact scale for these items.

An example of LGB's streamlined passenger equipment, in approximately 1:26 scale.
Photo courtesy of Ernst Paul Lehmann Patentwerk

Although most Large Scale rolling stock is supplied in ready-built form (with a few detail parts that must be added, in some cases), several of the above-listed manufacturers do offer rolling stock in undecorated form so the hobbyist can paint and letter the item for his or her own railroad, or for a particular prototype railroad not offered in the regular line.

• Whimsical, theme, and brand-related rolling stock

As was noted in the locomotives section above, many Large Scale manufacturers also offer whimsical, theme, and/or brand-related items for railroaders with special interests. Some of these cars may be decorated in convincingly prototypical ways, while others may be purely fanciful in concept. Whatever the case, these Christmas, circus, and brand name cars are very popular with the garden railroading community, and many of them are especially sought-after by collectors of Large Scale items.

• Rolling stock wheels

Although the situation is rapidly changing, many Large Scale manufacturers still equip their rolling stock items with plastic wheelsets. In part, this measure is taken to help keep the overall cost down. That's all well and good, but the fact is that plastic wheels simply do not roll as smoothly or hold up as well as metal wheels, especially on a large outdoor railroad or in a situation where the equipment will see a whole lot of use.

You should seriously consider replacing any/all plastic wheels on your rolling stock with metal wheelsets. Metal wheels perform much better then plastic wheels, and they do not leave a plastic deposit or coating on the track as they wear. Metal wheels, because they weigh more, also tend to lower the center of gravity of the car, which helps it to track better. A side benefit of metal wheels is the familiar and pleasant clickity-clack that these wheels make when passing over rail joints.

Metal wheelsets are available from nearly all of the major manufacturers, and a few after-market suppliers. The best procedure to follow is to plan on buying a set of metal wheels each time you purchase a new car, if the car you're buying is not already so equipped. Just assume that the cost of the wheels is part of the purchase price—that way it doesn't take such a big bite out of your wallet. What to do with the leftover plastic wheels? Paint 'em a weathered rusty color, and stack them beside the locomotive repair facility on your layout, or make them into flat car or hopper car loads.

• Couplers

Couplers are another subject deserving of your attention, especially if you intend to mix and operate rolling stock made by a number of different manufacturers. Couplers are, of course, what hold a train together, so they serve a most critical function. You'll discover that for yourself the first time a coupler releases when you aren't paying attention, and the head-end

of your train eventually plows into its own rear end!

Couplers on Large Scale trains generally differ from the prototype in at least three significant respects. First, couplers on model train cars, and some model locomotives, are often mounted on the trucks, so the couplers move in the same direction that the truck and wheels move. This permits the cars to negotiate relatively sharp curves. On the real railroads, where curves are much wider, couplers are mounted on the frame of the car itself, independent of the trucks and wheels.

Second, Large Scale knuckle couplers—the type that most closely resemble prototype railroad couplers—are generally not true to the scale of their real-life brethren. Almost all are at least twice the size of standard knuckle couplers used by railroads in the United States.

Finally, another characteristic of Large Scale couplers that distinguishes them from the prototype relates to compatibility, or the lack of it, between different brands. Certain types of couplers offered by different Large Scale manufacturers may or may not mate well, depending on, first, the type of coupler being used and, second, on who manufactured the cars you are planning to couple. This will all become a bit clearer if we first examine the most common types of couplers used in Large Scale model railroading.

Basically, the locomotives and cars you purchase will come equipped with one or the other of two types of couplers, although the second type may also be packaged separately with the item:

The first type of Large Scale coupler is known as the hook-and-loop type. As the name implies, hook-and-loop couplers consist of a rigid horizontal loop section and a movable hook that is shaped like an "L" lying on its side, with the short hooked end facing up. The hook is held firmly against its corresponding loop, as well as the loop of any car coupled to this car, by spring tension. Cars provided by certain manufacturers may come equipped with a complete hook-and-loop assembly at both ends of the car, while others are supplied with a hook-and-loop at one end, and just a loop at the other end. The latter type is a bit easier to work with when uncoupling, simply because only one hook needs to be depressed to separate the two cars. This can be done by hand, or by means of a spring-loaded uncoupling ramp that fits between the track ties at whatever location you want uncoupling activity to occur. If both adjoining couplers happen to be complete hook-and-loop types, it's a bit harder disengage the couplers by hand, since both hooks must be depressed at the same time—a difficult feat to accomplish on two closely coupled cars. Two uncoupling ramps, placed end to end, can also be used in this instance.

The hook-and-loop couplers are somewhat universal, and they generally perform both consistently and reliably, regardless of who made them. That's all well and good, because it sure helps to avoid a lot of train wrecks! However, there is a down side to this universal compatibility: Hook-and-loop couplers don't really look at all prototypical! The fact is, you'll never see a real train, in this country or elsewhere, equipped with anything that quite resembles a hook-and-loop coupler. As your involvement in model railroading increases, you're apt to become increasingly dissatisfied with this non-prototypical appearance. Another problem with the hook-and-loop is that it generally precludes you from being able to "shunt" an uncoupled car in order to move it into a siding, or elsewhere. As soon as the locomotive or car doing the shunting contacts the shunted car, the two will couple, and you're right back where you started!

The second type of Large Scale coupler is the knuckle coupler. Knuckle couplers are very similar in design and function to the standard couplers seen on all locomotives and cars in the United States, and they generally avoid both of the difficulties associated with hook-and-loop couplers. So named because they resemble a hand closed make a fist, when viewed from above, the knuckle coupler has been a part of prototype railroading since the late nineteenth century, when it replaced the old link-and-pin couplers that had caused injury or death to a great many brakemen in the years preceding its development.

Knuckle couplers are certainly the way to go if you want your train to "look right" in that visually obvious respect, and they do make it easier to accomplish switching moves because some types will not automatically lock whenever they contact another coupler. Furthermore, in many instances today, knuckle couplers come either attached to, or supplied with, many Large Scale locomotives and cars, so you may not have to rush out and buy a new set of couplers. For example, nearly all USA Trains, Aristo-Craft, Bachmann, and Lionel Large Scale products come from the factory with knuckle couplers, along with a separate pair of hook-and-loop couplers for those who wish to convert to that option. Nevertheless, all is not sunshine and roses in knuckle-coupler land! Although most knuckle couplers from the various manufacturers look very much alike, there really are no industry-wide standards for these devices in Large Scale model railroading, and there are minor variations between different products which cause some makes of couplers to not mate easily or properly with other makes.

Actually, many, if not most, of the knuckle couplers offered today will fit together, if you don't mind using the "five finger method"—meaning your hand—to fiddle with them a bit while performing the coupling

Kadee couplers mounted on a whimsical passenger car that was scratchbuilt by Gary Buchanan. Gary used parts left over from another project, and mounted the car on an Aristo-Craft heavyweight passenger car wheelset. This car is used by the Raccoon Creek & Gully Railway's president during his inspection trips.
Photo courtesy of Gary Buchanan

and/or uncoupling operation. The problem is that certain brands may not couple properly if you gently "bump" the cars together, much as the real railroads do. So, what should you do if you really don't want to contend with this brand-incompatibility problem?

One realistic solution is to select a specific brand of knuckle coupler, and then stay with that brand. Say, for example, that most of the rolling stock on your roster is comprised of Aristo-Craft cars. If that's the case, you may want to consider converting any non-Aristo-Craft locomotive and cars over to Aristo-Craft couplers. The coupler assemblies are available from most manufacturers as stock parts, and replacing couplers on most rolling stock and many locomotives is a procedure that usually requires only a few basic tools and a few minutes of your time.

Another solution employed by some garden railroaders, especially those who prefer things to be as prototypical as possible, is to convert all couplers, on locomotives and cars alike, to Kadee brand couplers. Kadee is a firm whose primary business is couplers for model railroad equipment in all scales from Z scale to Large Scale, and everything in between. Kadee offers Large Scale couplers in two sizes: #1 gauge and "G" gauge. The #1 gauge couplers are somewhat smaller, and are often preferred by those modeling in 1:29 scale or 1:32 scale, but both sizes look very much alike, both are very reliable, and both operate in the same way. Kadee also offers a choice between truck-mounted couplers and body-mounted couplers. Body-mounted couplers are what the real railroads use, and they do allow the cars to couple more closely together, but some modification to your rolling stock may be necessary if you choose to

go that route. Be aware, too, that body-mounted couplers generally require wide-radius curves, and that may be an important consideration if you decide to convert to this type of coupler after your railroad has already been constructed.

Kadee couplers generally resemble most other knuckle couplers, but they also possess a unique and very useful automatic uncoupling feature. The couplers are fitted with a curved metal rod—more or less resembling a disconnected air hose on a real railroad car—which extends down from the bottom. A permanent magnet, which can be easily placed and anchored just about anywhere along the track (although along straight sections is best), is the second necessary component of Kadee's automatic uncoupling system. When two cars equipped with Kadee couplers are stopped over one of these magnets; then shunted backwards just a bit to allow for some slack; the force field of the magnet pulls on the metal rods, offsetting them to each side, and the couplers disengage. Once the couplers are released, they will snap aside even further and remain in that position so the uncoupled car can then be shunted or spotted on a siding, or wherever.

Regardless of which type of coupler system you prefer, and no matter whether you elect to use plastic or metal wheels, or even a combination of the two, you'll find a large assortment of rolling stock items available in Large Scale, and you'll also soon discover that, irrespective of scale differences, most of these cars will look just fine operating together in your garden setting. Furthermore, the variety of durable, reliable, and attractive freight and passenger cars available keeps growing, almost on a daily basis.

A hard-charging K-4 Pacific locomotive glides along a sweeping curve on Charles Bednarik's "Triple-R Route" garden railroad. Employing the widest possible curves on any model railroad—particularly when long locomotives such as this 4-6-2 are part of the roster—adds aesthetic appeal in addition to enhancing smooth operations.
Photo courtesy of Charles Bednarik

Chapter 6

TRACK AND TURNOUTS FOR GARDEN RAILROADS

It's probably safe to say that properly constructed, supported, and maintained trackwork is the single most important consideration in creating a reliably operating and trouble-free model railroad, regardless of scale.

Without track, there can be no railroad. Without well-constructed trackwork, there can be no smoothly functioning railroad—a situation that both the real railroads and the modeled variety can ill-afford. With that in mind, it's a good idea to exercise care and good judgment in selecting track components that will perform well on your railroad, and in the prevailing conditions of your particular climate and geographic location.

As was noted earlier, the track most commonly used for garden railroading in the United States and many other nations is gauged at 45mm (approximately 1-3/4 inches) between the running rails. This track is designated #1 Gauge, a term applied to that 45mm track gauge by the German firm, Märklin, many years ago. You may also hear it sometimes referred to as "G Gauge" track, although that description is used more for convenience than accuracy. For the purposes of our discussion here, we'll continue to refer to it as #1 Gauge track, which, in fact, is what it really is.

The #1 Gauge track commonly used in garden railroading generally conforms to the profile of prototype railroad track. That is, most of what is offered and intended for outdoor use consists of solid metal rails (with some exceptions) which are more or less T-shaped, when viewed from the end. The distinguishing difference between prototype and model track lies in the supporting structure for the rails.

Real railroad rails are anchored to wood or (more recently) concrete ties to maintain the proper rail spacing, while commercially available #1 Gauge model rails are most often affixed to plastic ties. The use of plastic is dictated by the requirement that the model track, if it is to be used outdoors, be able to withstand the prolonged effects of exposure to the elements, and even an occasional tramping-on by human or animal feet or paws. In the small segments needed for #1 Gauge track ties, plastic simply holds up better than wood, over time. Likewise, where real railroads use metal fittings such as spikes and fishplates, etc. to anchor the rails firmly to the ties, #1 Gauge model track most often uses plastic fittings molded into the ties to accomplish this important task.

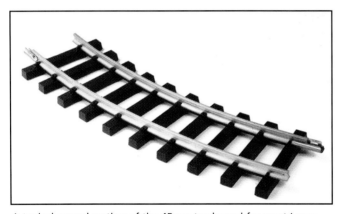

A typical curved section of the 45mm track used for most Large Scale garden railroads. This example is from the track assortment offered by USA Trains.
Photo courtesy of USA Trains

Even if you're new to the model railroading hobby, you may already be aware that most electric train sets—the type you may have placed around your own Christmas tree over the years, for example—come complete with a number of pre-made and pre-formed sec-

tions of track that are designed to join together to form a complete circle, or perhaps even a simple oval. Logically enough, this is called *sectional track*, and it is available for model trains in all scales and gauges, including #1 Gauge.

Sectional track is by far the most common type of track used in model railroading, because it is readily available and is the easiest to work with in most situations. This is as true of garden railroading's 45mm #1 Gauge track as it is of track made for other scales. Nevertheless, sectional track is not the only type of model railroad track that you might use, and it does have its limitations, so it's useful at this point to compare sectional track with the alternatives, and to consider the respective advantages or disadvantages of each type. First, though, let's take a look at the most common materials from which typical garden railroad (#1 Gauge) track is made.

• Types of rails

Brass rail

Brass is a very good conductor of electricity and it is relatively inexpensive, hence its popularity as the material-of-choice for affordable model railroad track. Brass rail exhibits a kind of shiny gold color when it is new, but exposure to the elements tends to "weather" it to a pleasingly acceptable dull brownish-gold color that approximates the rusted look that prototype steel rails acquire even before they are spiked in place. Brass also accepts solder well, and, as you shall see, this can be an important consideration when it comes to constructing a track-powered outdoor railroad.

A disadvantage of brass rail is its only-moderate resistance to oxidation—the natural molecular change that occurs in metal exposed to the elements and pollution in the environment. Oxidation affects conductivity, and the oxidation that forms on brass is non-conductive, which means that the railheads must be cleaned and shined on a fairly regular basis to remove the oxidized coating. You can largely avoid that problem by resorting to batteries to power your trains, or by operating live steam locomotives, but both of those solutions can add to the start-up expense for those who are new to the hobby.

Most "starter sets" in Large Scale come complete with enough sections of brass track to form a complete circle or an oval. If you're looking for the most affordable and available type of track for your garden railroad—and track that is relatively easy to work with—you may very well want to stick with solid-brass sectional track.

Nickel Silver rail

In the smaller model railroading scales, nickel silver track—there's no actual silver in it—is far-and-away the preferred type. Although it is not nearly as conductive as brass in terms of its ability to pass an unrestricted flow of electric current, nickel silver rail is somewhat more resistant to oxidation, which adversely affects conductivity, and it can easily be soldered. Additionally, unlike brass oxidation, the oxidation that forms on nickel silver is conductive, and is, therefore, less of a problem. Nickel silver track is a shiny silver color when new, but it normally weathers down to a dull silverish tone.

The major disadvantage of nickel silver track, as far as #1 Gauge track is concerned, is its relatively high cost. At the present time, only a few manufacturers offer nickel silver track in #1 Gauge, and the high manufacturing costs must ultimately be passed along to the consumer, resulting in considerably more expensive rails on a per-foot basis.

Stainless steel rail

In recent years, #1 Gauge track made of stainless steel has appeared on the scene. The primary advantage of stainless steel is its high resistance to oxidation, which results in less operator time being devoted to keeping the railheads clean. Although stainless steel track is more expensive than brass track, it is not nearly as expensive as nickel silver. Aristo-Craft recently introduced a line of stainless steel sectional track, and the ready availability and growing acceptance of these components is likely to bring stainless steel track prices more in line with the cost of brass track.

On the downside, stainless steel track is not as good an electrical conductor as either brass or nickel silver. Moreover, stainless steel is highly resistant to soldering, and this is an important consideration for many garden railroaders who prefer to solder jumper wires across each rail joint of their permanent track installations. These "jumpers" assure a more reliable flow of current from one track section to the next. The use of jumper wires will be discussed in more detail further along in this section.

Aluminum rail

Aluminum is a relatively "soft" metal when compared to brass, nickel silver, or especially stainless steel, but it is nevertheless suitable for most model railroad applications. Dull gray in color both when new and when it weathers, aluminum track is a good conductor of electricity, and it is the least expensive of all the track types. These two advantages can be a real benefit to modelers planning large garden railroads.

Perhaps the major disadvantage of aluminum track is that it cannot be soldered. Although soldering is not always required or necessary in building a garden railroad, the ability to hold a soldered joint is important to those garden railroaders who prefer to solder jumper wires across each track joint to help assure more dependable operation. If you decide to use aluminum rail, you'll probably want to consider applying rail clamps to each joint in lieu of the soldered jumpers. Aluminum also oxidizes rapidly, but the resulting oxide

layer is quite thin, so those who operate trains on a regular basis should experience few problems with oxide buildup. Another disadvantage that should be considered, depending on the region you live in, is that aluminum tends to expand and contract more in temperature extremes, and this can lead to warped rails or loose rail joints. Aluminum also tends to become brittle in extremely low winter temperatures, and this can lead to fractures or breaking. Finally, the relative "softness" of aluminum results in rails that are not as robust as their brass, stainless steel, or nickel silver counterparts.

• Types of track

Now that we have examined the metals customarily used in the manufacture of the rails for #1 Gauge track, it's appropriate to take a look at the alternative forms in which this track can be purchased.

Sectional track

As was noted earlier, sectional track is the most common type of track used in model railroading, regardless of scale. Sectional track is certainly what you'll find when you purchase a complete "starter set" in any of the popular scales.

A typical Large Scale starter set, such as this one from LGB, usually comes complete with enough track sections to form a circle or a small oval.
Photo courtesy of Charles Bednarik and Star Hobby

Sectional track for #1 Gauge is offered by nearly all of the leading manufacturers, although LGB, Aristo-Craft, and USA Trains track items tend to dominate the garden railroading scene. The track components made by these significant players in the Large Scale arena are largely interchangeable, and they look pretty much alike in most respects. Be aware, though, that some sectional track has U.S.-style ties and tie spacing (smaller ties, spaced closer together), while others have European-style ties and tie spacing (wider ties, spaced further apart), so you can generally stick with one manufacturer's product or go ahead and conveniently mix the different brands.

Most of the sectional track packaged with Large Scale starter sets is manufactured in segments that measure about one-foot in length for the straight sections. Be advised, however, that a wide variety of both shorter and longer sections are also available. Longer sections can be conveniently used to reduce the number of rail joints--always a good thing on lengthy straight segments of your railroad. The shorter-than-one-foot sections are customarily called "filler sections," and they can be employed wherever needed—to widen curves, for example, or to fill a small gap left when that final section of track to be laid is just a bit too long. LGB even offers a short expandable track section for use in that last odd gap where nothing else seems to fit.

Curved sectional track in #1 Gauge is available in a variety of radii. For some undetermined reason, Large Scale manufacturers tend to label their track products in terms of the diameter of a full circle, rather than radius, whereas the standard for measuring the curvature of model railroad track in other scales is based almost solely on radius. The diameter of a circle of #1 gauge track is measured, in inches or in millimeters, from the center of the track (between the rails) on one side of a complete circle to the center of the track directly opposite (180-degrees from) that initial measuring point. Large Scale starter sets normally come complete with enough curved sections (usually twelve) to form a full circle of about four feet in diameter. The number of curved sections needed to form a complete circle can vary, depending on the diameter of the circle itself. Four-foot, five-foot, and ten-foot diameter circles generally require 12 sections of track in the proper radius, while eight-foot and twenty-foot diameter circles are usually made up of 16 sections. Knowing just how many curved sections to buy may come in handy if you plan to construct a circle somewhat larger than what was provided with your starter set.

When it comes to curves on your model railroad, be it in the garden or elsewhere, bigger is almost always better! In other words, you should strive to create the largest-diameter curves that your available space will allow. Short, two-axle locomotives and cars will certainly be able to navigate four-foot diameter or tighter

curves, but all locomotives and rolling stock will look a whole lot better, and will often perform more reliably, on eight-foot, ten-foot, or even wider diameter curves. Larger and longer locomotives and rolling stock definitely require wider curves—the widest you can possibly give them—in most instances.

The German firm, LGB, had a long-standing policy that all of its train items be able to navigate the firm's smallest four-foot diameter curved sections. That policy may even still be in effect, but most of the larger locomotives—as well as the long passenger and freight cars—offered by LGB and others sure look awfully silly when they're negotiating such tight curves. And, a few of the more modern diesel locomotives offered by USA Trains, among others, specify on the packaging labels that eight-foot diameter or even ten-foot diameter curves are needed for proper operation. It's worth repeating again: Always use the largest-diameter curves that your layout will allow!

The major disadvantage of sectional track, if that is what you intend to use, is that the layout must be constructed to conform to the restrictions imposed by the pre-formed curved sections. There's little option for "customizing" the configuration to more precisely fit the existing landscape.

Another disadvantage in using sectional track— especially in short sections— is that the multitude of slip-on rail joiners on the ends of each track section can be a source of potential power-loss problems. For outdoor use, in particular, the application of a coating of conductive grease on each rail joiner before the track is put in place is highly recommended. Suitable conductive grease or paste is available from any LGB or Aristo-Craft dealer, or from your local electrical, builder supply, or automotive parts store. The conductive grease helps to inhibit corrosion, and to assure the uninterrupted flow of electricity. In fact, as has previously been noted, many experienced garden railroaders take things one step further, and in addition to using conductive grease, they also solder jumper wires around each rail joint. This allows the joints to expand and contract slightly with temperature changes, while still assuring a continuous flow of current. Garden railroaders who do not relish the thought of soldering jumpers across each joint may resort to special rail clamps, also coated with conductive grease, that screw onto the ends of adjoining sections to provide a secure connection. However, the rail clamp alternative can be a somewhat expensive proposition if you're building a large layout.

If you're building your first garden railroad—and that is really what this book is all about—sectional track is probably the easiest, fastest, and most affordable way to go because it's relatively inexpensive, easy to work with, and quite reliable as long as all of the connections are secure. Additionally, you can always replace all or part of your sectional trackwork with flex-track or hand-laid track sometime later on as your needs and interests evolve.

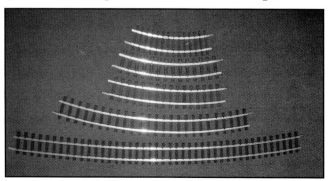

Curved section of 45mm track in five radii: (from top) 2', 2.5', 4', 8', and 10'.
Photo courtesy of Charles Bednarik and Star Hobby

Flex-track

Flexible track is offered by several #1 Gauge track manufacturers. "Flex-track," as it is commonly known, generally comes in five-foot or longer lengths, with the ties packaged separately in strips that can be slid onto the rails after they have been bent to the desired curvature. To be sure, flex-track isn't quite as flexible as the term may imply. It can be bent by hand if you're strong enough, wear a pair of heavy gloves, and devise a template of some sort to define the required curvature, but the much easier way to bend flex-track is to remove the individual rails and use a specially designed rail-bending tool to handle the bending chore. These rail benders are somewhat costly to purchase, but they're well worth the investment if flex-track is what you want to use in any significant way. You may also be able to locate an experienced garden railroader in your area, or perhaps a local garden railroad club, willing to lend you a rail-bending tool for a short period of time.

The primary advantage of flex-track is that it can be custom bent to just about any curvature needed for trackwork that must conform to existing obstacles at the garden railroad site. Another advantage is that a single long length of flex-track, or longer lengths of regular sectional track, can be used to replace several shorter pieces of sectional track, thereby reducing the total number of rail joints on the railroad—always a very good thing! In fact, longer lengths of sectional track can easily be "converted" into flex-track by simply removing the ties; bending the rails to the desired configuration; and then reinserting the ties.

Del Tapparo uses a rail-bending tool, mounted on a small workbench, to form curves for the D&L Lines garden railroad. A finished section can be seen in the foreground. The construction of the D&L is also detailed in Chapter 9.
Photo courtesy of Del Tapparo

When you use flex-track, you'll need to first bend each of the individual rails to the desired curvature (unless you're using the track for a straight section, of course) and then slide the rails back onto the ties—a simple task because rail-holding "spikes" are already molded into each tie. Some additional trimming (cutting) of the inside rail of a flex-track curve will also be necessary, because that rail, when bent, will end up being somewhat longer than the outside rail. A hacksaw, razor saw, or motor tool with cutting disk will do the job nicely (be sure to wear eye protection when cutting anything with a power tool). You'll also need to file the cut ends smooth to eliminate any burrs, and then you're ready to go!

Aside from the expense of purchasing a rail-bending tool (if you can't borrow one), and the work involved in actually bending the rails and getting everything ready for placement on the roadbed, there are no real disadvantages to using flex-track on your railroad. In any case, the advantages far outweigh the disadvantages, especially if you have a track plan that you are happy with and intend to keep in place for a long time.

Hand-laid track

The best-looking—meaning most realistic—trackwork you can possibly construct on your garden railroad features track that you construct yourself. Although not really recommended for the first-time garden railroader unless he or she has employed the technique in some other modeling scale, hand-laid track provides all of the advantages of flex-track, plus the more true-to-prototype appearance that results from using real wood ties affixed to the rails with miniature rail spikes. It's about as close to real railroad track as you can possibly get in the modeling world since the materials and techniques are pretty much the same.

As with flex-track, you'll need a rail-bending tool to curve the rails of your hand-laid track. In addition, you'll also need several (at least two, and preferably three or more) high-quality rail gauges to help assure proper alignment and spacing of the rails before you spike them down. And, you'll also need spiking pliers or a similar tool to drive the spikes home. All of these items are available from suppliers listed in the appendices of this book.

The step-by-step procedures for hand-laying track won't be covered here, based on the assumption that the novice garden railroader is far more likely to start out with sectional or flex-track, or a combination of the two. If hand-laying track appears to be something you might like to tackle, you would be well advised to gather the "raw materials" described above; obtain a short length of rail along with some wood ties and spikes; and then try your hand at mastering the techniques. Again, consult an experienced modeler and/or the web sites and suppliers listed in this book for more details relating to equipment you'll need and the best techniques to use.

A pair of hand-laid turnouts constructed by Gary Buchanan. The rail is Code 330 aluminum, which has been spiked to pressure-treated ties with stainless steel spikes. Pictured at left is a wide-radius curved turnout, and the photo on the right depicts a three-way turnout.
Photo courtesy of Gary Buchanan

that even though all Large Scale trains will operate satisfactorily on Code 332 rail, some trains will not perform properly on smaller rail sizes because the wheel flanges on some commercially available Large Scale locomotives and cars may be too deep, causing the equipment to bounce along on the spike heads and/or ties. For that reason, it's probably best to start out your garden railroading activity with the "norm"—Code 332 rail, in this case. You can always switch to a smaller profile rail once you've gained some experience in the hobby, and have had a chance to experiment a bit to determine that the wheel flanges on your favorite locomotives and cars will clear the spikes and ties on a smaller rail. If not, you'll have some serious reworking or replacement of wheels to attend to!

• Track sizes

If you're just starting out in Large Scale model railroading, and have purchased a starter set and perhaps some extra track from one of the leading manufacturers, chances are that the track you now have on hand is equipped with what is known as Code 332 rail. This number designates the height of the actual model rail, in thousands of an inch. Code 332 rail is considerably larger in scale than it should be to represent prototype railroad track, but it was intentionally designed this way to meet the requirement for a substantial track size that would hold up well under the changing and sometimes adverse conditions that an outdoor model railroad is subject to. Code 332 rail truly is tough, durable, and long-lasting (LGB even depicted an elephant standing on it in one of their advertisements), and it has become something of a standard for the majority of Large Scale garden railroads in the U.S. and elsewhere.

However, you should also be aware that Large Scale rail is also available in other, smaller sizes, including Code 250, Code 215, and Code 197. Märklin, for example, packages its MAXI line of Large Scale starter sets with the firm's smaller Code 250 #1 Gauge track. Although the smaller rail size has a more true-to-prototype appearance, and can certainly be used outdoors, it's important to keep in mind that the smaller rails are not as tough and durable as the significantly larger Code 332 rail. In addition, you also need to be aware

• Ties

Ties are the essential devices that hold rails in proper alignment—an absolutely critical function. The rails are generally held in place on the ties by means of L-shaped metal spikes, the heads of which grip the rail when the pointed shank of the spike is driven into the tie. On prototype railroads, ties are generally made of creosote-treated wood, although increasing numbers of major railroads now use cast-concrete ties, similar to what you may have seen on most urban light-rail systems, because they last much longer.

Not all ties are created equal! In the very early days of railroading, ties were often made of irregular roughly-hewn logs that could vary in width, depth, length, and even the spacing between individual ties. Contemporary wood ties (and their concrete cousins), are generally uniform in size and spacing on a given railroad, but be advised that many overseas rail lines use ties of a different size and with different spacing.

In the world of Large Scale garden railroading, the ties most often seen on model track are made of plastic, with a molded-in wood-grain effect. This is almost universally true of sectional track, although both plastic and real wood ties (generally redwood), are available for those who might prefer flex-track or hand-laid track. Plastic ties are normally molded in color and form to closely resemble wood, but the plastic sheen, particularly when new, reveals their true composition.

In buying additional ready-made track to expand your garden railroad, you'll want to make sure that the spacing of ties matches that of your existing trackwork. Some manufacturers offer both "American-type" and "European-type" track, and although the rails are the

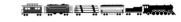

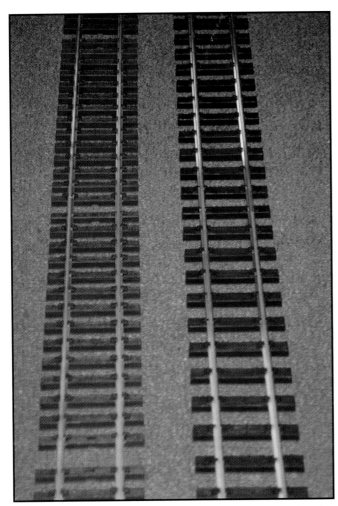

Comparison of Code 332 rail fitted with U.S.-style ties (left) and European-style ties (right). The U.S.-style ties are more square in shape, and are spaced closer together.
Photo courtesy of Charles Bednarik and Star Hobby

same in all respects, the ties of the European-type track may be wider than those used on the American-type track, and the European ties may also be spaced further apart. It's fine to use all of one or the other type, regardless of whether you are modeling an American or European railroad, but things won't look quite right if you try to mix the two.

• Roadbed and ballast

In the real world of railroading, track is constructed on a packed-earth sub-roadbed topped with a roadbed comprised of loose crushed rock or cinders that measure from about one to three inches or so in diameter. The rock material used may vary from one geographic region to another, and be dependent on such factors as availability and the weight of loads to be carried over the rails, but the basic functions of all roadbed materials are pretty much the same: To provide a level load-bearing surface; to evenly distribute the weight of passing rail traffic; and to provide for adequate drainage.

Properly done, a garden railroad's roadbed serves much the same purpose. It provides a firm and level surface that supports the trackwork and trains, and it helps to promote proper drainage and inhibit erosion. For that reason, many, if not most, garden railroads feature a raised, ballasted roadbed that is constructed much like the real-life counterpart. The major visible difference is that garden railroad ballast is much smaller and lighter than its prototype, and it is more easily displaced by the actions of wind and rain. In fact, if the ballast on our garden railroads was made true-to-scale, the individual rocks would only measure about 1/32" to 1/8" in diameter. From a practical point of view, this is a bit too small for most outdoor situations, and somewhat larger-than-scale 1/4" diameter rocks are more often used because they tend to stay in place whole a lot better when pounded by heavy rains or winds.

It's worth repeating several times over that a properly ballasted roadbed to support your track network is fundamental to smooth and reliable operations. All that you do to assure the proper alignment of your track, and the uninterrupted conductivity of electricity through it (assuming track power is the way you choose to go) will be to little or no avail if the track's supporting foundation—the sub-roadbed and ballasted roadbed in this case—isn't able to support and distribute the train's weight, and hold together properly despite being subjected to rain, snow, wind, and other natural occurrences.

Over the years, various ballast materials have been tried and tested by garden railroaders throughout the nation and around the world. These include such things as crushed rock, chicken grit (crushed granite), and commercially available model railroad ballast, among other materials. What works best for you may depend on several variables, including climate, seasonal changes or the lack thereof, and the materials most readily available in your particular area. For outdoor use, the manufactured model railroad ballast materials are undoubtedly the least practical and most expensive way to go because their small (albeit correct-to-scale) size may be something of a disadvantage in wet climates where the ballast will tend to blow around and wash away.

Many garden railroaders consider crushed rock to be the best ballast material—after all, that's also what the real railroads use, in much larger chunks, of course. Crushed rock of the type best suited to a garden railway is normally available at any local quarry, although it may be known by one of several names: Crusher Fines, Screenings, Quarter Minus, #5, or some other name. We'll refer to them all as "Crusher Fines" here, since that seems to be the most common nomenclature.

Crusher Fines are the combination of rocks and rock dust that remains after the larger mined rocks or slabs have been crushed and refined. Crusher Fines come in a variety of colors, depending on the type of rock that produced them, but any color will do as long

Nicely-ballasted trackwork on Ronald Wenger's still-under-construction Apple Valley Railway. Crusher fines, which are available in most areas, provide near-scale ballast that holds together well over time. Granite chicken grit is another good ballast material.
Photo courtesy of Ronald L. Wenger

as it pleases you and isn't particularly garish. Fines also come in a variety of sizes, and what you're looking for are small Crusher Fines, with individual rocks measuring about 1/4" or so in diameter.

The most important consideration in selecting Crusher Fines, or any other material that you choose to use for ballast, is that the material you select not be smooth, round, or polished. Small pieces of rock with sharp, irregular edges are really what want because these pieces will tend to bind together as they settle, yet still allow for proper drainage. This ability to self-bind will save you much time and effort in re-ballasting the roadbed later on.

• All about turnouts

In the world of model railroading, the proper designation for the device that enables one set of tracks to smoothly and safely merge with another set of tracks is *turnout*. Turnouts are what enable the model railroad to have spur (dead-end) sidings, passing sidings, and converging (or diverging) branch lines. Turnouts are often called "switches" in the modeling world (and, indeed, that's what they are known as in real-world railroad-

ing), but that term may easily be confused with an electrical switch, such as an ordinary on/off switch or a three-way toggle switch, so it's best to start out with the correct terminology, and then stick with it!

You can certainly construct a fine garden railroad without installing a single turnout, but these devices add operational capabilities and variety to your railroad. Ultimately, they add to the fun you can have by enabling you to operate more like the rail railroads do. For that reason, it's useful to consider incorporating turnouts in your garden layout—perhaps just two or three for a passing siding and a spur at the start, and more later on as your interests and needs develop.

As previously noted, the function of a turnout in both real railroading and model railroading is to allow a train to safely pass from one track to another. That being the case, at least two track systems are normally incorporated in every turnout—one set for the through route (normally straight), and one set for the diverging route (normally curved). There are even some more complex variations of turnouts available, such as the "three-way" type and "double-slip" type, but those are somewhat beyond the scope of this entry-level book.

You can best think of the *through track* as the mainline track—the route that the train would follow if no turnout was positioned at that particular location. The other track is the curved *diverging track*, so named because it is diverging from (or merging with) the through track at the turnout's location. If the diverging track branches off to the left side of the through track, when viewed from the entry (single track) end of the turnout, that turnout is called a left-hand turnout. If the diverging track branches off to the right, it's obviously a right-hand turnout.

Several essential components are part of every turnout, no matter how simple or complex, with the frog and the points being, perhaps, the two most obvious ones.

The *frog* is a fixture so-named because it more or less resembles a flattened-out reptilian critter of the same name. Normally constructed of forged steel on the prototype railroads, and of metal, plastic, or cast resin on model turnouts, the frog is the device that guides flanged wheels smoothly from one track routing to the other without leaving a significant break or gap in either route.

The *points* consist of a properly gauged pair of movable rails, beveled at one end to fit tightly against the stock rails, and pivoted at the other end so they can be shifted to align either for the through route or the diverging route. Movement of the points may be initiated manually, mechanically, or electrically by means of a *throw bar* on both the real railroads as well as on their modeled counterparts.

Stock rail is the term applied to the actual running rails of a turnout. A normal turnout with one diverging track would have a total of four stock rails, with the innermost stock rails ending at the frog. In prototype railroading the inner rails from the frog to the points themselves are called *closure rails*.

Other important components of a turnout are the *guard rails* that keep the flanges of passing wheels in the proper orientation and alignment for safe passage through the frog. And, of course, there is the necessary linkage that connects the throw bar and its movable points to a *switch stand* (hand-operated), or to mechanical or electrically controlled mechanisms some distance away so the turnout can actually be positioned for one route or the other. It is, by the way, called a "switch stand," and not a "turnout stand" even in model railroading!

In the world of garden railroading, an important consideration you'll face when it comes time to acquire your first turnout is the size of the turnout. In this case, size does not refer to the physical dimensions of the turnout, but rather to the angle determined by the frog and/or the degree of curvature of the diverging route.

In most railroading—real world and model—a turnout's size is determined by the angle established by the turnout's frog. The higher the number the better, in nearly every instance. Prototype turnouts are generally No. 12, No. 16, No. 20, or even higher. In the world of Large Scale and garden railroading, things are a whole

lot tighter, with most ready-made turnouts ranging from a No. 2 to a No. 4.5. The curved portion of a No. 2 turnout, for example, is designed to match a "normal" curved section of LGB or Aristo-Craft two-foot radius (four-foot diameter), track. A No. 3.5 turnout matches the four-foot radius (eight-foot diameter), commercially available curved sections, and a No. 4.5 turnout conforms with the five-foot radius (ten-foot diameter), sections. As is readily apparent, these turnouts are really a whole lot tighter than even the tightest prototype railroad turnout!

Again, the thing to keep in mind is the higher the number, the less severe the curvature of the diverging route, so you should always try to use the highest number (widest radius) turnout you can fit into the space you have available!

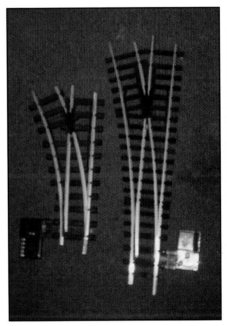

A typical small-radius turnout (left), and large-radius turnout (right). These two turnouts are representative of the ready-made products that are currently available. If you desire or need special curvatures for your turnouts, you may need to hand-lay some yourself, as Gary Buchanan did in the examples illustrated earlier. *Photo courtesy of Charles Bednarik and Star Hobby*

If this seems a bit perplexing, don't be overly concerned! Basically, if ready-made turnouts are your choice, you'll find only two general categories in the world of Large Scale model railroading: "normal" turnouts and "wide radius" turnouts, in both left-hand and right-hand versions, with perhaps an occasional design variation—a "Y" turnout or a "double-slip" turnout, for example—for use in special applications. Use the "normal" turnouts on your layout if space is at a premium, and use the "wide radius" turnouts—as wide as you can get—if/where space is not a major concern. Just remember to take the size of your turnouts—as well as their location—into account in planning your railroad.

Another choice you will face is how to activate or "throw" your turnouts. There are three common ways to do this: by hand, or remotely, by electric current or compressed air.

Many garden railroaders choose not to fuss with wiring their turnouts for remote control, preferring instead to follow along with their train and throw the

turnout lever by hand. There's absolutely nothing wrong with this approach, because it does provide the opportunity to observe the trains from different vantage points, and to gain a little exercise in the process. Hand-throwing the turnouts works especially well if there are few turnouts to operate on the layout, and, most importantly, if all of the turnouts are accessible from outside the perimeter of the layout area. You don't want to be tramping through your creative landscaping in order to divert the Silverton Limited into a passing siding, and risk damaging the scenery or a structure or two in the process. So, if you do plan to stay with hand-thrown turnouts, be sure to take this into account in the early planning stages, when the railroad is still a vision on a sheet of graph paper.

Electric-powered turnouts are another viable option, and they allow the operator to activate the turnout from a remote location, either through conventional wiring linked to a switch box of some sort, or by means of radio control. Both LGB and Aristo-Craft turnouts, for example, come either fitted with an electric activation capability, or they may easily be fitted with the appropriate device. If you do elect to remotely control your turnouts, you'll need to plan for buried conduit or coated wire to make the necessary connections from your power source to the turnout motor.

Again, this is another consideration that should be weighed in the track planning phase of garden railroad development.

A third alternative, which is basically the creation of a firm called Del-Aire Products, makes use of compressed air, passed through flexible tubing of the type used for home aquarium filtration systems, to activate an "Air Motor," which, in turn, causes the points on the turnout to move. When air compressed to 40 psi is passed through the line, the points are thrown, and then held there. When there is no pressure in the air line, a spring returns the points to their most-used position (usually the straight route). The pressurized air can be supplied by a compressor equipped with a regulator, or by bottles of compressed air. The "Air Motor" is small, and has only one moving part, so it is easy to conceal and maintain. Del-Aire's system was originally developed for conventional indoor model railroading scales, but it is very capable of handling the more rugged requirements of Large Scale railroading in the great outdoors. Since the system does rely on air tubing to function, this tubing, like electrical wiring, needs to be buried in conduit of some type. In recent years, increasing numbers of garden railroaders have turned to this innovative turnout activation system, and have reported good results.

Ready to lay some track? One good way to check alignment is to get your head down as close to track level as possible, and sight along the rails. Any kinks, bends, or curvature will be readily apparent. There doesn't appear to be a problem on this section of Peter Thornton's line!
Photo courtesy of Peter Thornton

• Track-laying and turnout tips

Following are a few useful tips that will help you achieve solid, dependable, and long-lasting trackwork. Several of these tips may cover points that have already been discussed, but they're well worth repeating again because they are critical to successful track-laying and, thereafter, consistently reliable operations.

• *Keep things straight, tightly joined, and level.*

Throughout the process of track laying, take time to assure that each section you put in place is as level as possible, both from end-to-end and from side-to-side, and tightly fitted to its adjacent sections on both ends. If you're laying a long, straight section of track anywhere on your railroad, place your eye down as close to the railheads as possible, and sight along that stretch of track from one end to the other, and/or from both directions anywhere in between. Any bends or kinks, however slight, will be readily visible, and this time-tested method for assuring straight trackwork is as reliable as any more scientific method.

• *Provide adequate spacing between parallel tracks, and between the track and any trackside objects.*

If you plan to have tracks running parallel to each other at any point on your railroad, you'll need to allow for adequate separation between the adjacent tracks to avoid having passing trains sideswipe each other. At minimum, allow for 6-1/2" between straight sections of parallel trackwork (measured from the center of one track to the center of the adjacent track), and increase the separation even more on curved sections. Before running any trains on this parallel trackwork, take a few pieces of your longest rolling stock, and/or a couple of your longest locomotives, and give them a slow hand-assisted "test run" over the track to assure that everything will clear properly.

You'll also want to pay attention to how close to the track you place any structures, signals, or other trackside objects. As a rule, you should allow for 2-1/2" from the center of the track to the near edge of the object along straight sections, and about 3-1/2" from the center of the track to the near edge of trackside objects on curves.

• *Check to assure that you have sufficient vertical clearance at tunnel entrances, bridges, and the like.*

Generally, about 9" of vertical clearance, measured from the railheads to the lowest point of the object in question, will work well enough, unless you are planning to operate modern "high-stack" cars or other especially high items of rolling stock on your layout.

• *Plan for transitional curves and for easements on graded sections.*

Transitions are gently curved sections of track (normally constructed with flex-track) that help to ease a train into a sharper and more well-defined curved area of trackwork. Although the real railroads use a mathematical formula to construct their transitions, we really don't need to resort to such precise measures on our garden railroads. Simply allowing for a gently curving section of track—several feet in length, if possible—where a curve both starts and ends will help prevent your rolling stock from jerking into and around the curved areas.

Care must also be given to points on your layout where level track begins an uphill climb, and to points where the track levels out again at the summit of the grade (or downgrade). The real railroads use easements—a very gradual change in elevation over a considerable distance—to accomplish a gentle and progressively steeper incline. You'll have little problem constructing proper easements if you use long sections of straight track at both points, and allow the trackwork to just naturally ease itself (supported by ballast, of course) into the grade.

• *Avoid combining grades with curves.*

Trains have to work harder going up a grade, and they also have to work harder pulling a string of cars through curved sections of trackwork. So, if you combine both grades and curves, you're asking your locomotives to do even more work. For this reason, you should try to avoid the combination of grades and curves wherever possible.

• *Use conductive paste on all rail joints.*

We've provided this tip in other sections of this book, and it's certainly one that merits repeating. The use of a conductive paste on all of your rail joints and/or rail clamps will help to inhibit corrosion and maintain good electrical conductivity. Plan to use this paste, which is available from several manufacturers, as well as at auto supply and home improvement stores, on every outdoor railroad, regardless of whether or not you also plan to solder your rail joints with jumper wires across all of your rail joints.

• *Solder jumpers across all rail joints, if at all possible.*

Speaking of soldering, it's a very good idea to take the time and effort necessary to solder a jumper wire across each of your rail joints along all points on the railroad, except where you have installed a turnout. Use a heavy-duty soldering gun and heavy gauge stranded wire, and allow the wire to "sag" just a bit so it can expand and contract as the rail itself expands and contracts. In fact, allowing for some expansion is why using soldered jumpers on rail joints is preferable to using rail clamps on all joints, especially if you live in a climate that is subject to extremes in temperature. Rail clamps may provide too tight a joint if they are used throughout the layout, and rails that cannot expand or contract a bit may possibly buckle. These short lengths of jumper wire will allow for the necessary expansion

and contraction, while still assuring that electricity flows from one rail to its adjoining partners in an uninterrupted manner.

• *Use rail clamps on all turnouts.*

You'll want to be able to remove your turnouts from time to time to service and maintain their moving parts. That's the main (and only) reason that soldering jumper wires across the rail joints of turnouts is not recommended. However, you still want to assure a steady flow of current through the turnouts, and rail clamps, in place of, or supplementing, the usual slip-on rail joiners, will help to assure that everything stays tight and true along the entire track network.

Rail clamps are designed to grip both adjoining rails with side-mounted screws. They provide a secure and properly aligned rail joint, and enable you to install and remove your turnouts without risking damage to the adjoining track since the clamps themselves can be loosened, then removed or slid back on the rails until the joint itself is unobstructed. Being made of metal, the rail clamps also conduct electricity, and they do not impede the flow of current through the turnout. Some rail clamps are even made to slip over existing rail joiners, to assure that the joiners stay tight. However, that's not a real advantage when it comes to easily replaceable turnouts, because it's the joiners that make them hard to remove.

When installing rail clamps, whether on turnouts or elsewhere along your trackwork, be sure to liberally coat the clamps with conductive lubricant or paste before installation, just as you would do with any track joint. That simple step will help prevent any corrosion over time.

Rail clamps are not overly expensive, and they are readily available from any well-stocked Large Scale retailer—Split Jaw clamps and Hillman's Railclamp are two of the more popular brands. Check the ads in *Garden Railways* and *Finescale Railroader* magazines to see what's currently offered, since several manufacturers produce rail clamps for a variety of rail sizes and specific applications.

• *Apply the final layer of ballast* after *the track is in place.*

Although most of your ballasted roadbed should already be down when you start laying track, you'll want to apply the final layer of ballast after the track is positioned to help lock the track in place; to fill in any

gaps; and to cover the open areas left between the ties. Here's what you should do:

After you have all the track in place and properly connected, fill a convenient-sized container with ballast and move along the right-of-way, depositing a small pile of ballast between the ties every couple of feet or so. Then, go back an re-check the level of your trackwork, adjusting it up or down by allowing the track to "float" on, or nestle into, the small ballast piles that you distributed.

Next, arm yourself with a bucket of ballast, and apply the ballast mix between the ties over the full length of the trackwork—use enough ballast to completely cover the track.

Finally, take an inexpensive two-inch paintbrush (just wide enough to conveniently fit between the rails), and working carefully in relatively small sections, use the brush to distribute the ballast evenly between the rails and ties. You'll want the rails and just the top of the ties to be visible when you've completed that step.

After you're satisfied with the overall appearance, "seat" the track a bit more firmly by wiggling it in place with your hands every couple of feet, and then take a small tamping tool (a small square of plywood with a handle nailed on will do nicely) and tamp the ballast to pack it along the slopes of the roadbed. Then go back and recheck the track level and cross-level one more time; clean out all of the flangeways and moving parts of your turnouts; apply a good mist of water to soak the ballast mix if you've added cement; and then you should be ready to run some trains!

• *Provide a firm foundation for your turnouts.*

For smooth and dependable operation, turnouts must be properly installed wherever they are used on your garden railroad. "Properly" first means perfectly level, or as close to perfectly level as you can possibly get them. And, because there are moving parts on a turnout, a second step well worth taking is to install a firm base support under the turnout to help assure consistent and reliable performance. This supporting base, made large enough to protect the full bottom area of the turnout, could be constructed of metal, treated wood, or, preferably, cut from a heavy sheet of Plexiglas. Plexiglas is preferred here simply because it is pretty much impervious to the elements, and will serve reliably for a very long time without any additional care or maintenance.

Ben Kreke uses a radio control unit to adjust the speed of the "Grizzly Flats Special" as it chuffs along the powered loop of Jan and Ric Golding's Kaskaskia Valley Railway.
Photo courtesy of Richard Golding

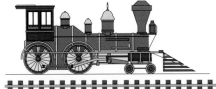

Chapter 7
POWER AND CONTROL SYSTEMS FOR LARGE SCALE TRAINS

A train without power from some source, be it internal or external, is a train with a place to go, but no way to get there. In garden railroading, you have a selection of power sources to choose from that is more extensive than that available in virtually any other model railroading scale, ranging from electrical power through the track (still the most common method), to live steam power, which operates just like the prototypes do. Because it ranks as something of a "special case," we'll discuss live steam power in more detail later in this book, and for now will focus attention on the more conventional sources of power most often used on garden railroads. These include conventional track power, radio-controlled track power, battery power with radio-control, and digital command control (DCC).

Each of these power and control systems have their own distinct advantages and limitations, but the primary function of each is to allow you to effectively and efficiently regulate the flow and direction of electric current reaching your locomotive's motor(s) so the units perform as you want them to.

• Track power

At this date, it's probably fair to say that the majority of garden railroads in this country, and probably throughout the world, are powered by low-voltage electricity fed to locomotive motors through the rails of the track. This is a somewhat logical approach for several reasons.

For one thing, electricity is readily available in nearly all households in most areas of the nation and the world, and it just makes good sense to exploit this convenient and reliable source. Since most Large Scale starter sets come complete with a power pack for providing track power, and with locomotives designed by their manufacturers to handle this method of tried-and-true track power, it stands to reason that many model railroaders are content to stay with this standard.

Also, track power, in its basic form, is very easy to install and control. Ordinary household line voltage, in the form of 115 volts of Alternating Current (AC) is fed into a device called a power pack. The power pack, which resembles the toy train transformer that you may have used for your around-the-tree Lionel train set at Christmas, converts dangerous high-voltage AC current from your household lines to a safe level of controllable Direct Current (DC) with a range of about 0-22 volts or so. The only real difference between a transformer and a power pack is that the transformer reduces (transforms) high-voltage AC to low-voltage AC, while a power pack converts high-voltage AC to low-voltage DC. In other respects, the two devices are very similar. Both are normally equipped with, at minimum, a speed control knob or lever, an on/off switch, a reversing switch for changing the direction that your locomotive is moving, and a circuit breaker. Some power packs also sport other features, such as momentum control, sound activation buttons, accessory terminals, and the like. Although some model locomotive motors are capable of operating efficiently with either AC or DC, you should be aware that the majority of electrically powered Large Scale locomotives are designed to operate on low-voltage DC.

Connecting and operating a conventional power pack is a simple task. First, two wires are connected from the two output terminals on the power pack to each of the two running rails anywhere along the trackwork. The wires can be soldered to the outside edges or bottom of the rails, or they can be attached to the rails by means of screw-on connectors supplied by the manufacturers or by using special rail clamps or joiners made for that purpose. Then, all you need do is plug the power pack's AC cord into a grounded (three-prong) household outlet, and you're ready to go! The amount of electricity provided to your model locomotive's motor(s) is regulated by the control knob on the power pack. A small switch, or some alternate configuration of the speed control knob, also allows you to reverse the flow of current, thereby causing the locomotive to reverse direction. It's really as simple as that!

Traveling through the metal rails of model track,

the current provided by your power pack is subsequently transferred to the locomotive's motor(s) via the wheels, and perhaps through sliding contact shoes fitted to the locomotive's underframe. The type of motor most commonly used in Large Scale locomotives is known as a "can motor"—a self-contained, sealed motor unit resembling a small tin can, which has a drive shaft protruding from the end. This shaft rotates as current passes through the electrical field within the motor itself, and the rotation is then transferred, via a series of fittings and gears, to the powered wheels of the locomotive. When the current flows in one direction, the locomotive moves forward; its rate of forward movement dependent on just how much current you provide when you move the speed control knob on your power pack. If you reverse the flow of current to the rails—a process accomplished by simply flicking a switch or rotating the speed control knob past a center-off position on the power pack—the locomotive will begin to move in the opposite direction.

Be aware that the power pack that came with your starter set, if that's what got you started in this hobby, may not be adequate for powering the full extent of your outdoor garden railroad, depending on its planned or actual size. Unless you plan to run only one small locomotive at a time, with very few powered trackside accessories, you'll likely want to invest in a power pack that will provide more total power, designated as volt-amps or VA (volts x amps= VA). Additional VA capacity or amperage is needed for multi-train operations, or for running single trains headed by dual- or larger-motor locomotives, and for operating trackside lights and/or accessories simultaneously with running your trains.

Aristo-Craft #5460 "Ultima" Power Supply and #5401 Speed Controller. With 10 amps of power, the "Ultima" system is able to meet the needs of even a large garden layout.
Photo courtesy of Aristo-Craft

Your starter set power pack is probably rated at somewhere in the neighborhood of 1-2 amps, and what you'll really need for a modest-size or larger garden railroad is something rated at 5-10 amps. Although the controllable output voltage of these larger and more robust power packs generally remains in the same 0-20 volt range of the smaller packs (with some exceptions that provide even more high-end voltage), the additional amps, when multiplied by a given voltage, are what provide the total output power needed to operate larger layouts most efficiently. Additional capacity for accessories is also provided by the larger power packs.

Aside from certain locomotives that you might purchase, a good power supply is likely to be the most expensive single item you'll acquire for your garden railroad. Nevertheless, it is an investment well worth the cost. You may want to do some research and a bit of "asking around" before deciding which power pack is right for you, because there are a number of reliable units available. Some of the units recommended by experienced garden railroaders include:

• Aristo-Craft "Ultima" (10 amp power supply unit and separate speed controller, used together, provide all the features of a conventional power pack. A 13.5 amp unit is in the planning stages).

• LGB "Jumbo" (10 amp)

• Model Rectifier "ControlMaster 20" (5 amp)

• Blue Streak (12 amp)

• Bridgewerks "Magnum 200" or Magnum 400" (each is rated at 15 amps)

One very important point to keep in mind regarding any use of track power outdoors:
You MUST keep the power supply itself—both the housed unit and its AC household voltage cord and plug—fully protected and shielded from any moisture!
Water and electricity are a very dangerous combination! The low-voltage output from your pack doesn't pose any real danger, so you can still safely operate your trains in the rain or snow, if you so desire, but the 115 volt AC current feeding into the power pack is extremely dangerous and you must take appropriate steps to prevent injury, or worse, to yourself and other operators! Among other considerations, the AC outlet that your power supply connects to should certainly be equipped with a Ground Fault Circuit Interrupter (GFCI), which functions as a circuit breaker to instantly disable the circuit whenever a short occurs. Unless the weather is clear and dry, you should always keep the power supply itself indoors, or contained in a dry, waterproof structure of its own. One garden railroader reports that he houses his power supply in a large picnic cooler, kept near the layout. An AC cord running from a wall outlet in the garage to the cooler's location is properly encased and buried, and it is fed into the cooler through what originally was intended to be the water drain plug. The plug opening was then tightly sealed with silicon caulk. All of the power equipment is kept securely housed inside the cooler when not in use, and it sits on the lid/shelf when trains are operating.

The cooler was even spray-painted dark green to better blend into its environment.

Regardless of how you elect to shield your power source, it MUST be protected from moisture at all times. This requirement should by no means dissuade you from using and enjoying conventional track power on your layout, because countless thousands of garden railroads are safely powered in this way, and have been for years. It is certainly easy enough to take the appropriate precautions, and that's all you need do.

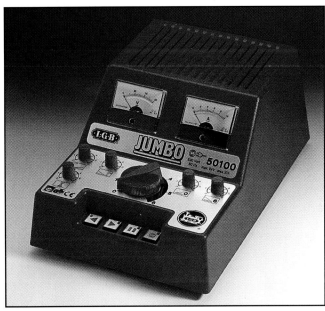

LGB's "Jumbo" power pack, rated at 10 amps, will handle the power requirements of virtually any garden railroad. *Photo courtesy of Ernst Paul Lehmann Patentwerk*

Advantages of track power:

• Except for live steamers, most Large Scale locomotives are already pre-wired to operate from track power.

• Track power is the least expensive of the power and control options, since all that is required is a suitable power pack and some wire.

• Trains can operate continuously and indefinitely off track power without any additional operator attention, aside from regular maintenance of both the track and the locomotives.

• There are no real power limitations, as long as the electricity flows, since there are no batteries or other components to be replaced or recharged. A good power pack should last a lifetime, and beyond.

• No special installation or additional wiring is needed to activate other features in the locomotives or cars, such as sound systems, lights, smoke, etc.

Limitations of track power:

• Track must be kept as clean as possible for reliable and efficient operations.

• Locomotive wheels and pickup shoes (if so equipped) also need to be kept clean.

• Trackwork must be properly secured at all rail joints. For outdoor use, this involves soldering jumper wires across rail joins, or using rail clamps.

• Installation may involve a considerable amount of underground wiring and the construction of relatively complex control panels, which must be protected from the weather and any moisture.

• Reversing loops, wyes, and turntables require special wiring and control.

• Track power with a conventional power pack may require the operator to stay at or near the pack to control speed, direction, and other functions. Some power packs have walk-around control units, but these are generally connected to the pack itself by a wired tether of some sort.

• Only one locomotive can operate along the same section of track at any one time. A system of insulated "blocks" is needed to operate two or more trains on the same line.

• Radio-controlled track power

Arguably, the most popular and commonly used method for controlling train operations on garden railroads in the United States today involves a combination of track power and radio signals. Radio-controlled track

Aristo-Craft's Basic Train Engineer (#5480) is designed for single train control on a small layout. It is ideal for remotely controlling your around-the-tree train at Christmas, for example, or for use on a small indoor layout. For a larger layout, you'll want to consider the full-feature Train Engineer system.
Photo courtesy of Aristo-Craft

power essentially involves placing a radio-controlled receiver between the track connection and the power source (which, in most cases, can be any conventional power pack). The receiver, which gets its instructions via radio signals issued from a hand-held control unit, has functions for controlling speed and direction of a locomotive, and, in some cases, for activating other features on the locomotive or even other accessories. The real advantage, of course, is that this system affords walk-around capability, allowing full control of a train from a relatively remote location.

The best known of these hands-off control systems is the "Train Engineer," developed for Aristo-Craft by Crest Electronics. The "Train Engineer," which can also be used in other scales as well as Large Scale, is very simple to set up and operate. All that's required, in addition to a conventional power pack, are a receiver and a hand-held transmitter/throttle that's not much larger than a full-featured remote of the type used to control your TV/VCR/stereo system, and much easier to use.

Two wires from your track—one from each rail—are connected to output terminals on the receiver. Two similar wires are then connected from the input terminals of the receiver to the track power terminals on your power pack. Almost any power pack rated up to 10 amps can be used, so compatibility is usually not a problem. Since the "Train Engineer" passes pure filtered DC through its circuits, the system is safe to use with any manufacturer's DC-powered locomotives and all pre-installed or after-market sound systems.

After the necessary connections are made, you simply turn on the power pack and use it's built-in speed control knob or lever to set it at the full power setting. It's really a matter of set-it-and-forget-it! All of the subsequent control functions relating to your locomotive's speed and direction can now be regulated via the hand-held, wireless transmitter/throttle. Perhaps best of all, no modification to the locomotive is required, unless you plan to operate multiple locomotives along the same track.

With the addition of a Onboard Mini-Receiver in each locomotive, the "Train Engineer" system can provide independent control of up to 10 locomotives operating on the same track, or anywhere else on the layout. Adding a Onboard Accessory Board will even permit you to activate smoke, lights, and sounds—up to a total of five such additional features—on each locomotive independently.

Two other related components—the Accessory Receiver and the Switch Receiver—can be used to control the function of operating accessories, or to align the points of turnouts. Each of these devices, which are placed near the objects they control, can operate five accessories or switches, up to a combined total of fifty such items.

Aristo-Craft Train Engineer Walk-Around Control System (#5470). Both the hand-held Transmitter (#5473) and Receiver (#5471) are needed for this system, in addition to a conventional power pack. The receiver connects between the track and the output terminals of the power pack, and interprets radio signals relayed by the transmitter through the track network.
Photo courtesy of Aristo-Craft

Aristo-Craft Remote Accessory Receiver (#5474) provides remote control of turnouts, lights, and sound features through the Train Engineer's hand-held transmitter.
Photo courtesy of Aristo-Craft

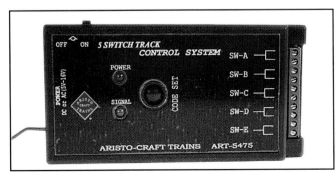

The Aristo-Craft 5475 Switch Control device allows for remote control of up to five turnout motors.
Photo courtesy of Aristo-Craft

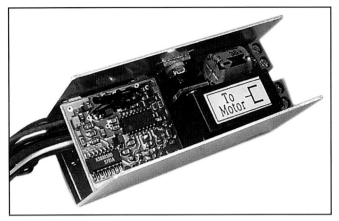

The 5490 On-board Mini-Receiver for the Aristo-Craft system mounts in the locomotive, and can operate with either AC or DC motors.
Photo courtesy of Aristo-Craft

There's even a low-cost "Train Engineer Basic" available for those who want to operate a single train on a small or temporary layout, such as a Christmas layout, and who don't really need all the features of the full-blown system. The "Basic" version is designed to operate with smaller power packs which are rated at 2.5 amps or less.

Because the radio transmitter operates on an FM (Frequency Modulation) frequency in the 27 MHz band, obstacles between the transmitter-equipped operator and the receiver do not normally interfere with the signal. Likewise, other radio-emitting sources in the vicinity of the "Train Engineer" will not interfere with its signal, thanks to special coding that is applied to the FM carrier system. Distance permitting, you could even run your trains while sitting in your living room, since walls and other such obstructions will not adversely affect the transmitted FM commands over the unit's specified range.

Buttons on the hand-held transmitter control all of the available functions. A "fast" button causes the locomotive to increase speed, while the "slow" button decreases the speed. An "emergency brake" button causes the locomotive to come to an immediate stop. And, a direction button allows you to reverse the direction the locomotive is heading.

There are also a number of other features built into the system, including momentum control (the ability to automatically and very gradually increase or decrease a locomotive's speed); a safety pause feature that prevents a locomotive from being switched from forward to reverse abruptly (which could damage working components of the motors); and a track channel selector switch, which allows a single hand-held transmitter to control two trains operating on separate or isolated tracks, as long as two power packs and two receivers are used. Other features include a Linear/Pulse Width Control (PWC) selector switch on the receiver (PWC helps to provide cooler operation and smoother power transitions), and accessory control buttons on the transmitter keypad that allow the operator to activate up to fifty accessories and their related functions.

Advantages of radio-controlled track power:

• Easily adaptable to most locomotives. Some systems do not require any locomotive modification whatsoever for single locomotive operation.

• Moderate cost. The most commonly used Aristo-Craft "Train Engineer" system can make use of the hobbyist's existing power supply in many instances.

• Trains can be controlled from a remote location, up to several hundred feet away.

• No complex wiring or special skill is required to install the system.

• Constant high voltage supplied to the track minimizes rail oxidation, and reduces track cleaning effort, although track must still be kept clean.

• Other features, such as whistles, horns, locomotive sounds, lights, and bells can all be activated by radio control, if so desired.

• Multiple locomotives, if equipped with separate on-board receivers, can operate along the same track.

Limitations of R/C track power:

• Track must still be kept clean for most efficient operations.

• Locomotive wheels and pickup shoes (if so equipped) also need to be kept clean.

• Trackwork must be properly aligned and tightly secured at all rail joints, just as with conventional track power.

• Reversing loops, wyes, and turntables still require special wiring and control, just as with conventional track power.

• Battery power with radio control

In its original form, battery power ranks just behind live steam as the oldest means of powering model trains. Of course, things were considerably different back in those pre-twentieth century times, since the batteries employed then were large, caustic, wet-cell versions that actually provided power to the track, rather than directly to the locomotives, in the days before electricity became a commonplace household commodity.

Today we've come full circle, and the use of battery power to operate Large Scale model locomotives is quickly coming of age for the second time as components become more technologically advanced, compact, and affordable, and as increasing numbers of hobbyists

discover that, once installed and equipped with radio control, this power system is a reliable approach to hands-free operation.

You'll note that we're discussing battery power used in concert with radio control (R/C) here, rather than considering the two as separate components. In fact, they are separate components, and it is entirely possible to operate a battery-powered locomotive without any external radio control apparatus, and it is possible to use radio control with other power sources. Nevertheless, the use of battery power alone limits flexibility of the control functions available to the operator, so it's best to view batteries and a radio control apparatus as two related parts of a total control system.

If you feel that battery power with radio control may be the way you would like to go with your railroad, it's perhaps wise to make a firm decision before you begin actual construction of your layout, if you possibly can. An early decision may save you considerable time, labor, and expense in the long run.

First, you'll avoid the labor and expense of constructing trackwork that is up to the high conductivity standards required for electrically powered layouts. Although your trackwork still needs to be level, aligned, and properly connected at the rail joints, you won't have to bother with soldering jumper wires at each of these joints, and you can likely avoid the expense of costly clamp-on rail joiners, although these are still recommended for use on all turnouts so they can be easily removed for servicing.

You also won't have to fuss with buried cables or the other wiring needed to make your railroad operate, aside from the wiring needed to power accessories, water features, layout lighting, or remote-controlled turnouts. Nevertheless, it's important to note that many battery power enthusiasts still do elect to maintain a track power capability on their layouts so visitors can run trains on occasion, and so new locomotives can be run-in and tested prior to converting them over to battery power.

Finally, an early commitment to radio-controlled battery power will help you to spread out and better manage your expenditures on the trains themselves. You'll be able to equip each locomotive for battery power, whether it is internally supplied or provided by a trailing car that houses the batteries, as you make your individual locomotive purchases. This results in far less up-front expense than if you were to decide later on to retrofit an entire fleet of locomotives.

The use of battery power in combination with the Aristo-Craft on-board receiver is just one way many operators achieve a battery-powered radio control capability. This technique negates the need for track power (and track cleaning), but the battery packs themselves, which are usually NiCads or Gel Cells, require a considerable amount of space. They often must be mounted in a trailing car behind the locomotive, unless the locomotive has sufficient interior space. Even if there is enough space, recharging or changing battery packs can be somewhat problematic if they are difficult to access

inside the locomotive. Aristo-Craft plans to release a specially designed and ready-to-run battery car, in both old-time and more contemporary configurations, to accommodate the dimensions and weight of the firm's Gel Cell battery packs.

Today, the leading radio-controlled battery power systems suitable for Large Scale model railroads include Aristo-Craft's "Train Engineer," Keithco's "Locolinc," Remote Control System's "RCS," and Reed Hobby's "Instant R/C." Each of these systems has its own set of advantages, limitations, and features, so you should plan to explore the capabilities of each before deciding on a purchase. You'll find these suppliers, including their web site addresses, listed in the manufacturers/suppliers appendix of this book.

Advantages of battery power:

• There is no need to wire the trackwork, since both power and control components are independent of the track system. No special wiring is needed for reversing loops, wyes, or other such configurations.

• Electrical conductivity between track sections is not a consideration. Solid rail joints and good alignment are still necessary to assure smooth operations, but there's no need to solder jumper wires across the joints to assure an uninterrupted flow of electric current.

• Little track cleaning is needed, aside from removing obvious obstacles from along the line. Some operators even assert that somewhat dirty track actually improves operations by providing better traction.

• If radio-controlled battery power alone is to be used to power the locomotives on your railroad, layout construction is simplified, and can be accomplished in a shorter time.

• An unlimited number of battery-equipped locomotives can operate on the same track section, consistent with between-train spacing considerations and/or the number of independent frequencies assigned when radio control is used.

• Battery-powered locomotives can operate on any other Large Scale layout, regardless of whether it is set up to run off track power or some other method.

• The combination of battery power and radio control permits hands-off walk-around control of a train. You can operate your equipment from any location around the layout. If you've planned your layout properly, you can operate turnouts and perform coupling and uncoupling operations while walking along with your train.

• Many of the available radio control devices can also activate whistles, bells, lights, locomotive sounds, and other features.

• Batteries need not be installed in the locomotive. Installation in a car coupled directly behind the locomotive allows the same battery system to be used with any number of locomotives, with only minor modification to the locomotive itself. Regardless of whether the batteries are located in the locomotive or in a trailing car, the additional weight provides greater tractive effort.

Limitations of battery power:

• Batteries have a limited useful operating life between recharges, which limits running time. They also have a somewhat limited functional life overall, and require replacement when they can no longer take and hold a charge (usually after several hundred charging cycles).

• Depending on the type of system selected, the time needed to recharge batteries can be quite long. The usual types of batteries used for Large Scale operations are generally either sealed lead-acid (gel cell) battery packs or nickel-cadmium (NiCad) packs. Both types can be recharged.

• Effective and constant speed control of a battery-equipped locomotive requires a radio control system.

• Battery power systems, particularly when they are equipped for radio control, can be costly.

• Options for installation in certain locomotives may be limited, since the battery systems require a good amount of space, and such space is often at a premium in smaller locomotives, in particular. A trailing car to hold the batteries may be necessary.

• The extra weight of a battery system can limit overall train length. This may become an important consideration if you have grades on your layout, or enjoy operating very long trains.

• Digital command control (DCC)

Advancements in computer technology, and especially in the computer chips that control this technology, have made it possible for model railroaders in all scales to enjoy reliable, independent control of locomotives and accessories in a way not known as recently as a decade or so ago. Today, some eighteen manufacturers and after-market suppliers are known to produce Digital Command Control (DCC) systems that are suitable for use in Large Scale locomotives.

In essence, a DCC control system is very much like having a small computer on-board each locomotive so equipped. This micro-computer is what controls motor speed and other functions, such as lights, smoke, and sound systems. As most computer enthusiasts know, a

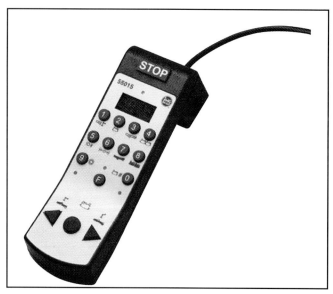

LGB's #55015 Universal Remote for the firm's digital Multi-Train System.
Photo courtesy of Ernst Paul Lehmann Patentwerk

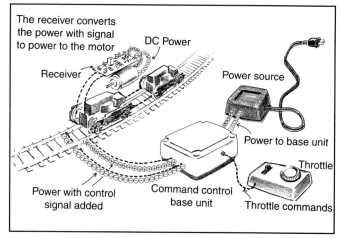

A typical DCC system consists of a throttle, a power source and command control base (which may be combined in one unit), and a miniature receiver mounted in the locomotive. Receivers are available for nearly all scales, from Z to Large Scale. Commands from the throttle are fed to the control base; then relayed via the track feeder wiring to the track; and then on to the receiver that is mounted in the locomotive. The receiver interprets the command signal and thereby controls the locomotive's motor speed and direction, as well as other functions, such as lights, smoke, and the like.
Illustration by Dennis Auth

computer's ability to process and use information is really quite simple, in theory at least, and is based on a system that makes use of "bits" (a 1 or 0), and "bytes" (composed of 8 bits), in nearly infinite combinations to direct that a specific action be taken in a given sequence. These bits and bytes are bundled together in what are know as "packets," with each packet providing a specific instruction to its affiliated decoder.

In 1995, the National Model Railroad Association promulgated a standard DCC protocol that assures compatibility between DCC products made by different manufacturers. Therefore, even though you may buy several different brands of components—decoders made by different firms, for example—you can take comfort in knowing that everything will work together properly when you install the complete system on your railroad, provided that what you buy carries the NMRA certification.

Basically, a DCC system consists of two primary components: a command base system, which is the "brains" for interpreting and issuing operator-initiated instructions, and a decoder, which is mounted in the locomotive, car, or accessory to read these instructions and to convert them into specific actions. If remote operation is desired and available, whether tethered or by radio or infrared control, a hand-held throttle is also used. The electric current needed to perform each action is provided by full track power, furnished in the same way that it is with the radio-controlled track power method previously discussed. In most cases, the operator's existing power pack can be used for DCC applications. With DCC control, the rails also normally carry the digital command signals to the decoders that have been installed in each locomotive.

The decoders themselves are quite small, so installing them in virtually any Large Scale locomotive

presents few problems. The only real concern with decoders used in Large Scale trains relates to the amount of current, or amps, that the decoder can provide. Some Large Scale motors may require two or more amps to function properly, and this power requirement for one motor alone may exceed the total power requirements of a small HO or N scale layout. For this reason, before you rush out and purchase a decoder, you will need to determine the maximum current requirements of the locomotive in which it will be installed. The dealer or manufacturer can generally tell you which decoder should be used for a particular locomotive model, so be sure to ask.

Remember, too, that various on-board functions such as lights, horns or whistles, bells, engine sounds, and other such features also require current to operate, so the current drawn by these functions needs to be considered in addition to the motor's power needs. Again, the decoder manufacturers can provide information that will help you make the right selection.

The point is: Any decoder you select must be able to power your locomotive without the decoder itself overheating. That is the first and most critical criterion to be applied in choosing a decoder capable of performing consistently and well in Large Scale applications. Suitable decoders are available for nearly all Large Scale locomotives at this time, so doing some homework and asking a few questions before you buy will certainly get you headed in the right direction.

Digital Command Control, in light of the practically limitless flexibility and control it provides relating to the various functions of today's Large Scale locomotives, is a viable and attractive control system.

Nevertheless, there are some significant limitations to DCC, particularly when used for outdoor operations, and these need to be carefully considered before you commit to this type of control system. DCC is not for everyone, of course, but it is a fine way to take advantage of current and ever-improving technology to efficiently and creatively operate your railroad in a very realistic manner. If you're interested in exploring the subject of DCC in far more depth, consider visiting the following two web sites on the Internet:

www.trainweb.org/largescaledcc/

www.trainweb.org/girr/tips5/dcc_tips.html

Together, these sites provide a valuable must-read introduction for anyone interested in exploring the world of Digital Command Control. Between them, you'll find full descriptions of DCC features and decoder operation; detailed lists of available equipment and decoders appropriate for Large Scale; tips for DCC decoder installation in a number of the most popular locomotives from a variety of manufacturers; and a wealth of other practical and technical information. If you're at all interested in what DCC is, and in learning more about what it does, these two web sites, in particular, should be considered as primary reference sources.

As noted earlier, a number of manufacturers currently offer DCC decoders the are suitable for Large Scale locomotives. These include: Arnold, Digitrax, ESU, HAG, Heller, Itelec, Lenz, LGB, MRC, North Coast Engineering, PSI (Dynatrol), Ramtraxx, Soundtraxx, T. B. ITEN, Umelec, Wangrow, Zimo, and ZTC Systems. Contact information for most of these firms can be found in the manufacturers/suppliers appendix of this book.

Advantages of Digital Command Control (DCC):

• Allows for fully independent control of speed and features on multiple locomotives.

• Performs well in multiple-unit operation, where you may want to double-head two locomotives or lash-up several diesel locomotives to pull long trains.

• Affords unlimited run time.

• Most DCC equipment is made to conform to National Model Railroad Association DCC standards, and therefore is largely interchangeable.

• Reverse loop, wyes, and turntable wiring is greatly simplified.

Limitations of Digital Command Control (DCC):

• High initial cost for the equipment and professional installation. If walk-around radio control is desired, the cost goes even higher.

• Each locomotive requires installation of its own decoder. In some cases, this installation can require some level of expertise with such devices, especially if the user wants the decoder to control auxiliary functions such as lights, horns or whistles, bells, engine sounds, and other features. Professional installation may be necessary. You should also be aware that installation of a DCC decoder may void the locomotive manufacturer's warranty.

• As with conventional track power, the track must be kept clean and securely joined.

• Some systems may require that your layout be all-DCC, meaning that conventional track-powered locomotives may not be able to operate on the layout.

• Some DCC-equipped locomotives may not be able to operate on non-DCC layouts.

So, aside from live steam power, those are the power and control choices! It's obvious that there are, indeed, a varied number of ways for the garden railroader to power and operate his or her trains. The system you ultimately choose should really be based on what you expect your railroad to do; how big you expect it to eventually be; and the restrictions imposed by your own hobby budget. There are no "right" or "wrong" choices, since individual needs and expectations can vary widely. You may even want to consider some combination of options that will allow you to operate your trains via one mode of power—battery power, for example—while still affording friends and visitors the opportunity to operate their trains on your layout in a more conventional way.

Regardless of which power system you choose, there are obvious benefits to weighing all of the options carefully before you become too involved with the actual construction of your garden railroad. Plan ahead, study the alternatives, and don't hesitate to ask questions. As with any other area of the hobby, this approach will pay off in the long run.

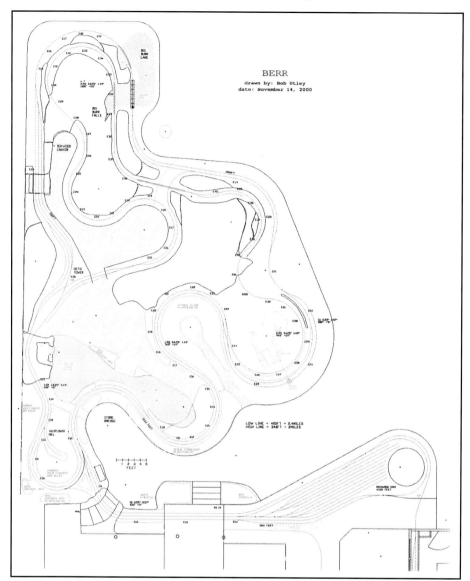

The completed site plan for Bob and Ellen Utley's BERR garden railroad. Bob used CAD software on his home computer to design, modify, and re-modify the plan several times. A garden railroad of this size and complexity is an ambitious project, and the Utleys are doing as everyone is advised to do: Building the layout in manageable phases.
CAD drawing courtesy of Bob Utley

Chapter 8
GARDEN LAYOUT PLANNING AND SITE PREPARATION

The temptation is *so* great! You receive a Large Scale train set as a gift, or have purchased one for yourself, and you're anxious to get some track laid and to get the train up and running. After some initial exploration, you determine that you don't have room inside your home to do justice to the layout you envision, so you check around outdoors; locate what you feel is a suitable plot of relatively level ground; rush out to buy some additional track; and then set about constructing the layout of your dreams.

Sound familiar? Although slightly exaggerated here for the purpose of driving home a point, that is, indeed, the way that many garden railroads begin. There's nothing terribly wrong with this get-'em-up-and-running approach, of course, because it does help to maintain a certain level of interest and enthusiasm, at least for a while, and it does allow the hobbyist to see how his or her equipment actually might perform in real-world conditions. Nevertheless, this somewhat hasty, albeit well-intended, approach overlooks an important step: Layout planning. And, because this important step was bypassed, either intentionally or otherwise, a good many dreamed-about rail empires never really advance beyond this somewhat rudimentary stage, except in the imagination of their creators.

Time devoted to properly planning your layout, regardless of whether it will be located in the garden or elsewhere, is time well spent. In fact, this important step will save you time, effort, money, and possible frustration later on as your interests develop and as your knowledge of railroading in both prototype and miniature form grows. Planning will help you avoid pitfalls that might otherwise become apparent only after you are well along in the construction phase, and which are time-consuming and often costly to correct. Proper planning will also assist you in developing a railroad that can expand as your equipment roster grows, and as you learn more about both the advantages and limitations of operating miniature trains in the great outdoors. Also, careful planning will help you identify exactly what is needed to develop a realistic rail operation consistent with any theme you may already have chosen for your railroad.

One bit of sage advice is warranted before we proceed with discussing a step-by-step approach to planning and building a garden railroad:

Start simple and small; plan for expansion; and always use the broadest curves possible.

Although there really are no hard-and-fast "rules" governing track planning or layout construction, these words provide a very useful guideline well worth keeping in mind as you prepare to venture into the world of garden railroading. If you can resist the temptation to become overly ambitious in the early stages of your railroad's planning and execution, you'll likely achieve a greater sense of satisfaction in the long run; have some trains up and running sooner; and you'll benefit from learning a few new techniques, tricks, and short-cuts along the way. It is, therefore, strongly recommended that you get your feet wet before you attempt to take a full-fledged plunge into the hobby.

Starting small; keeping things simple; and planning for future expansion (if space permits), is just good common sense. A small layout will enable you to get up-and-running in a much shorter time, and the things you learn at this early stage will serve you well as the layout continues to grow. Keeping things simple means avoiding complex track plans and multitudes of turnouts, at least when you're initially starting out. Rarely, if ever, will you see a garden railroad—even a large and fully developed one—that in any way resembles the complex layouts with dozens of turnouts and a spaghetti-like network of track that you so often see in the smaller scales. Garden railroaders seem to generally prefer operating their trains rather than fussing with intricate layouts, and perhaps that's one reason why the outdoor-oriented folks are such a laid-back and stress-free group! An added benefit of keeping things small and simple is that you can subsequently expand your layout in manageable phases without fear of interrupting your train-running activities, save for those times when you're installing a new turnout somewhere along the line, or performing a bit of maintenance.

That final point about "always use the broadest curves possible" really applies to model railroading in any scale. If you simply must use four-foot diameter (2' radius) curves on your garden railroad because of space limitations, then by all means do so. Just keep in mind that such tight curves are best suited to small, short-wheelbase locomotives and cars. Even though some larger and longer equipment may negotiate these curves (many certainly will), these items will look kind of strange in doing so, and they may even tend to balk or slow down a bit in the curved areas. For your outer mainline, in particular, try to use eight-foot, ten-foot, or even twenty-foot diameter curves if at all possible. Then, as your railroad grows you can always employ some tighter curves, if necessary, for a secondary mainline, branch lines, or various sidings.

So, with that bit of time-tested wisdom in mind, let's examine, step-by-step, a viable approach to planning an outdoor railroad. Keep in mind that this is just one of several possible ways to proceed. The approach you take, and the sequence of the steps involved, may be slightly different in your particular circumstance. For example, you may want to design your layout as part of an existing garden. In that situation, steps such as site selection and a considerable amount of the site clearing and preparation have already been accomplished. In general, however, the following are the basic steps you'll need to consider in planning a garden railroad, regardless of its final size or configuration:

Step #1: Select a site for the layout.

Step #2: Clear and prepare the site.

Step #3: Create a site plan, complete with measured distances, elevations, and the plotted location of any permanent obstacles.

Step #4: Develop a track plan.

Of course, there are other steps, such as actually constructing the layout, providing power, landscaping, and the placement of structures and other accessories, that will necessarily follow after the track is down and the trains are operating. These steps or stages will be covered in subsequent chapters. For now, our focus is on getting the basic railroad planned and prepared for smooth and reliable running.

• Step 1—Selecting a site for your garden railroad

We have to start our layout planning somewhere, so deciding on a location for the railroad is a logical first step since the location pretty well defines the overall dimensions of your rail empire. Site selection involves actively exploring the area surrounding your home to determine the most suitable location for your proposed railroad. Keep the guideline noted earlier in mind while you're doing your exploring: Start small; keep it simple; and plan for future expansion. This one guideline, if followed faithfully, will definitely help to keep your hobby from becoming a laborious chore rather than a labor of love.

Perhaps you have already given some thought to a general location for your new garden railroad—a corner or one side of your back yard, for example. If so, you have completed a rudimentary "site evaluation," in a manner of speaking, and you may feel that you're ready to move on with drawing up a track plan and beginning construction. Ah! If only things were all that simple! But, because a garden railroad is somewhat more permanent than many indoor model railroads,

and because its construction involves dealing with a variety of special considerations such as terrain, weather, security, and the like, it's worthwhile to devote a bit more time to evaluating the true suitability of any prospective site. And, if you have not yet carefully weighed all of the inherent advantages and limitations of your location of choice, now is surely the best time to do so.

A back yard is, quite naturally, the preferred location for a great many garden railroads. There are a number of reasons for this, not the least of which is the privacy and security that a back yard provides, especially if it is already fenced, or able to be fenced.

Depending on the proximity of neighboring homes, privacy may or may not be a major issue. However, if your neighbors live close enough to be affected by the sounds of your favorite Mogul chuffing through the garden with whistle screaming, or your SD40-2 roaring through the evening calm with horn blaring, you may want to take some precautionary steps to assure that your own leisure activities don't intrude on your neighbor's right to peaceful coexistence. You've probably heard it said that "good fences make good neighbors," and there's likely more than a bit of truth to this if you're planning to regularly run trains equipped with all the bells, whistles, and other sound effects. Any barrier that will help to shield your neighbors from what may be perceived as unwelcome noises—be it physical distance or an actual barrier such as a fence—will help to maintain peace and tranquillity in the neighborhood.

A fenced-in area, regardless of where it is around you home, also makes good sense from the standpoint of security for your railroad and its equipment, especially if it is a solid fence that shields the railroad from

David Snow laid track sections on his proposed layout site to see how things might eventually look, and to determine any elevation changes along the track's route. He then traced the perimeter of the layout with white play sand, allowing enough room for some track adjustments later on. David is fortunate to have a good amount of area available for future expansion of his layout, but note that he chose to start small—a good way to begin any new venture into garden railroading.
Photo courtesy of David Snow

outside view. Although it's not likely that you'll leave locomotives and rolling stock outdoors at all hours of the day and night, you certainly may prefer to leave many or all of your structures in place, and you surely will keep the track, bridges, tunnels, and landscaping features right where they are. That being the case, you'll want to take steps to assure that these costly items are reasonably well protected from vandalism, curious passersby, and even the damage that can be caused by wild or stray critters that may roam the neighborhood. It should be fairly obvious that constructing your railroad on a piece of real estate that is, or can be, protected by a high, opaque, well-constructed fence certainly provides long-term benefits.

A solid fence along one or more sides of your railroad may also help, in many instances, to shield the railroad from strong gusts of wind and blowing debris. This is an added benefit, but it can be an important one if you live in a particularly windy region of the country. And, while we're on the subject, there's one more point about fences that's worth noting here:

It's not a good idea to place any of the sides of your garden railroad right up against a fence line. If you do so, you'll likely have to climb all over your layout at some point to perform routine landscape or track maintenance chores in those against-the-fence sections, and you'll risk damaging the landscaping, trackwork, bridges, and modeled structures in the process. Plan to allow for a three-foot-or-wider aisle between the perimeter of your layout and the fence. This will provide enough room for you to move about without unduly disturbing your existing handiwork. Keep this in mind when you get to the site map phase of layout planning, described below.

Yet another distinct advantage of a back yard location is that this is a somewhat customary area for a family's outdoor recreational activities—playing ball, holding a barbecue, planting a vegetable garden, entertaining guests, and that sort of thing. So, a garden railroad in the back yard is a rather logical addition to the scene, since the railroad and its landscaped garden will nicely complement other family-oriented pastimes.

Of course, there are viable alternatives to a back yard garden railroad. The railroad could just as well be built in an open area alongside your home, if space permits, or even on a deck or porch if suitable terra firma is not available elsewhere. For that matter, some garden railroads have even been constructed in the front yards of homes, and a few individuals with very little or no out-of-doors real estate available have constructed realistic garden railroads—complete with living plants and operating water features—inside their homes. If these are the only options available to you in your particular situation, there's no need to rule them out. Remember, though, that you'll certainly want to give due consideration to privacy concerns, and especially to the security issue, before electing to locate your railroad in any area that provides open and easy view, and access to outsiders.

• **Step 2—Clearing and preparing the terrain**

Once you have pretty well determined the general area where your garden railroad will be built, it's time to take a good, hard look at the terrain and the existing landscaping, and to get on with the chore of clearing your site—assuming, of course, that at least some clearing will be necessary.

Clearing is the process of stripping the existing terrain of anything that will not be included as a permanent fixture on your railroad. It's certainly not a whole lot of fun to dig out rocks, shrubs, weeds, and bushes, but it is work that must be done. In fact, it's preferable that you attend to this chore at an early stage—first, to get it over with, and, second, because a totally cleared and properly leveled area will make things much easier when you get to the actual track planning and track installation phases. Keep in mind, too, that simply cutting back overgrowth isn't quite enough—you also need to dig out an offending plant's root systems wherever possible. Some hardy varieties of unwanted weeds and other plant life have a nasty habit of regenerating themselves in areas that can cause persistent problems later on, after the trackwork is in place.

As part of the land clearing process, take a good, close look at all of the permanent landscape features—whether natural or man made, and regardless of whether they are existing or planned—that will likely impact the final configuration of your layout. You're probably not going to chop down that stately ninety-year-old oak tree that has provided the family with cooling shade over the years, and you're not likely to consider relocating an in-ground swimming pool just for the sake of establishing a garden railroad right-of-way. However, you may very well want to consider adding a water feature to your layout at some point—a small pond, perhaps, or even a pond with a waterfall—and now is the best time to at least think about the size, shape, and location of such major landscape-altering projects. Your railroad will have to work around or over all of these obstacles, and it's never too early to begin giving some thought to how that might be done with the least amount of effort and reconstruction.

For that matter, you may already have an attractively landscaped garden in place, and perhaps your railroad is destined to become a integral part of that existing feature which has been lovingly nurtured by you and/or your spouse. If that's the case, you'll want to give additional thought and attention to blending both the garden and the railroad together in such a way that the two complement, rather than compete with, each other.

• **Step 3—Creating a site map**

Once you have cleared your selected piece of real estate, you're ready to begin the next phase of layout planning. This involves, first, creating a rough pencil

A foot-high retaining wall made of landscape blocks was constructed along the front of David Snow's layout to account for the slope of the terrain, and a leveling board was used to guide placement of the backfill soil needed to get everything close to level. *Photo courtesy of David Snow*

sketch of the overall area that depicts the actual shape of the intended layout location, including such peripheral objects as the walls or corners of nearby buildings, fences, swimming pools, walkways, and other permanent fixtures that surround the site.

Measure the width, length, breadth, and distances to other objects for each of these permanent fixtures, and jot these measurements down on your rough drawing. You can begin your site survey by using a tape measure to accurately determine distances between the four or more corner points that define the perimeter of the area you have available for your railroad. It's a good idea to place surveyor's stakes in the ground to physically mark each corner point for future reference, and you may even want to join each stake with string to more visibly define the full perimeter.

Then, starting at one corner stake, which will serve as a primary reference point, measure the exact distance between that stake and one on either side of it, and note that measurement on the rough drawing of your layout area. Repeat this measuring-and-recording process around the full site until you have measured, documented, and sketched the full perimeter of your proposed layout area.

Next, repeat this measuring process in order to identify and record the location of each fixed object within your site plan (objects that cannot be moved, or that you prefer not to move). This may include any large trees or bushes that will stay in place; obstacles such as swimming pools, cabanas, decks, and walkways, rock formations, and any other natural or man-made features that will not be disturbed or relocated to make way for your railroad. To be most accurate, be sure to measure distances to each object from two or more fixed points, approaching the object from different directions. For example: Start at one known reference point (a corner stake, or a marked or flagged point on

the string defining the perimeter, for instance), and measure from that point to the object itself. Then, repeat this process by making another measurement to the same object from a different direction and a new reference point. Repeat this process as often as needed to accurately "fix" the location of each object that is within the proposed layout site. After all preliminary measurements have been made and recorded, you'll end up with a crude but accurate sketch of the plot of land where your railroad will operate, with all obstacles and exact distances to these obstacles penciled in.

The next step is to transfer this preliminary information to a sheet of ruled graph paper. If your proposed layout is a relatively small one (a very good idea if it's you first layout), everything will probably fit onto a single 8-1/2x11 sheet of graph paper. If the layout is large, or especially long and narrow, larger sheets of graph paper are also readily available. Depending on the size of your layout, and the size of the graph paper you have to work with, you can use the pre-printed ruled squares on the graph paper to represent any scale that is convenient for your purposes. For example, one small square on the graph paper could represent six inches, or even one actual foot. Or, you could use some other number of squares to represent one foot. You can pretty much use whatever scale works best for you, consistent with trying to keep everything plotted on the single sheet of paper that you're working with, if possible. And, of course, it's a good idea to try to plot these things as neatly and accurately as possible, since this will be considered your finished site map, and you'll need these accurate measurements later on.

As you transfer information from your preliminary sketch to the graph paper site map, be sure to check and re-check carefully so each permanent feature is truly depicted in its proper location, and in its proper relationship and distance to other nearby objects. Once

With the retaining wall complete, and the fill soil in place and reasonably leveled, David Snow again laid down the track. He marked the track's route by pouring white sand between the ties; then removed the track once again so he could dig a trench, which was subsequently filled with crusher fines to provide a solid and level supporting roadbed. After the power leads were connected, a couple of "track testing" trains were run just to make sure everything was operating as it should. Adjustments to track level were made by adding or removing crusher fines, as necessary.
Photo courtesy of David Snow

you have this drafting work done, you'll end up with an accurate-to-scale rendering of the proposed railroad's location, and everything that is in and adjacent to it.

At this point, it would sure be nice to be able to say that our site mapping project is completed, but there's still one very important step to attend to. That step involves determining and recording any changes in elevation that occur throughout your layout site. Changes in slope and elevation are important, not just for the effect they may have on your trackwork, but also because some sloping of the terrain may be needed to assure proper drainage on the layout as a whole.

Unless you're planning to build your garden railroad atop a paved parking lot, chances are that the now-bare slice of real estate you envision for your layout is going to require some additional work to make it—or at least the areas where track will be placed—as level as possible. In the real world, sad to say, perfectly level terrain is a rare thing—so much so that even most of the aforementioned paved parking lots aren't usually all that level, although they may appear that way at a casual glance.

The real railroads go to great pains to construct level and smooth trackwork for efficient and safe operations, and your garden railroad is more than likely going to require a bit of back-bending labor on your part to achieve those same goals. Grades—the increase or decrease in track elevation over some measured distance—are something that railroad engineering departments strive mightily to avoid, wherever possible, and you would be well advised to follow their example. That does not imply that your entire garden railroad has to be as flat as, say, a typical toy train layout con-

structed on a sheet of plywood. That's not the case at all! In fact, a perfectly flat garden layout would more than likely invite drainage and erosion problems—something the indoor table-top layouts never have to contend with. What is does mean, however, is that the roadbed portions of your garden railroad should be as close to perfectly level as possible, along the length of the track as well as crosswise.

If any grades are necessary, or desired, they should be gradual, and restricted to no more than about three percent in elevation—that's three inches of elevation change over a distance of 100 inches (slightly less than three yards) of linear measure. In fact, if you think of an acceptable grade as being anything less than a three-inch elevation change over three-yards of linear measure, you'll end up with gentle grades that will generally serve you well regardless of the type of equipment you plan to operate. In any event, strive not to exceed three percent, if at all possible, since even that seemingly gradual grade is considered a bit steep in the world of real railroading. Some experienced garden railroaders even insist on two percent as the maximum allowable grade for their layouts. But before we get too far into the subject of grades and how to determine them, there's one more idea that you may want to seriously consider at this point.

Some garden railroads—and especially many smaller ones—are constructed on elevated layouts. That is, the entire layout, regardless of the configuration of its final topography, is elevated a couple of feet, more or less, above the level of the surrounding terrain. A perimeter framework made of brick, stone, concrete, wood posts, old railroad ties, or some other suitable retaining material provides the structure that holds

everything in place, as long as you remember to provide for proper drainage. The area inside this perimeter retaining wall is then completely filled with compacted soil, bringing the entire layout up to a predetermined, and relatively level, above-ground elevation. There are real advantages to this type of layout construction, the most important being that significant portions of the elevated layout can subsequently be worked on without a whole lot of bending over or kneeling on the ground. Also, an elevated garden railroad provides an attractive and unified appearance in relation to its environment. It becomes a distinctive feature—a stage, if you will—that attracts and holds the viewer's eye, and places the trains and other objects in a more natural closer-to-eye-level perspective. At the same time, an elevated layout discourages trespass by some small critters who would otherwise be prone to pawing their way through your rail empire in wild abandon. As an added plus, you'll be able to start your layout and landscaping with an area that's fairly level to begin with, because you made it that way, and which can later be configured to a varied topography that best suits your needs and interests.

Tom Ruddell chose to elevate part of his Bethlehem Central Railroad well above ground level. This type of construction would be ideal for many live steam operators, who need to be work in close proximity to their locomotives, and who may be more inclined to the mechanical, rather than landscaping, aspects of garden railroading.
Photo courtesy of Tom Ruddell

However, there is a downside to this higher-than-ground-level layout concept. Depending on the size of your planned layout, it may require lots of dirt and topsoil—many tons of the stuff, in some cases. If you have a ready supply source for free soil and the related transport of that soil to your site, you're in good shape. If you have to pay for the stuff, you may find that this idea is cost prohibitive. The same can be said for the cost of the materials and labor that might be involved in building the retaining structure. It may be that this type of garden railroad, as desirable as it might be, simply has too great a negative impact on your railroad's bottom line!

That said, the important thing at this point in the planning stage is to determine and record any significant changes of elevation within your planned site, which leads to the natural question: "How can I accurately determine if, when, and where the ground is truly level?" Indeed, that's an entirely reasonable question, in light of the somewhat critical need for constructing a level roadbed.

Actually, there are several good methods that can be used for determining the slope of a section of terrain, ranging from the simple but reliable carpenter's-level and water-level techniques to the more sophisticated and costly laser surveying techniques used by engineering crews. Since this is a book that's primarily intended for the first-time garden railroader, we'll keep things as basic as possible here, and will cover two of the most simple slope-measuring methods that work well for the majority of small and medium-size layouts.

One method involves little more than a carpenter's level; a long, straight length of 2x2 or 2x4 lumber; a few wood stakes; and a couple of other around-the-home items. The second method requires a long length of garden hose or, preferably, clear vinyl tubing, along with some water and a few other supplies, to accomplish the same slope-measuring task.

With either technique, you'll start by locating and marking, both on your site map and on a stake planted in the ground at that exact location, a sort of "ground zero" reference point. It's best if this reference point is determined by the highest elevation on your chosen plot of real estate.

• The carpenter-level technique for determining slope

For a small garden layout, the carpenter-level technique of determining changes in elevation will certainly work well, and it is easy enough for one person to manage when working alone, if necessary, although the measuring and recording process does go a bit faster if two people are involved. Here's a list of the supplies you'll need, followed by a description of the procedure:

Items needed:

• **Eight-foot length of straight (no bows) 2x2 or 1x4 board or two-inch aluminum angle.**
• **Short scrap piece of straight 2x4 board.**
• **Three-foot-long or so 1x2 board or stake— pointed at one end if you're working alone and will need to drive the stake into the ground.**
• **C-clamp to attach the level-measuring board to the stake.**
• **Carpenter's level--any length will do, but the longer, the better.**
• **Yardstick or carpenter's rule.**
• **Pencil or felt-tip marker.**

1. Start at the highest point on your proposed layout site. Place the 2x4 scrap piece flat on the ground so the two-inch dimension is vertical, and then support the uphill end of the eight-foot leveling board or metal strip on the wider top surface of the 2x4.

Adjust leveling board up and down until it is level. Mark the stake; then subtract the height of the upper level stake.

Carpenter's level

8' length of <u>straight</u> 2x2

Carpenter's level method of determining changes in ground elevation.
Illustration by Dennis Auth

2. Rest the downhill end of the eight-foot board on a C-clamp that you have attached to a vertical stake that has been driven into the ground (a stake about three or four feet long should do fine). If someone is assisting you with these measurements, you won't really need the C-clamp, since he/she can hold the end of the board against the side of a free-standing vertical stake, and mark the level point with a pencil or felt-tip marker.
3. Place a carpenter's level anywhere along the length of the 8-foot board, and then move the board and its C-clamp (or have your assistant move the end of the 8-foot board) up or down along the vertical stake at the low end until the bubble on the level indicates that the board is perfectly level.
4. With a yardstick or tape measure, determine the distance from the bottom of the leveling board to the ground, measuring along the vertical stake you're using at the lower end.
5. Subtract the vertical thickness of the scrap of 2x4 that you placed under the upper end (it may be something less than exactly two inches) from the above measurement to account for the thickness of that piece of wood. Because the 8-foot board you are using is nearly 100-inches long, the number of inches remaining after you subtract will be very close to the actual percentage of grade or slope at that particular point on the terrain. For example, say that at the low point you are plotting, the distance from the ground to the bottom of your measuring level measures 4-1/2 inches. At the upper end, the scrap piece of wood you used measures 1-3/4 inches from the ground to the bottom of the measuring level. Subtract 1-3/4 from 4-1/2, and the result is 2-3/4 inches. That is the approximate slope of your land at that point: 2.75%. That would be an acceptable downgrade for your roadbed (under 3%), assuming that the actual terrain between the upper point and bottom point is flat and smooth.

6. Repeat this process until you have plotted the actual changes in slope or elevation for all sections of your planned layout area. Place a short surveyor's stake in the ground at each location where you take these measurements. Assign each stake a number, and label each stake with the distance between the two stakes, the height of the stake as measured from the ground to the level mark, and the percent of grade to that point.
7. Record the location of each survey point, along with the applicable data, on your site map. Then, repeat this process for any area of your planned layout space that is not perfectly level, and the end result will be an accurate elevation plot of the entire area.

• The water-level method for determining slope

The water-level method of determining slope or grade is simplicity itself, and it has some advantage over the carpenter-level method, particularly for larger layout areas, because you are not restricted to the eight-foot distance—the usual length of a carpenter-level measuring board—from your reference point to the lower elevation point. So, just what is a water level, and how does it work?

Think back to your school days, when you learned in physics class that "water always seeks it's own level." For example, if you partially fill a container with water, the water always remains perfectly level, regardless of how much water is in the container, and no matter how much, or in what direction, you tilt the container. This leveling action results from atmospheric pressure being exerted equally on all areas of the water's surface. This same principle can be applied to reliably determine how level (or not level), your piece of terrain actually is. Here's how it works:

Items needed:

• **Surveyor's stakes, or other long, straight, thin, pointed sticks.**
• **Length of clear, flexible plastic tubing (roughly 3/4-inch diameter), long enough to reach at least half the length of your planned layout. An ordinary garden hose will also work, if fitted with some clear tubing at each end.**
• **Two short (one foot or so) lengths of clear 3/4-inch diameter tubing to provide extensions at both ends if you're using an opaque garden hose.**
• **Hose end repair kit (for attaching the clear extensions to each end of the garden hose, if that is what you decide to use).**
• **Yardstick or tape measure.**
• **Clamps or duct tape to attach the water level tubing to the stakes.**
• **Pencil or felt-tip marking pen.**
• **Optional: food coloring to make the water easier to see.**

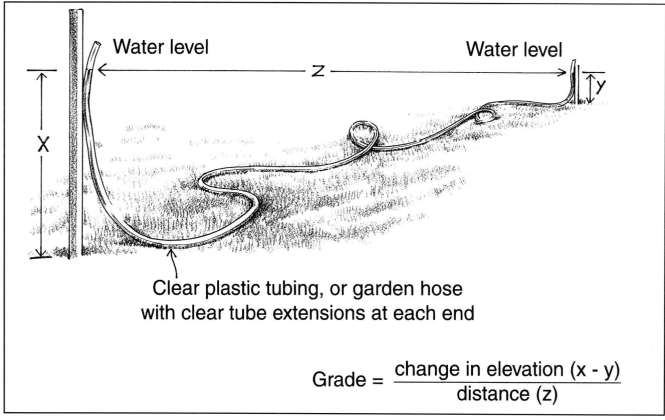

$$\text{Grade} = \frac{\text{change in elevation (x - y)}}{\text{distance (z)}}$$

Water-level method of determining changes in ground elevation.
Illustration by Dennis Auth

A water-level device, of the type to be used for determining grades on a garden railroad, simply takes the water-in-a-container concept described above and extends it to cover a much greater distance. The "container" in this case will be a long section of clear, 3/4-inch (or thereabouts) flexible vinyl tubing, or an ordinary garden hose. To first see for yourself how the process will actually work, take a couple of feet of garden hose or clear tubing and hold both ends in one hand so it's in the shape of a "U". Pour enough water into the section of hose or tubing until you almost fill it up to the ends. You now have the makings of a perfect leveling system! The water levels itself, regardless of the length of the hose or tubing, because, as noted earlier, atmospheric pressure is being exerted equally at both ends.

You can now use a longer version of this same simple apparatus to check the level at any point on your garden railroad, as long as the tubing or hose you use is long enough; doesn't have any kinks; and has both ends left open. If your planning to use an ordinary garden hose, you'll want to attach a clear vinyl tube extension to each end of the hose—that's where the hose repair kit comes into play. Use about a two-foot length of clear, 3/4-inch vinyl tubing for each end section, and attach those sections to the hose using the fittings supplied with the hose repair kit. Preferably, use clear vinyl tubing for the entire apparatus, and forget about the garden hose. You can buy this tubing at a reasonable

price at just about any home improvement. You may want to add some food coloring to the water you will use, because this will make it far easier for you to see just where the water level is, even from a distance. After you've prepared your tube or hose, here's how you should proceed:

1. Take two stakes, and plant them in the ground—one to serve as a high-level reference point and the other to serve as a low-level reference point. If possible, the first high-level stake you place should be at the corner of the planned layout area that marks the highest elevation on the chosen plot of land. That way, this stake can be labeled "#1," and all others used can refer to it in terms of their distance and degree of slope.
2. Tie or tape the vinyl tube (or vinyl hose extension) to the high-level (#1) stake so at least a foot of the vinyl tube/extension is in a vertical position.
3. Tie the other end of the vinyl tube/extension to the stake you planted at the low-level point for this particular measurement.
4. Fill the tube with water (colored water, if you prefer), until the water level reaches within an inch or two of both ends of the tubing. This procedure may require a little up-or-down adjustment of the lower-end tube so the water does, indeed, remain within the tubes at both ends.
5. Measure the distance from the ground to the water

level on the high-level stake, and then repeat the process by measuring the distance from the ground to the water level on the lower-level stake.

6. Subtract the measurement taken at the high-level stake from the measurement taken at the low-level stake. (This gives you the actual change in elevation, as determined from ground level.)

7. Measure the distance, in inches, from one stake to the other stake.

8. Divide that distance by the difference in the height of the two stakes, as determined in Step 6, above, and the resulting number will be the percentage of slope or grade. Say, for example, that the two stakes are 200-inches apart, and that the water level on the upper stake is 3 inches above the ground, while the water level at the lower stake is 24 inches above the ground. Subtract 3 from 24, which gives you 21. Divide 21 by 200 (the distance from one stake to the other), and the result is 10.5 percent. No train, real or model, can handle such a grade, so you know that there's going to be some work in store for you to get that measurement down to around 2 percent or so!

9. Place a surveyor's stake in the ground at each location where you made the measurements. Assign each stake a number, and label each stake with the measured distance between the two stakes, the height of each stake, and the percent of grade.

10. Record each stake's location and elevation on your site map.

Either of these two methods described can be used successfully for plotting elevations on a garden railroad, but the water-level technique, although it involves a few more steps, will probably work best if your railroad is going to cover a fairly large expanse of land. The question now becomes: "What do I do with this information?"

• Types of track plans

The next pre-construction phase of garden railroad planning involves merging the on-site information previously gathered with a functional track plan. However, before we get too far into the development of a track plan, it's worth taking a bit of time to review some of the options available in terms of types of track plans.

When it comes right down to it, virtually all model railroad track plans fall into one of four basic categories or types, regardless of how complex the completed trackwork may appear, and despite the fact that some final plans may combine more than one of the basic types as part of the overall scheme or even as a separate and independent line. These four basic track plans include the closed loop, the dogbone, the figure eight, and the point-to-point.

Closed loop:

The closed loop is perhaps the most common of the basic track plans for model railroads in all scales, and this is the type of plan selected for the majority of garden railroads. The track sections that may have come packaged with your starter set already form a closed loop—a circle or an oval—that affords continuous running of the train in what amounts to an around-the-Christmas-tree manner. You can subsequently add straight and curved sections to expand this circle or oval into a wide variety of sizes and distorted shapes, but it will still be a closed loop. Think of it in this way:

Say, for example, that you label one of the two running rails of your track as "+" and label the other running rail as "-". In a closed loop track plan, the "+" rail will always be "+" and the "-" rail will always be "-". If you're using electricity through the rails to power your trains, this basic principle is very important, because a "+" rail meeting a "-" rail anywhere along the line will result in a dead electrical short, meaning that nothing will run. A train on a closed loop is, in fact, always chasing itself around the loop, much as it did when it ran around your Christmas tree, and it will eventually end up right back at its point of origin, still facing in the same direction as when it began its journey.

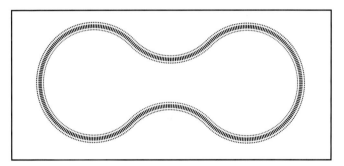

Closed loop track plan.
Illustration by Dennis Auth

The closed loop track plan is generally preferred by folks who enjoy sitting back, perhaps with their favorite beverage in one hand and a control unit in the other, watching their trains run continuously without any significant human intervention. That preference may even apply to the majority of us, which likely accounts for the overall popularity and acceptance of this type of track plan in one contorted configuration or another.

The only real disadvantage of the closed loop type of plan relates to the fact that watching a train chase itself in endless abandon can become a bit boring, particularly if the layout is a very small one. With a somewhat larger layout, the closed loop can be more or less disguised by adding various twists and turns to the route, so the track skirts the edge of a pond or tree, then curves around a bed of azaleas, and so forth. Another thing to keep in mind is that a closed loop is certainly not the way the real railroads actually operate. None of the major railroads you may be familiar with run in even a very large circle, including those that cover a good number of states or regions.

Dogbone:

The closed loop track plan described above may, of course, be configured into the shape of a dogbone—two long parallel straight sections connecting curved "bulges" at both ends—but that would still be a closed loop. A true dogbone track plan is one that consists of a single length of straight track (or an extended mainline section comprised of both straight and curved sections), that is connected to what are known as *reversing loops* at each end. For that reason, this track configuration is also sometimes called a loop-to-loop type of plan. The reversing loop that forms each teardrop-shaped end of a dogbone does just what its name implies: It causes the train to traverse that loop and then head back, now moving in the opposite direction, along the same straight route that it had previously traveled. At the opposite end, the turn-around activity repeats itself, by means of yet another reversing loop.

In certain respects, the dogbone type of track plan more closely emulates the routing of a real railroad, some of which still do have a means for turning a complete train around at the end of its journey. A few railroads actually use what amounts to a large reversing loop, of sorts, to accomplish this task. Others may use a very long Y-shaped structure of trackwork (described in more detail below) to reverse a train's orientation. Today, however, most major railroads have little or no need for turning entire trains. They may wish to turn a locomotive around so it is facing forward along the intended route, but it really doesn't matter much which end of a freight or passenger car is considered the "front end."

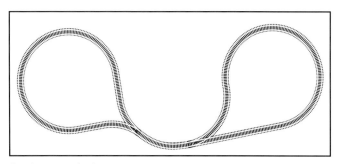

Dogbone track plan.
Illustration by Dennis Auth

The principal disadvantage of the dogbone track plan is the somewhat complex wiring that may be required if you intend to use track power to supply the operating voltage to your trains—the most common way of powering model railroads in all scales. What happens is that each reversing loop creates a dead short at the turnout where it diverges from, and subsequently reconnects with, the straight section or mainline. Again, as was demonstrated above, you can rather easily see how this occurs if you draw two parallel lines to represent the running rails of track, and then curve each of these tracks around in a loop so they come back and connect to the original straight section. Again, label one

of the "rails" as "+" and the other one as "-". Where a "+" joins with a "-" (or vice versa), you have the makings of a dead short! There are ways to get around this problem, including devices that activate automatically to change the flow of electric current in the reversing loop, and some wiring schemes that can be controlled manually to accomplish the same thing, but many model railroaders much prefer to avoid potential reversing loop problems whenever and wherever possible—a good idea if you're new to the hobby.

Figure Eight:

In it's simplest form, a figure eight track plan requires the use of a special section of track known as a 90-degree crossing to allow the track in what otherwise would be a simple oval to cross over itself on the same level, thereby creating a route that resembles the number "8". Actually, the track is crossing through itself— an action made possible by the crossing section. If space permits, a 45-degree or even a 30-degree crossing can be used to extend the length of the closed loops at the top and bottom of the "8".

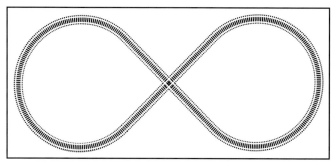

Figure eight track plan.
Illustration by Dennis Auth

A figure eight track plan can also be created without the use of a crossing, if the plan is intentionally designed so that the track passes over instead of through itself. To accomplish this, a significant number of track sections need to be gradually and progressively elevated until there is sufficient clearance at the point where the tracks cross to allow for unobstructed passage, underneath this crossing point, of your tallest locomotives or cars (about nine inches of clearance above the railheads is recommended for most Large Scale locomotives and cars). Of course, the same consideration must be given to the downgrade portion after the train has reached the crossover point. The upgrade and downgrade portions of such a configuration require carefully planned and properly executed gradual grades—something the real railroads prefer to avoid, wherever possible. If you decide that this type of plan is really what you want, you'll need to allow for plenty of space to achieve the upgrade and downgrade segments without exceeding, for example, a two- or three-percent change in elevation in either direction (four percent, a very steep grade in the world of railroading, is definitely the maximum you should consider using on a garden railroad). One way to achieve more gradual grades in a somewhat restricted space is to lower the elevation of the lower line as you increase the elevation of the upper line.

Figure eight track plans offer the primary advantage of a closed loop plan— continuous running of a train—without quite the level of boredom that comes with watching a train chase itself around a continuous circle or oval. Depending on the topography of the location selected for your garden railroad, this track plan may also permit you to take better advantage of existing changes in elevation at your selected site, and if the over-and-under type is used, it will afford you an opportunity to try your hand at a bit of bridge building.

Point-to-point:

If true-to-prototype operations are what you want to duplicate on your garden layout, or if a long but very narrow space is all you have available, then a point-to-point track plan certainly deserves your consideration. Real railroads almost invariably operate with a point-to-point track network.

As the name implies, a point-to-point railroad consists of little more than a line, be it straight or full of twists and turns, drawn between two points. A train starts at point "A", or somewhere in between, and ends up at point "B", or at some intermediate destination. There may be passing sidings along the main route, to allow a train heading in one direction to bypass a train heading in the opposite direction, and there may be numerous sidings, spurs, or even interchanges with other railroads along the way, but the basic goal is to deliver loads in the most direct manner possible from point of origin to final destination.

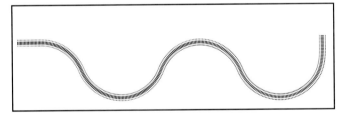

Point-to-point track plan.
Illustration by Dennis Auth

An inherent problem with the point-to-point scheme, at least as far as model railroad operators are concerned, is the inability to conduct continuous running. Operators of a point-to-point rail line can't just sit back and watch the trains run around and around. They must be in control of their trains at all times, particularly when the train approaches one end of the line or the other. The railroad must also be equipped with some means of actually turning the locomotives around at the end of the line, unless the operator is content with having trains operate in what is known as a push-pull fashion (seen in real life on a number of commuter lines, where locomotives or locomotive control units are

at each end of the train).

In the days when steam power ruled, a turntable at each terminus, and even at service points in between, was used to turn locomotives so they would be facing in the right direction. Even diesel-electric locomotives were turned in this way. An alternative to the turntable, in areas where sufficient real estate was available, was a long Y-shaped network of track, called a "wye", which could be used to turn either the locomotive or an entire train around. A train heading up the stem portion of the wye would move into one or the other of the branches. When it neared the end of the branch line, it would reverse direction; a switch would be thrown; and the train would then back through a "saddle" route that connected the two branches. After it had moved fully into the opposite branch, and had cleared the opposite switch on the saddle, that switch would then be thrown and the train would head back onto the stem en route back to the main line.

In model railroading, either the turntable or the wye, or perhaps a combination of the two, offers a lot of fun and challenges for those who truly want to operate trains in a realistic way. However, a good many model railroaders, including many garden railroaders, still prefer the comfort and ease of watching their trains operate in a continuous and uninterrupted manner, and neither the turntable nor the wye allow for much lemonade sipping when you reach the end of the line!

A "wye" that will allow a locomotive or a short train to turn around so it can head in the opposite direction is under construction on Peter Thornton's garden railroad.
Photo courtesy of Peter Thornton

Keep in mind that all of the basic track configurations outlined above are just that: basic! They can be embellished in any number of ways to increase operational capabilities and to enhance the fun you have with your layout. In some instances, two or more types of track plans might even be combined on a single layout. You might, for example feature a closed loop configuration for your main line, but supplement it with a point-to-point commuter or trolley line elsewhere on your layout—especially since many trolleys and commuter trains do not need to be turned around. And, of course, all of these basic track plans can easily be made considerably more complex and interesting by adding a

variety of turnouts almost anywhere along the line, thereby allowing you to incorporate passing sidings, branchline routes, and various types of diverging routes to serve stations, locomotive servicing facilities, and an assortment of industries.

• Step 4—Developing a track plan

Now that you have some idea of the basic types of track configurations, it's time to put this information to use in creating a viable track plan. You already know the physical dimensions and topographic makeup of the land area you will be working with, and have pretty much prepared that area to accommodate your railroad, so now we need to see if and how the garden railroad of your dreams can be accommodated by the real-world plot of ground that awaits it!

A well-thought-out track plan will permit you, in advance of actual construction, to determine how to make the best use of your available space, and it will enable you to explore various options relating to operational characteristics that are most important to you. Perhaps most important, it will help you to determine just how much track and related items such as turnouts and rail clamps you will actually need to make your dream a reality.

One approach to track planning is to simply conjure-up a rough sketch of what you envision; haul boxes of shiny new track out to your prepared site; and begin placing track sections on the ground to see how everything will fit. Not unlike working with a jigsaw puzzle, you can manipulate individual track sections to your heart's content, rearranging and reconfiguring things until everything "looks right" and appears as if it will go together reasonably well. And, this approach may work well enough for you if (1) you have a fairly simple track plan in mind; (2) have the time and the physical energy to contend with all of the repetitive gyrations that will be involved in bending over to pick up and reposition lots of individual track sections; and (3) you are very good at guessing just how much track you will really need. However, it's a whole lot easier and far less tedious if you give a bit of advance thought to what you want your railroad to be, where you want it to go, how you would like it to operate, and how much "stuff" you will need before you forge ahead in wild abandon and start laying-down and connecting the track.

A related on-site track planning technique that some garden railroaders have employed with reasonable success involves using a number of 50- or 100-foot lengths of ordinary, disconnected garden hose to form an outline of the proposed track plan. This is accomplished by simply laying the garden hose directly on the site, then moving it around until it approximates a track plan that fits the space and suits your purposes. A tape measure, string, and a good supply of short wood stakes are useful in helping to get the curves properly configured, and once everything is satisfactorily in place, additional stakes can be driven into the ground

every couple of feet or so to mark the route that the track is to follow. An advantage of this technique is that when the hose is properly laid, and assuming you have enough hose to cover the full route that your railroad will take, you'll have a pretty good visual representation of what the rail line will actually look like without having to deal with lots of individual track sections. An obvious disadvantage is that you still won't know exactly how much track you will need unless you do some very accurate calculations. And, it may take a whole lot of garden hose and a considerable amount of time to create and mark the complete track plan, unless you are proposing to build a relatively small layout (which, again, is not a bad idea at all).

But even though either of these two on-site track planning methods may work well enough in some situations, a far better approach to layout planning involves doing things in a somewhat easier and more systematic manner. That involves sitting down with pencil and paper in hand, or in front of your computer screen if you have access to design software for model railroads and are somewhat computer literate, and then

David Winter's proposed Winter Valley Regional Railway site started out as a steeply sloping area of terrain with rocks, trees, and a variety of other obstacles that would need to be cleared to make way for the railroad.
Photo courtesy of David Winter

Seen here after some initial clearing, leveling, and tree removal had been attended to, David's site is starting to take shape. That truss bridge sitting on the ground is a dead giveaway to David's future plans for this piece of real estate.
Photo courtesy of David Winter

A lot of back-breaking labor on David's part has culminated in a functional and attractive garden railroad that will soon be filled in with additional vegetation.
Photo courtesy of David Winter

taking a bit of time to consider what it is that you want your railroad to be, and how you want it to operate. Initially, all you need to get the process rolling are some ideas, a basic understanding of the general types of track plans that might be considered, and some photocopies of your site map.

Start by conceptualizing what you would like your railroad to look like, from the standpoint of operational capabilities. If you don't have anything special in mind in this early stage, aside from a theme that you might like to follow, take the time to do a little research. Browse through some model railroad magazines and track planning books to gain inspiration and to develop a few ideas. It doesn't matter if a good plan you find is not drawn specifically for Large Scale trains or for a garden railroad. What you're seeking at this stage is simply some idea of what can be done, and what has worked for others, regardless of their scale-of-preference. There will be ample opportunity to fret over space limitations and other considerations later, but for now the important thing is to find a general track plan or concept that appeals to you, for whatever reasons. This concept will serve as the launch pad for developing your own track plan—one that has been tailored to your specific location and needs.

At this point, you would also be well advised to review the list of track planning tips that follow this section. Although some of these are simply helpful tips, a good number cover specific points that really do need

to be adhered to when you get to the actual construction phase. Try to fix as many of them in your mind as you possibly can—especially those that relate to placement of track and turnouts.

Once you have a general concept in mind, and have reviewed the track planning tips listed below, you're ready to begin committing things to paper. Start by drawing a rough pencil sketch of your proposed mainline on a photocopy of your site map. Don't worry about getting things to scale at this point; just see if and how the ideas you have developed will work on the plot of land that you have available. Then, draw in the location of one or more passing sidings, if possible, followed by however many other spurs, sidings, and yards you might want to have. Keep in mind that each siding or yard track should be there for a purpose—to serve some industry or to gain access to an engine servicing facility, or the like. Whatever you do, remember to keep things simple! Use your eraser and/or additional photocopies of your site map until you have developed a rough track plan that will satisfy your needs and particular interests.

The next step is to merge your proposed track plan with your site map in a drawn-to-scale version. The easiest way to do this is with the aid of a plastic track planning template, which will allow you to trace individual straight and curved track sections, turnouts, and other related items to an predetermined scale. Both LGB and CTT offer Large Scale track planning tem-

plates, and one or both of these is generally available at any hobby shop that stocks Large Scale equipment and supplies. Or, you can refer to the manufacturer/supplier appendix at the end of this book for addresses and contact information.

If you exercise some care in using the template—properly matching the ends of each track section, for example—the result will be an accurate, to-scale rendering of your proposed track plan. You can then add up the total number of straight sections, curved sections of various radii, and turnouts, and you'll have a very good idea of exactly how much trackwork, rail clamps, and other items you will need, and with that information at hand you can determine how much everything will cost.

Once you have the scale track plan drawn to your satisfaction, it's a rather simple process to transfer data from your site map to the final track plan. Just be sure to use the scale of the track plan as the scale for determining the position of site map objects drawn onto that track plan. For example:

Say that a two-foot diameter tree trunk is indicated on your site map, and it is located eight feet from the fence that runs alongside your yard, and ten feet from the wall of your garage, as measured on the ground. Your site map shows this object's location in accordance with whatever scale you used to construct the site map—perhaps one ruled line on the graph paper was supposed to equal six actual inches, or something along those lines. But, your final track plan may very well have been drawn to some other scale—say 1/4 inch equals one foot, for instance—depending on which track planning template you used. When you transfer this particular tree's location to the final track plan, make sure that you use the 1/4 inch = one foot scale (or whatever) assigned to the template. Following this example, the tree would be placed two inches from the indicated position of the fence, and 2-1/2 inches from the indicated location of the garage wall.

Transfer data from your previously completed site map—again being careful to keep everything to scale if the track plan and site map are in different scales, as they likely will be—and the end result will be an accurate depiction of your layout site, including an equally accurate track plan. And, if you plotted the various elevation changes within your layout site, as you should have, you'll be able to see how the track plan conforms to those changes in elevation, and where some additional soil removal or fill might be needed.

Garden railroaders who are somewhat high-tech oriented, and who like to tinker with what many model railroaders call "confusers" instead of computers, may enjoy taking advantage of some of the sophisticated and fun to use track planning software that is available to model railroaders.

RR-Track, 3rd PlanIt, and Abracadata, among others, provide sectional track layout software that helps you to design and redesign your entire layout, be it indoors or outdoors, from the comfort of a seat in front of your home computer. Your computer's mouse does most of the work, and all you really need do is keep moving things around until you're satisfied with the results. Then hit the "print" button, and you'll have a properly scaled version of your entire layout, complete with all of the landscaping features and even a list of the individual track components needed!

Some of these track planning and layout design programs are available for either PC or Macintosh operating systems, and they generally come equipped with complete "libraries" of images that not only include different makes of track, but also accessories of all types and even landscaping features such as trees, structures, and so forth. Certain of these programs will also provide a 3-D view of your completed project, so you can see how it looks not only from a top view, but also from various lower angles. If you're comfortable with computers, these applications can be a whole lot of fun to play with!

OK! Now that the track plan and site plan have been merged into a single document, it's time to get "down and dirty" and begin some actual construction. But before moving on, it's appropriate to review some important tips that apply to both track planning and track laying.

• Track planning tips

• Restrict any grades on your railroad to 4% or less. Actually, around 3% or 3.5% is a much preferred upper limit—something less than 3% is even better! While some narrow gauge railroads actually had grades of around 4%, this was avoided wherever possible. And, most standard gauge railroads today rarely have grades in excess of 2%, with 1% being far more common. Model railroad grades steeper than 1% or 2% generally require some control by the operator to give the trains more power on the upgrade and to slow them on the downgrade, so if you prefer to just turn on your trains and let them run relatively unattended, you should plan for grades that do not exceed 2%. The base and summit of each grade should also include a transition section to gently start and end the inclined area (see transition tip below).

• Avoid sharp "S" curves wherever and whenever possible, unless these curves are very broad, and unless the section where the two curved sections meet can be separated by a considerable length of straight track, preferably equipped with easements at both ends (see easement tip below). "S" curves, particularly tight ones, tend to invite derailments. Furthermore, most trains look very awkward weaving their way through such convoluted trackwork.

• Place your turnouts where you can most easily get at them. If you're ever going to experience trouble with your trackwork and/or derailments, the problems will most often occur at or near a turnout. For that reason, you should strive to place all of your turnouts in as

accessible a location as possible. Ideally, you should be able to get to your turnouts without having to walk or crawl all over the railroad to get to them. Placing turnouts as close as possible to the layout's perimeter is always a very good idea. NEVER place a turnout inside a tunnel or similar enclosed feature—that's just begging for trouble!

• Even on a small and very basic layout, try to include at least one passing siding. Passing sidings, which require both a left-hand and right-hand turnout, make it possible for two or more trains to operate over a single mainline track. When one train approaches or draws too close to the other, the leading train, or the closest of the two approaching trains, can be diverted into the passing siding and held there until the second train passes. After the main route is clear again, the second train exits the passing siding and proceeds on to its destination.

• Plan to have at least one or two spurs or sidings on your layout. Spur tracks (also referred to simply as "sidings") are dead-end sections of track that divert from the mainline by means of a single turnout. The curved, or diverging, section of the turnout can face either left or right, depending on where the spur needs to go.

• Plan to include *easements* and *transitions* on your track plan and actual trackwork. Easements are stretches of slightly curved track that gently ease a train into a more pronounced curved section. You've probably seen how toy trains tend to jerk around the curved corners of a simple oval of track. Easements help to reduce or eliminate the "jerk." You can use a length of flex-track, in place of several ordinary straight sections, to provide a gentle easement. If the real railroads didn't use easements, they would likely suffer some very hefty damage claims from shippers and passengers! Transitions are very gently elevated stretches of track that are constructed at the beginning and end of a grade to help a train move smoothly from a level to an inclined position (and back again). In planning and execution, a transition should require at least three feet of track length at both the base and the summit of the grade.

• Allow for adequate separation between parallel tracks and between the track and any trackside signals or structures. As a general guide, allow for six inches (6") from track center to track center along parallel straight sections of track, and increase that center-to-center distance to at least eight inches (8") or more on curves. These separations are important to avoid having a train on one track sideswipe a train passing on the adjacent track, especially on curves where there is some overhang of the ends of locomotives and cars.

• Provide for adequate vertical clearance between the track and any overhead obstructions. Allow for at least nine inches (9") of vertical clearance when measured from the top of the railheads to the bottom of the overhead obstruction (tunnel portal, bridge framework, and the like).

• Avoid placing turnouts on or near curves. A turnout on a curve is just a problem looking for a place to happen, since any slight discrepancy with point alignment or some other adjustment on the turnout will simply be compounded by the fact that wheel flanges are riding harder against one rail or the other on curved sections. In some model railroading scales, the manufacturers do offer curved turnouts, but, to date, these are not commercially available in #1 Gauge track.

• Related to what was noted above, try to have at least one straight section leading into and out of each segment of a turnout. This helps to direct locomotive and car wheels along a smooth path through the turnout, reducing the chance of derailments.

• Consider elevating the entire railroad above ground level, if that is at all feasible. This point was mentioned earlier, but it's worth repeating. It's a whole lot easier to both admire and work on your trains if you can get them even a bit closer to normal eye level. When a garden railroad is constructed on the ground (and most are), the view a standing person gets is pretty much an aerial view—kind of as if they were in a low-flying airplane. In real life, we rarely see trains from an airborne perspective. Anything you can do to elevate your rail line—even if it amounts to just a foot or so—will help to provide a more realistic feel to the overall setting.

• Employ various scenic features to mask portions of the layout so not all of the track can be seen from any single vantage point. Ideally, a viewer should be required to at least turn his or her head, or even walk around a bit, to take in the complete railroad. Hills, rockwork, trees, shrubs, and other landscaping features, properly planned and placed about twelve feet apart, can help provide the visual break that is needed to effectively separate one scene from another. This technique will also help to make the railroad appear longer and larger, since the trains will disappear, and then reappear, throughout the course of their journey.

• Wherever possible, use broad, sweeping curves that follow the contours of the terrain. This advice is closely related to the "always use the widest curves possible" theme that is preached throughout this book, but it differs in some respects because here we're talking about aesthetics rather than operation. The course a real railroad follows is generally defined by the terrain, not the other way around. Railroads try to find ways around mountains, if possible, rather than punch through them. Railroads prefer to follow a waterway rather than bridge the waterway. Plan your railroad as if the terrain and landscaping was there first, even though it may not be. Then, make your track plan conform to the requirements posed by these features.

After freeing the locomotive seen trapped in a snow drift in the Introduction section of this book, the crew of a Suleski Transportation Inc. plow train stops to inspect their equipment and enjoy a hot cup of coffee at a small depot along the line.
Photo courtesy of Scott Suleski

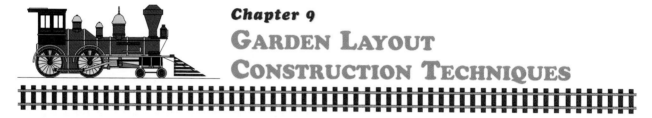

Chapter 9
GARDEN LAYOUT
CONSTRUCTION TECHNIQUES

With the planning and preliminary site preparation attended to, it's time to get on with actual construction of your roadbed and the other fixtures needed to get the trains up and running. The techniques and steps described in this chapter are among the most important you'll find anywhere in this book, because all of your previous planning and preparation will be to little or no avail if the railroad itself is not firmly and securely constructed and wired. A case in point:

Not long ago, I had an opportunity to visit one of the most attractive garden railroads I have even seen. It was a huge layout, set on a sloping hillside, and it featured a spectacular cascading waterfall, lush vegetation, gigantic bridges and trestles, a variety of interesting structures, and a track network that would enable several trains to run for long distances without ever having to pass the same point twice. Yes, it *would* permit this level of operation, if only the railroad operated! The fact is, not a single train was running during my visit, simply because they couldn't run. Somewhere along that extensive network of track and turnouts the gremlins were at work, and not a single train was able to operate despite the repeated efforts of a several-person crew to identify and remedy the problem or problems. There were problems with grades and turnouts, too, so even the live steamer that was available for service couldn't perform. In effect then, what I saw before me was not a garden railroad at all, but rather a large and beautiful garden with a lot of track weaving its way throughout. It was a disappointment for me and, I'm sure, for the owner of the layout.

This chapter—this entire book, in fact—is designed to help you avoid such frustrating and even embarrassing situations. The goal is to make building your first garden railroad a fun-filled learning experience so that operating and expanding the completed layout will provide a lifetime of even more fun. But this goal can only be achieved if proper care and attention is given to each phase of construction, thereby assuring that what you build is, indeed, a garden railroad, and not just an attractive garden adorned with track.

How well your trackwork performs over time depends in large measure on how well the roadbed supporting that track was constructed. The fact is, there are probably as many ways to construct supporting roadbed as there are ways to landscape the garden railroad, but a select few methods have been time-tested, proven, and generally accepted for their long-term reliability. That being the case, the focus here will be on several of those methods. You can certainly feel free to explore other alternatives—that's even recommended—but chances are you'll find that one of the three roadbed construction techniques described below will work well in your circumstances.

Following some preliminary discussion relating to garden railroad roadbed, track laying, and electrical construction techniques in general, this chapter will also explore the real-life experiences of two garden railroaders who explain, step-by-step, how they went about building their layouts, each of which was constructed in a very different region of the country. One of the layouts is located on the East Coast, in Virginia, and the second layout is located in northern Colorado. The two garden railroaders who built these layouts necessarily followed somewhat different approaches in terms of planning, construction methods, and even the materials used, but both have achieved the same result: A garden railroad that that is a joy to operate as well as a joy to behold. There's much to be learned from the first-hand experiences of others, and these two accounts provide splendid examples of how that works.

First, though, it's worthwhile to explore some of the commonalties that exist for garden railroads in general, no matter where they are located and regardless of how they are constructed. It's pretty much a given that most garden layouts will, at one time or another, have to contend with the effects of wind, water in different forms and amounts, temperature variations, weeds, and wandering critters, among other things. Short of encasing the entire layout in a greenhouse (which a few have actually done), there's really no way to completely avoid having to cope with these influences. Moreover, why would you really want to do so, since a real-world environment is part of the challenge and fun of garden railroading in the great outdoors?

Nevertheless, we can take certain steps to minimize the impact that most of these natural events have on the railroad, and the best place to start is with sound and solid construction techniques to support our rail line. Of course, we'll still have the forces of nature to deal with from time to time, but the end result of following proper construction procedures early on is that far more of our future leisure hours will be available for actually operating trains rather than fixing things so we can operate later.

We'll assume at this point that your layout site has been properly prepared, and that all of the basic dirt hauling, rock moving, tamping, and other major back-breaking labor has been pretty much completed. If you built your layout above ground level, the retaining walls are in place, and the general area where your track will be located has been leveled and marked with flags or stakes every couple of feet or so to indicate both the route and the elevation.

If you haven't already done so, this is a good time to make some provision for the electrical wiring that will be used to power the railroad. You may need wiring for such things as lights (floodlights for night-time running, as well as interior lights in any structures), water pumps that might be used for ponds and streams, and track and turnout power feeds, among other things. Buried PVC conduit, with appropriate junctions and inverted U-shaped end fittings installed where needed, can be used to protect any and all of this wiring. Just be sure to select pipe of a wide enough diameter to accommodate any future expansion needs, such as more lights, additional turnouts, a turntable, and that sort of thing.

Constructing the supporting roadbed:

The supporting roadbed for your track is no less important than the track itself. In some ways, it's even more important than the track, because without proper support, you'll very likely experience track-related operating problems down the road as track alignment shifts or as track level changes with the passing of time.

As noted earlier, there are a number of ways to build a solid supporting roadbed, and they range from ballast poured into a trench all the way to a formed concrete roadbed, with lots of variations in between. The three methods described here are just a small sampling, but they have been selected because they seem to serve well in the most broad range of circumstances and conditions.

• Trenched roadbed

By far the most common way to support track on a garden railroad, and perhaps the easiest way, is to do it the way the real railroads do, with just a few minor variations. The prototype railroads cushion their track on a firm and level roadbed made up of crushed rock ballast. The ballast provides a solid supporting foundation for the track and the trains, and it also helps to promote proper drainage. Furthermore, it is easy enough to replace or repair the ballast where and when necessary. Aside from the fact that garden railroad ballast is

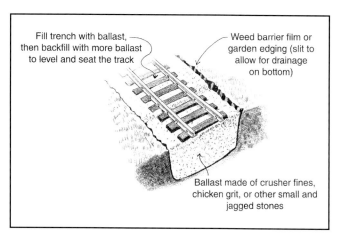

Trenched roadbed
Illustration by Dennis Auth

Fill trench with ballast, then backfill with more ballast to level and seat the track

Weed barrier film or garden edging (slit to allow for drainage on bottom)

Ballast made of crusher fines, chicken grit, or other small and jagged stones

much smaller, and therefore subject to more disruption from wind and rain, there's no reason that the same technique shouldn't work well enough with our smaller #1 Gauge track.

However, there are differences in the way the real railroads build their roadbed and the way it is done in a garden-size scale. On the full-size railroads, an embankment of ballast is constructed directly on top of a graded land surface. On a garden railroad, the ballast, because of the much smaller size of the individual rocks, must be handled somewhat differently. Generally, a trench is dug into the ground to retain the bulk of the scale-size ballast, while a small embankment above ground provides a firm support surface for the track.

The supplies you'll need for constructing a trench roadbed are fairly simple: the right tools for digging a shallow trench, enough ballast to fill that trench, and, as an option, rolls of garden weed barrier or plastic sheets of weed barrier, if you elect to go with that option. You'll also need your leveling devices, for confirming that everything is smooth and level, both with the roadbed and with the track itself.

Here are the basic steps for constructing trenched roadbed:

1. Start by digging a trench about four inches deep, and about six inches wide, along the flagged or staked route that your track will follow. Before you start to dig, it helps to mark where the edges of the planned trench will be, so your digging will be as straight and consistent as possible. If your layout is a modest size (which it really should be), you might even consider laying the actual track on the ground, and then marking a chalk line about an inch or so outside the tie ends on both sides along the entire route.

2. Some folks prefer to line the side walls of their trench with garden edging to contain the ballast and prevent weed growth. Others choose to line the full trench—both sides and the bottom—with plastic weed barrier

sheeting. Still others contend that neither of these anti-weed measures is really necessary, and they simply pour ballast into the trench until it is level with the surface of the ground. This latter group will also argue that proper drainage may be restricted if an edging wall or weed barrier is used. They are right about that, to the degree that some drainage capability is necessary. So, if you're planning to use plastic weed barrier sheeting to line your trench, you should cut slits along the bottom to allow water to drain out. Any excess weed barrier sheeting that overlaps the sides of the trench can later be trimmed flush to ground level, where it won't be easily noticed.

3. Fill the trench with crusher fines, chicken grit, or whatever other ballast material you've chosen, to just below ground level (refer to the "Track and turnouts" chapter for a detailed description of suitable ballast materials). After the ballast is in place, distribute it evenly with a paint brush or small broom, as necessary, and then tamp the ballast firmly to seat and "lock" the individual stones. If you don't do this, the ballast will have a tendency to shift when it eventually settles. You can use the end of a piece of 4x4 or 2x4 as your tamping tool. Check to assure that the sub-roadbed is level (both lengthwise and side-to-side) in areas where it is supposed to be level, and that it gently eases into elevations in areas where you have planned for grades. You'll also want check to make sure that any grades along the line do not exceed three percent, if at all possible—less is even better.

4. Once you're satisfied that the sub-roadbed is smooth and level both lengthwise and crosswise, go ahead and place the track atop the ballast, checking to make sure that track sections are positioned where you want them to be, and that the track, too, is level. Connect track sections securely, using conductive paste on all rail joiners and any other track-connecting devices, such as rail clamps or screws (Aristo-Craft track comes with pre-drilled holes and small screws). In lieu of rail clamps, you can place small sections of wood under the ends of adjoining sections and hold the two track sections together by installing screws through the end tie on each section, driving the screws into the wood plate. Now, or at some early date, it would also be a very good idea to solder jumper wires around each rail joint if the wood plate method is used, since any loss of electrical current will result from the rail joiners themselves being loosened over time, and the wood support alone will not really prevent that from happening.

5. Now go back and pour more ballast directly over the track until it reaches the top of the ties, both inside and outside the running rails. Tamp the ballast with a small piece of wood to compact it tightly between each tie, and then check for level once again—both lengthwise and crosswise. As you may have discerned from reading to this point, level trackwork is as important as properly connected trackwork!

One good way to confirm level is to lay a carpenter's level lengthwise on a flatcar, and then push the car along the track as you work from one point to the next. You can also lay a small line level across one end of that same car, or place it on a following car, to check cross-level of the track. If you find that the track is too high or low in some spot, or on one side, you can gently lift the section and add or remove some ballast; then re-seat the track by wiggling it a bit as you place it back into position. When everything is just right, go back along the entire route and add a bit more ballast, where necessary, to fill any gaps.

6. After you're satisfied that the track is level with ballast supporting it properly in all areas, give the entire roadbed a gentle but thorough soaking with a water spray. Don't blast it with your garden hose, because that will scatter the ballast. Once wetted, dust and fine particles in the rock will act as a sort of adhesive, helping to bond everything in place.

7. Allow everything to dry for at least a day, then give the rails a good cleaning to remove any rock dust or other residue deposited during construction. At this point you're ready to connect the power feeds (be sure to coat the connections with conductive paste!); set a locomotive on the track; and throttle up for the inaugural run!

• Wood roadbed and supports

If you live in a fairly moderate climate, where hard frosts are not a frequent occurrence during cold weather months, and you enjoy doing carpentry work, there is an alternative method of roadbed construction that may work well for you.

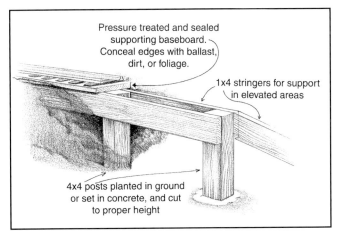

Pressure treated and sealed supporting baseboard. Conceal edges with ballast, dirt, or foliage.

1x4 stringers for support in elevated areas

4x4 posts planted in ground or set in concrete, and cut to proper height

Wood-supported roadbed
Illustration by Dennis Auth

This method involves supporting the track on a pressure-treated wood roadbed which, in turn, is attached to wood posts anchored into the ground. As with any other roadbed construction method, there are advantages and disadvantages to this approach. One

distinct advantage is that wood roadbed under the track provides a firm and stable support for the track-work, and is not subject to erosion or wind damage. Another advantage is that the track itself can be securely anchored to the roadbed with screws, thereby assuring and maintaining proper track alignment along the entire route. On the downside, wood is affected by long-term exposure to the elements, particularly moisture. Even pressure-treated and sealed wood is subject to some rotting or deterioration over time, especially if it is not occasionally re-sealed with a preservative. Also, a wood-supported roadbed may not be a viable option if you live in a climate where frost heave is likely to force the vertical supports upward during the change in seasons, although driving the supports into the ground below the frost line, or encasing them in concrete, will usually take care of that problem. Finally, this all-wood method is probably best suited to those who enjoy tackling a bit of carpentry work, and who have all the necessary power tools available.

The supplies needed to construct a wood roadbed supported by wood posts include pressure-treated or marine-grade plywood sheets or 1x6 boards for the roadbed base, 4x4 pressure-treated boards for the vertical supports, 1x4 pressure-treated boards for the horizontal support stringers, and screws of sufficient length to hold everything together. Depending on the specific approach you take, you'll also need an assortment of tools, including a hole digger, power saw, power drill with drill and screwdriver bits, carpenter's level, line level, and some measuring and marking implements.

Here are the basic construction and assembly steps:

1. If you're using pressure-treated plywood, begin by cutting six-inch wide strips, lengthwise, to place in areas where you have planned for straight trackwork. Trace your pre-assembled curved sections directly on the plywood sheets, (allowing for an extra inch on each side), in order to get the longest possible roadbed sections and to keep the total number of roadbed-to-roadbed joints to a minimum.

2. Assuming that you have previously marked the track route with surveyor's stakes, small flags, or chalk lines, you can begin placing your 4x4 vertical support posts in the ground, centered on your track line. Place each post about four feet apart in straight sections, and perhaps three feet apart on curves, depending on the degree of curvature of the roadbed and the thickness of the material used to make the roadbed. The tighter the radius, the closer together the posts should be placed. Again, you'll want to extend them below the frost line, or bury them in concrete, if you live in a frost-prone region. With a long, straight section of board and a carpenter's level, check level by resting the board atop two or more adjacent post tops, and then place the level

atop the board. Make any necessary adjustments by driving the higher supporting 4x4 a bit deeper into the ground. When you are satisfied that everything is level, you're ready to proceed.

3. Screw the roadbed strips to the top of the vertical support posts. One or two screws per post should do the job. Go back and again check the level along each stretch of the line.

4. The role of the horizontal 1x4 stringers that run from one or more support posts to adjacent posts is to provide horizontal stability to the roadbed strips. The 4x4 posts alone will not provide all the stability that is needed. The stringers also eliminate the need to install scab plates—small sections of wood used to join adjacent roadbed sections—along the line. Stringers are placed on both outward-facing sides of the posts, flush with the bottom of the roadbed. The stringers will need to be cut to fit. One or two screws should be adequate for attaching the stringers to each vertical post. Before you permanently attach the stringers, check for cross-level to see if there is any tilting of the roadbed across its width. If there is, the stringer on the low side can be forced upward to correct the sideways tilt. If you desire, screws can also be driven through the roadbed and into the top of the stringer, especially in areas where roadbed sections butt against each other, and in places where especially long stringers are used.

5. The final step is to backfill dirt against the outside surfaces of the exposed stringers, bringing the roadbed flush with its surrounding landscape. Small bushes or other groundcover can also be used to provide the necessary masking.

The roadbed is now ready to accept your track, which can be loosely screwed directly to the roadbed every few feet or so. There's no need to go overboard with the number of screws used, since their primarily function is just to prevent the track shifting out of alignment, and to keep the rail joints as tight as possible. Screw holes drilled through the ties should be a bit larger than the screw itself, to allow for a bit of "give" in all directions. Also, do not tighten the screws too tightly, or you may crack the tie or even force the rails out of gauge.

Some garden railroaders also insist that no roadbed is truly complete without a layer of ballast, so you can certainly add ballast right over your new roadbed.

• PVC supported roadbed

The PVC roadbed support method is simply a variation of the wood roadbed support technique. This involves the use of 1-1/4" diameter PVC pipe sections to provide the upright supporting structure for the wood roadbed. There are some real advantages to using PVC pipe for the vertical supports. First, PVC will

never rot, and it is impervious to termites and anything else that might harm a wood support. Also, PVC pipe is easy to cut. All in all, it is a method of roadbed construction well worth considering.

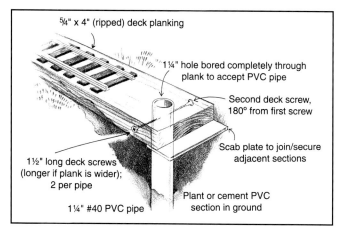

PVC roadbed support
Illustration by Dennis Auth

The supplies you will need for the PVC method include various lengths of 1-1/4" diameter, #40, PVC pipe; 5/4" thick x 6" wide deck planking (which you may want to rip into 4" wide lengths); a good quantity of 1-1/2" long deck screws (longer, if you don't rip the deck planking to a lesser width); and a 1-1/4" hole-saw attachment for your power drill. You'll also need some wood "scab plates"—short sections of pressure-treated plywood or 1x4s will do—to attach each section of deck plank roadbed to its adjoining sections.

Here's the procedure to follow:

1. Rip the 6" wide deck plank material into 4" wide lengths. This is just a bit wider than the tie lengths on most #1 Gauge track. If your planned curves are of a sufficiently wide radius, you can actually lay your curved sections of track on the uncut deck planks; trace the outline; and then use a saber saw to cut along the marked outline. Otherwise, you'll need to angle-cut the ends of a number of short sections of planking to accommodate the curved areas.

2. After all the planking has been ripped and cut to the lengths needed, lay the planks on the ground along the path that your track will follow. After all the planks are down, you may even want to place your track on top to make sure everything fits properly. Remove the track when you are satisfied that things are pretty much as they should be.

3. Now, work your way around the loose roadbed sections and attach a "scab plate" to the bottom ends of each adjacent plank. Three screws in each end should suffice. The result will be a joined-together wood roadbed that defines your track plan, sans its supporting structure and the track.

4. The next step involves using a hole-boring attach-

ment on your power drill to bore 1-1/4" diameter holes—spaced about four feet apart along straight sections, and closer together on curves—clear through the deck planking. Try to keep the holes centered on the width dimension of the planking.

5. After you have bored the necessary holes around the entire circumference of your roadbed, go back and drill pilot holes for the deck crews that will be used to affix the deck plank roadbed to the vertical PVC support posts. It's easier to drill these holes now, rather then later, when you're trying to get everything into final position. Drill clear through the side of the deck plank, on-center with the hole you previously cut through the top and bottom of the plank. Drill through from both sides of the plank. Later, after the PVC support post is in place and sticking through the hole that you bored, you'll confirm level and cross-level, and then anchor things in place by inserting screws into the side of the planking, and directly into the side of the PVC pipe.

6. Now it's time to prepare a hole in the ground to hold the PVC pipe. Perhaps the best way to do this is to use a three- or four-foot length of iron pipe, of the same diameter as your PVC pipe, as a sort of auger for hole-digging. You can place the iron pipe in the center of each plank hole, and then use a sledge hammer or similar tool to drive it into the ground until you hit a firm sub-layer that "feels" secure; then drive it in a bit further. Place a crayon mark on the side of the iron pipe were it emerges from the top of the plank—when the iron pipe is withdrawn from the ground, the distance from this mark to the bottom of the pipe will show the length of PVC pipe needed for that particular hole. If the PVC-supported roadbed is going to be more than a couple of feet above ground level, you may want to consider using a wider-diameter PVC pipe in those areas (in places where bridges or trestles might be added later, for example), to provide some additional support.

7. Next, cut a section of PVC pipe to the proper length, as determined above, and carefully drive it into the ground. Do not use a hammer to directly strike the end of the PVC pipe though, because it may crack or break. You can set or hold a short scrap of wood on the end of the PVC pipe, and strike the wood scrap with your hammer.

8. After all of the PVC support sections are in place, use the estimated point of highest elevation on the railroad's route as "ground zero," and, starting at that point, proceed around the railroad from one post to the next, leveling things as you go and attaching the plank to each PVC pipe section with just one of the two screws. That first screw is placed to assure that everything is level along the length of the roadbed. After one screw is in place along the full route, with everything leveled lengthwise, go back and check cross-level (side-to-side level) and when that is satisfactory, you can drive the second screw.

9. When everything is in place, you'll still have open holes every four feet or so along your roadbed where the PVC pipe sticks through the planks. You can leave them open, if you wish, or fill the pipes with ballast, dirt, or even a wet mixture of concrete before you lay the track in place.

At this point, you now have a firmly supported roadbed, complete with vertical supports that will never rot or be devoured by termites. Track can be screwed directly to the roadbed through the ties every few feet or so, with screws placed more closely together in curved areas. Be sure to drill pilot holes in the ties that are slightly wider than the shank of the screws being used. This will allow for some "play" without affecting track alignment. Also, do not tighten the screw too tightly, because that might crack the plastic tie, or force the rails out of gauge. All the screw really needs to do is help keep the track lined-up properly, and help to keep rail joints as tight as possible. Ballast can also be applied over the roadbed, if you desire to achieve a more finished look overall. Either before or after you lay the track, you can back fill around the edges of your supporting roadbed to convincingly blend it into the surrounding environment.

As further evidence that roadbed construction techniques are as diverse as most other aspects of garden railroad, here's another very simple roadbed support method as described by Illinois resident Ric Golding on the www.myLargescale.com Internet forum under the "Track and Roadbed" topic:

"I use concrete block (for my supporting roadbed), and you only have to level once. Put the first block at the lowest point and just barely get it in the ground. Dig the rest in the ground to be level with this first one. Fill the holes with ballast (I use crusher fines); set the track on top; then add more ballast. The track is level, and stays level, or at a grade, or however you want it. Where the block is above ground level, bring soil, mulch, or whatever up to it. Lay a little ridge of mortar along the top edge, and the ballast will stay in place. As I said, sounds like a lot of work, but you only do it once. I've got some in the ground that are the same as the day I put them there—six years ago."

Again, diversity, experimentation, and experience are three things you will certainly find in this hobby. The phrase "that won't work" just seems to challenge garden railroaders to prove that it will work!

Tunnels and tunnel portals:

A long tunnel that virtually swallows a train as it passes through an imposing mountain is certainly a much sought after feature model railroads of all scales, and no less so on garden railroads. The tunnel itself can be constructed either before you build the mountain, which simplifies things in many respects, or you can dig into an existing mountain later on if a tunnel was

not part of your original plans. That second option involves more labor, but it's certainly not a major obstacle that can't be overcome. However, there are some practical considerations to weigh carefully before you forge ahead and begin construction of a tunnel on your garden layout, regardless of when it's built.

A brick tunnel portal on Scott Johnson's garden railroad. Portals like this one are available as ready-to-install castings, or you can make them yourself. Although a turnout is right at the tunnel entrance, it nevertheless is accessible for maintenance. Sections of track inside tunnels should be straight and turnout-free, if at all possible.
Photo courtesy of Scott Johnson

A corollary to Murphy's Law might state that if something can possibly go wrong with trackwork at any point along your rail line, it will generally occur at the most inaccessible point. On a garden railroad, that point is most likely going to be right in the middle of a tunnel, right where the problem is most difficult to get to. Unless you have very l-o-n-g arms, or have planned for some sort of access panels or hatches to reach the interior of your tunnel, you'll have to resort to all sorts of tricks and gyrations to get at the source of the trouble. For that reason, it's important to restrict the length of any tunnel to about three feet. At that length, the average adult arm can reach to the middle of the tunnel, when needed, to perform routine track cleaning-chores; to perform any maintenance that might be required; or to re-rail an errant locomotive or car. If you

absolutely want and need a longer tunnel, you will need provide for side or top access to portions of the tunnel that cannot be reached by extending your arm through one or the other of the portals.

Speaking of portals, you can make them yourself out of wood, concrete, foam castings, or a variety of other materials, or you can purchase ready-made tunnel portals for Large Scale trains in a variety of styles that simulate wood, concrete, stone, and brick portals. Extra wide double-track portals are also available from a number of sources.

Another major consideration in tunnel planning involves clearances. Regardless of how you construct your tunnel liner, or the portals themselves for that matter, you will need to assure that there is adequate side-to-side and top-to-bottom clearance to accommodate your longest and tallest locomotives and rolling stock. In most situations, about nine or more inches of overhead clearance, measured from the top of the rails to the bottom of the portal or liner, should be sufficient, along with about three inches of side clearance on both sides, when measured from the ends of the ties. If the tunnel contains a curved section (which should be eliminated if at all possible), even greater side-to-side clearance will need to be provided.

Probably the easiest way to go as far as a rigid and reliable tunnel liner is concerned is to use a pre-formed product of some type. Del Tapparo's garden railroad, the construction of which is described later in this chapter, has a tunnel made of 3' x 13" square masonry chimney flue. Teya Caple-Woods, whose layout is also featured in this chapter, used 15" diameter culvert piping for two of the four tunnels on her rail line, with the remaining two being made from the same concrete mix used for building her mountains. These methods, as well as many others, will all work. It's just a matter of being innovative, and willing to make a mistake or two along the way. Remember: You don't have to wait for Mother Nature to change things; you can always beat her to it!

Bridges and trestles:

Bridges and trestles are both scenic and functional features. They are varied and attractive structures that add diversity to what otherwise might be hundreds of feet of open trackwork, and they allow your railroad to cross over streams, gullies, or depressions along the line. They also serve to promote proper drainage from high areas of your layout. Always remember, though, that the real railroads resort to bridges and trestles only as a last resort, and they will nearly always fill an area or construct an earth embankment if that will prevent resorting to far more costly and maintenance heavy bridge construction.

Actually, one type of structure that the real railroads frequently use is a culvert, which may be nothing more than a large pipe stuck through the earth embank-

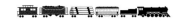

An LGB Mogul hauls its passenger consist through a wood truss bridge on Bob Maisey's garden railroad. Bob constructed the bridge with a hinge at one end so it can swing up and out of the way to allow access to interior portions of the layout.
Photo courtesy of Bob Maisey

Ray Jakabcin mounted this ornate covered bridge atop trestle piers on his railroad. The variety of bridge types available for a model railroad is wide ranging, but you'll want to be sure to match bridge construction styles to the general period that your rail line represents.
Photo courtesy of Ray Jakabcin

ment under the roadbed to promote proper drainage in low-laying or swampy areas, or perhaps to afford an uninterrupted flow to a very small stream. Garden railroad culverts can serve the same purpose, especially in regard to promoting drainage. If there are elevated areas along your rail line that tend to retain water in a dam-like fashion after a heavy rain, a simple PVC pipe culvert might be installed to take care of the problem. PVC is readily available in a variety of diameters, so you can match the pipe to your specific needs. The protruding end sections of the PVC pipe can be painted and left as they are, or they could be made to look more

complete by adding concrete, stone, or brick retaining walls on both sides along the embankment.

The types and styles of bridges and trestles used in prototype railroading are almost limitless, so when it comes to modeling these structures, the only real limitation is your imagination and creativity. Just be sure that the type of bridge you choose is appropriate to the era and type of railroad you are modeling. In other words, try to match the bridge to your overall theme. A wood trestle—always an imposing feature on any model railroad—is certainly very appropriate for those modeling nineteenth century railroads, regardless of whether the

This imposing wood trestle on Tom Ruddell's Bethlehem Central garden railroad measures nearly twenty feet long. The truss bridge at top left spans the deepest part of the chasm.
Photo courtesy of Tom Ruddell

focus is on narrow gauge or standard gauge lines. However, a spindly wood trestle may be less appropriate for those who elect to represent contemporary railroading. There are exceptions in every case, of course, but you would be well advised to select a type of bridgework that obviously supports your theme, rather than one that is apt to look out of place.

Some relatively short truss and girder bridges are available in built-up form or in easy-to-build kits, but most trestles and larger bridges are only available in kit form, or are constructed to fit the site based on plans that you can find in various model railroading publications. Pre-assembled short bridges can also be joined together to form longer bridges, if putting together a bridge kit is not your cup of tea. In some cases, bridges of different types can be combined to form a longer bridge—a truss bridge, placed where it crosses the deepest part of a waterway or ravine, may have plate- or deck-girder bridges on each end, for example.

Bridges do require supporting piers at each end, and at any point where one or more bridges join together to form longer spans. These support piers can be made of anything strong enough to support the weight of the track and the trains—wood, concrete, or even plastic that is molded or carved to resemble some other material, such as brick or stone. If you notice that soil erosion becomes a problem at either end of your bridge, or even around the supporting piers, you can do as the real railroads do and construct retaining walls to inhibit or redirect the erosion.

It should be fairly obvious that there's no need to wait for your bridges to be built before running trains on your layout. Temporary bridge supports, constructed of lumber scraps, can be placed under an equally temporary wood roadbed (or under the actual roadbed, if you have used wood as your roadbed material), so you can enjoy uninterrupted operations while the "construction crew" works on completing the final bridge at an off-site location.

If you are going to use wood to construct a bridge or a trestle, be certain to coat every part of the structure with a good wood preservative. Otherwise, these relatively small structures, with their numerous small and exposed parts, will be especially prone to rot and decay.

Powering the railroad

If you are building your first garden railroad, you'll likely want to keep any electrical wiring to a bare minimum, at least in the initial stages of operation, so you can spend less time fussing with installing and connecting wires (unless electrical things of that sort appeal to you), and have more time available to run some trains. Nevertheless, unless you have elected to go solely with radio-controlled battery power and/or live steam operation and hand-thrown turnouts, you will need to run at least some buried wiring to feed power to your

power pack's selected site, and from your power pack and accessory control boxes to the track, to insulated passing tracks or sidings, and to the various turnouts. Of course, you can also do as some enterprising garden railroaders have done, and use scale-size telephone poles to carry the wiring! You may also need some wiring for outdoor lighting of the layout, if you find evening operations appealing.

Tom Ruddell ran the wiring for his garden railroad through buried PVC piping, which, if installed properly, is virtually maintenance free.
Photo courtesy of Tom Ruddell

It has been noted elsewhere in this book, but it deserves repeating again: You *must* protect your power pack, and the wire connecting it to your household outlet, from moisture! **You also *must* assure that the household outlet you use to get power to your power pack is equipped with a ground fault circuit interrupter (also known as a GFI).** If you elect to have your power pack close to the railroad site, you'll need to provide some sort of enclosed, weatherproof housing to protect it, or resign yourself to disconnecting the pack after each operating session and storing it in the house, garage, or a garden shed until the next session.

If track power is how you are going to operate your trains, you'll also need to bury the wiring that runs from your power pack to the track, plus any additional wires connected to that pack or any additional pack, such as one that might be used to power any insulated track sections, turnouts, and lighted or operating accessories. Plan ahead, and use PVC pipe and fittings of a diameter large enough to handle not just your current wiring needs, but also those you may use in the future expansion of your railroad.

The gauge, or thickness of the copper wire used to provide electricity to the layout site is also something to keep in mind. The heavier the wire gauge (thickness), the greater its ability to provide a full flow of current that is less affected by resistance. The greater the distance between the power source and its destination, the heavier the gauge of wire that should be used. Remember, in determining wire gauge, lower numbers indicate a heavier gauge. For example, #12 gauge is

heavier than #14 gauge wire. The former should be used at distances of, say, 30 feet, while the #14 gauge would likely be fine for a 15-foot length. There is an advantage to using some lighter-gauge wire, where suitable and appropriate, because it is easier to feed through your PVC pipe or other conduit, and generally easier to work with.

Truthfully, wiring a garden railroad is not a terribly complex undertaking, *if* you plan ahead. The time to consider your wiring needs and where you will bury conduit is when the railroad is being planned on paper, and not the day before you are ready to drive your golden spike. Knowing and diagramming what you want to do, anticipating future needs, and accurately estimating the materials needed will go a long way to making this a far easier task. Once the wiring is properly installed, you should be able to sit back and enjoy many years of dependable, glitch-free operations.

A tale of two railroads:

The following accounts, written by the individuals involved, detail the creation of two garden railroads built in two very diverse regions of the country. Each of these dedicated garden railroaders employed somewhat different construction methods and techniques, based on their specific interests, goals, climatic conditions, and availability of materials. The intent here is to demonstrate, based on real-world examples, that garden railroading doesn't necessarily follow any one path, and that what you can accomplish with your own railroad is limited only by your imagination and resourcefulness. That said, here, in their own words, is how two folks approached their initial involvement in the hobby, and how they fulfilled their dreams.

Constructing the D&L Railroad in Colorado

by
Del Tapparo
President, Secretary, Chief Engineer, and Head Maintenance Man
and
Linda Tapparo
Vice President, Treasurer, Design Consultant, and Horticulturist

All photos of the D&L are by Linda and Del Tapparo.

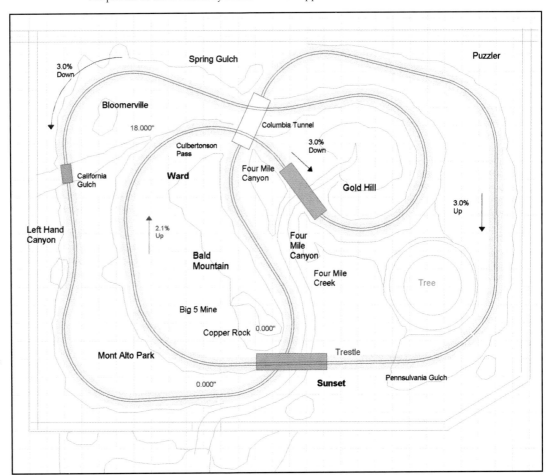

The site plan for the D&L garden railroad. The overall layout size is 29' x 22', with 147' of mainline trackage. Minimum radius of curves is 4', and maximum grade is 3%. The railroad is based on Colorado & Northwestern three-foot narrow gauge.

I had been involved in N scale model railroading since Christmas of 1989. This interest waned because I decided I didn't have the cash to remodel the basement prior to starting the N scale layout of my dreams.

The garden railroad seed was planted about May of 1998, when I received a complimentary copy of *Garden Railways* magazine and discovered that garden railroading was big here in Colorado. For some reason, I had earlier assumed that this was strictly a warm-weather activity! We have a nice big back yard that needed a facelift anyway, to remove a swing set and sandbox that the kids no longer use, so I decided to take the plunge!

Initial research involved large doses of *Garden Railways* magazine, joining the Denver Garden Railway Society to tour their layouts, and browsing the World Wide Web on the Internet to check out the many garden railroad sites that groups and individuals had set up there. This provided a convenient and very fine way to

Up and running! Track is down, bridges and trestles are in place, and the mountains are complete. The D&L is finally a railroad ready for some revenue traffic!

The evolution of the D&L over time and seasons. This first photo shows the site at an early stage, after the perimeter retaining wall had been constructed and a number of masonry blocks had been put in place to protect the large tree that would remain on the site. A few rocks have been added at this point to get a general idea of how things might eventually look.

Another season has arrived, as evidenced by the leaves which now adorn the trees. Gold Hill is taking shape, and Four Mile Creek is starting to take shape. The stream will eventually empty into Glacier Lake, which, at this point, was about to be relocated outside the perimeter of the layout proper.

see what others are doing, or have done. My research phase also led to the formation of a local club, the Northern Colorado Garden Railroaders, and a number of new friendships.

Many trial and error track plan designs were created using "3rd PlanIt" CAD software from El Dorado on my PC. I learned from my experience in N scale that what looks like it ought to fit, and what actually does fit, are often two entirely different things. My final track plan, a folded and twisted dogbone in a relatively small space, required careful planning to achieve enough vertical clearance at the tunnel and bridge crossings without exceeding my design goal of 3% maximum grades.

CAD software provided me with a lot of comfort, because I knew that most of the dirt and rocks on my garden railroad would only have to be moved one time. Railroad CAD can actually be a hobby unto itself, so just use it to the level you are comfortable with, or you may never get out of the planning stage!

The site for the first phase of the D&L (the origin of the railroad's name should be fairly obvious), was formerly occupied by a rather large sandbox and a raised-bed flower box. Site demolition required removal of a swing set that had been cemented in place; removal of a circle of vertical landscape timbers that had framed the sandbox; and removal of the raised-bed flower box.

Construction started with some rerouting of the existing sprinkler system, and trenching-out the sod in the area where landscape timbers used for framing the railroad would be placed. I used 6" x 4" brown landscape timbers to raise the base level of the planned railroad nine inches in front, and 18" in the rear, thereby providing a more elevated view of the trains. I was actually planning to go one timber width higher until I realized how much additional dirt and dirt-hauling would be involved! The timbers were spiked together and installed to give a level top frame all around the perimeter of the layout area. A three-foot access was left on the two fenced sides for both viewing and working purposes.

Then, some 115-volt electrical conduit and boxes were installed for future use with track power, pond pumps, lights, and whatever else I might eventually need on my railroad.

All elevations on the D&L were determined with a homemade water level, which essentially consists of a plastic container filled with water, along with fifty feet of clear plastic tubing.

After I had installed all the timbers, it occurred to me that I had an Ash tree in the middle of my layout! Actually, I knew that the tree was there all along, but I just hadn't considered how to handle the raised elevation around the base of the tree. Checking with a local nursery, and after browsing the Internet for information, I learned that adding a foot of soil around the base of the tree would possibly suffocate the roots. Too late now! So, as a solution to that problem, I installed a circle of masonry blocks around the tree to protect the trunk and provide some space for the roots to breathe. Two years later, the tree is still healthy!

The next step involved dirt—lots of dirt! Some 30 tons of dirt just to get the base fill! The demolition refuse was used as bottom fill, and the remainder was filled with tamped layers of topsoil. This dirt all had to be hauled in by wheelbarrow, one load at a time, to get it through the yard gate.

Next, with my CAD drawing in hand, I surveyed the site using a tape measure and the water level. Stakes were driven about every three feet to mark where the track would be. Track elevation at each point was also marked on the stakes, and then the stakes were cut off at the mark. The track would ultimately be laid right on top of the stakes, insuring it was in the proper location, and at the proper grade.

When you're modeling the area west of Boulder Colorado you gotta have a lot of Boulders! A small number of the many rocks that are a scenic attraction on the D&L are in evidence in this photo. The small yellow flags indicate the route of the future roadbed.

Rocks and dirt were then placed to form the grades and the basic foundation of what would eventually be a mountain. A tunnel through the mountain was con-

structed of 3' x 13" square masonry chimney flue. This tunnel came to be named Columbia Tunnel.

Retaining walls, comprised of granite rip-rap, were built up to define the mountain ledges for the roadbed and to contain the mountain soil.

Even more rocks are need for the area around Gold Hill Tunnel. That's the tunnel liner behind Del Tapparo, who is handling more of the heavy lifting and rolling.

Finally, the days of hauling dirt and rock were pretty much over—for the time being, at least! The grand total at this point came to 43 tons of dirt and 11 tons of rock, all of which was hauled by pickup truck, then transported to the site by the old shovel-and-wheelbarrow method. (This seemed like quite a feat to me, until I read somewhere that firemen on a steam locomotive often shoveled 6-20 tons of coal per 12-hour work day, and they often worked seven days a week.) After all that labor, I thought I had a wonderful landscape ready for track laying—until I decided to incorporate a stream, and Linda decided we needed a larger pond.

My original plans had called for a 50-gallon static pond to be incorporated inside the layout area. Now, a 100-gallon pond just outside the layout's perimeter would receive the stream. This allowed for an elevation drop for the stream, and helped to better integrate the "box" appearance of the elevated section with the rest of the yard. Of course, a section of the timber framing had to be removed to make way for the stream's flow into the pond.

Attention was next given to the stream itself, which I named Four Mile Creek. I decided to use lawn edging to shape the course of the stream, and to restrain the dirt that formed the stream's banks. The square sides will also keep the rock in the stream bed from moving around, like they would in a rounded trough. A sort of stair-step approach was used down the side of the mountain for the waterfall, so the water would eventually flow into a series of small pools, thereby creating some pleasing water noises.

Lawn edging was used along Four Mile Creek to shape the flow and retain the stream banks. The stairsteps down the mountain will form small pools to create more water noise.

A rubber liner was used in the stream bed. The folds were necessary in order to follow the curved areas, and rocks were used to hold the liner in place. A test of the water flow was then conducted using a water hose so any necessary adjustments were made before everything was permanently fixed in place.

Trim the liner back; add a few well-placed large rocks and a whole lot of smaller ones; and you end up with a pretty convincing stream.

Next, the rubber liner was installed. The curved areas of the stream bed resulted in some folds in the liner at various places, but after many adjustments and some fine-tuning, including widening the stream bed and making it a bit more shallow, things were pretty much as I wanted them to be. I had the most difficulty hiding the rubber liner in the area of the waterfall. Flat rocks on the bottom and sides of the stair-steps provided a fairly decent solution to that problem.

Once it was in place, the liner was trimmed back a bit, and disguised with rocks of various sizes along the course of the stream. Again, I had the most difficulty hiding the rubber liner in the area of the waterfall. Again, flat rocks provided the solution. To test everything out before proceeding further, a garden hose was placed at the highest point so I could observe the actual flow of water through the stream and into the pond. Further adjustments ultimately resulted in the appearance and flow pattern that I was hoping to achieve.

The actual water pumping system to be used was then tested. This system consists of a pre-planned buried pipe running from the pond to the top of Gold Hill, and a 1450 gal/hr recirculating water pump (probably about twice the capacity of what was actually needed for my situation). One problem I immediately noted was that the water from the pipe was just spraying all over the place because the recirculated water is under pressure at this point. What is needed is some means of converting this water under pressure to water flowing by gravity alone down the stream. The solution

was a small water reservoir at the topmost point, where the water exits the pipe.

My first attempt at creating a suitable reservoir involved inserting the flow pipe into a small mop bucket that had a nice flat pour spout. The plan was that the bucket would fill with water, and the water would then overflow out the spout and flow more gently into the stream. This idea worked, too, but only if the flow rate was kept very low—too low, in fact. If I cranked up the flow rate, the water volume became too great for the spout, and water ended up splashing all over the place. I really liked this bucket idea, because it was small and would be easy to conceal. Still, it didn't offer the solution that I needed.

So, I resorted to using a small pre-formed pond with a larger spillway to capture the water at the head of the stream. The nice wide spout works great! To hide this catch basin, I built a strong wood cover for the basin/pond, then stack rocks directly on top of it to form a mountain peak. Lava rock was also placed in the upper pond to help filter the water.

I was concerned about how I was going to drain the pond for the winter. No problem! It just so happens that when you turn off the pump, the water siphons out of the upper pond and returns to the lower, big pond via the pipe, and the stream just empties itself through natural gravity. The only real downfall I've found is that the pond level decreases by about two inches during the initial filling operation (when you first turn the pump on). If you attempt to fill the pond fully when

The trenched roadbed technique was used on the D&L. After the trench was dug, gray crusher fines were used to fill the trench with ballast. After the track was laid in place, more ballast was added to the top of the track, between the ties.

A paint brush was used to smooth-out the ballast, and gradient changes were checked by placing a carpenter's level lengthwise on a flat car, with a line level placed across the end of the car to check cross level. Adjustments to track level were made by adding or removing small amounts of ballast.

the pump is running, the lower pond will overflow the next time you shut the pump off. To minimize the drop in water level, I subsequently added a check valve to the supply line. This stops the backflow into the pond. Nevertheless, the water level in the pond still drops a bit though.

Now it was time to get to the train part—finally!

One task I had started earlier was to pre-bend my rails to the desired curvature needed for my track plan. I used brass LGB code 332 rail in five-foot lengths, fitted with LGB's flex ties. Istra Metal Craft supplied the rail bender, which worked great. A rotary tool with a fiberglass cutting disk was used to trim the rails to their proper length. Be sure to always wear safety glasses when you're using a power tool for this or any other purpose! I soon discovered that most five-foot lengths of rail required a compound bend to attain the desired shape; i.e., the rail might have a 48" radius at one end, while the other end might be a 60" radius, or even straight. A lot of trial-and-error fitting was involved in getting things right. It's just a good thing that rail benders also unbend rail! Getting the curves just right was a time consuming process, but it was also a lot of fun.

Three things guided my actual track-laying: my original computer drawing, the elevation stakes that I placed every five feet or so, and the final physical lay of the land.

The track location was first marked with small flags. Then, a 3" deep by 6" wide trench was dug with a garden hoe. I filled the trench with ballast (gray crusher fines); leveled the ballast to form the roadbed; placed the pre-bent rails directly on top of the ballast; added more ballast; then smoothed everything out with a fairly stiff paint brush.

Still using my elevation stakes as a guide, I only need to check local gradient changes between the stakes using a flat car with a plumber's level mounted lengthwise (1/8" per foot = 1% grade), and a cheap line level mounted sideways to check cross-level and superelevation of the track. Adjustments for level can be made by simply lifting the track a bit; adding or removing ballast as necessary; then laying the track back in place. When everything is just right, the track can be wiggled a bit to firmly nestle it into the ballast.

Rail sections were joined together using Split-Jaw rail clamps and a dab of "Ox-Gard" anti-oxidant paste. The track network is powered at two different places to minimize voltage drop.

Our Golden Spike Ceremony was held on April 16, 2000, and the fun has really begun! Although the D&L is far from complete, what model railroad is ever considered to be complete? The trains are up and running now, and the landscaping is taking hold. The Moss Roses we planted to temporarily fill in the many bare spots in the early stages of operations turned out to be beautiful throughout the summer. A passing siding is in the planning stages, as is an even bigger pond. Who knows what else might be in store for the D&L? We're now having so much fun running our trains that we even tend to neglect taking as many photographs as we should. Building the D&L was a labor of love, and the rewards have been great all along the way. Indeed, the important thing for every garden railway enthusiast to remember is: "A garden railroad is a journey, not a destination."

Cribbing was installed in areas where experience indicated that erosion might be a problem.

Of course, no model railroad—be it in the garden or indoors—is ever really finished! But trains are operating on the D&L, and Del and Linda Tapparo are now able to proceed with other additions to the line at a far more leisurely pace.

Constructing the Capleville & Sugkat Valley Railroad in Virginia

by

Teya "Happy Hogger" Caple-Woods

CEO, President, Chief Financial Officer, Road Foreman, Dispatcher, and Chief Engineer

All photos of the C&SV are by Teya Caple-Woods.

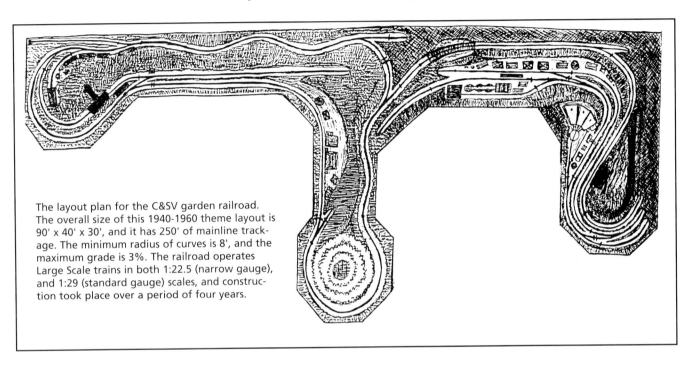

The layout plan for the C&SV garden railroad. The overall size of this 1940-1960 theme layout is 90' x 40' x 30', and it has 250' of mainline trackage. The minimum radius of curves is 8', and the maximum grade is 3%. The railroad operates Large Scale trains in both 1:22.5 (narrow gauge), and 1:29 (standard gauge) scales, and construction took place over a period of four years.

I'm a woman in what has been, and perhaps still predominately is, a man's hobby. I remember as a little girl watching my father build indoor toy train layouts for my brothers during the holidays. They seemed to enjoy playing with the trains at the time, but never showed any real or lasting interest in railroading as they got older.

When I moved to Hawaii in 1985, I decided it was time to build my first train layout. Because of space limitations, my first layout was in HO scale. The following year, I went to work for Honolulu Trains and Hobbies, Oahu's only train store. It was then that I became interested in what was then referred to as G scale. I worked at the store for three years, and purchased my first LGB set there.

I was working on my second HO layout when I moved to Chesapeake, Virginia, in 1993. Being a member of the National Model Railroad Association, I was fortunate to find that an NMRA division was active here. I decided to join the G scale group, and through them I learned of the existence of the Tidewater Big Train Operators club, which I joined a short time later. I have enjoyed the fellowship of the TBTO club immensely, and I'm extremely grateful for all the knowledge I have gained about this great hobby through my association with other members.

In the autumn of 1996, my mother suffered a severe stroke, and came to live at our home. I had to tear down my HO layout to accommodate her furniture and other possessions. Well, I had to have a layout of some kind, and my backyard was the only space left! At this point I began actively discussing garden layouts with other club members. I wanted to learn about things they had tried, and wanted to see what had worked for them and what didn't work. I also began re-reading back issues of *Garden Railways* magazine.

One club member, Buddy Stark, actually designed a layout for me, but I found that I wanted to take a more active role in shaping the planning and development of my layout. So, I borrowed enough track and turnouts to lay a preliminary track plan right on the ground of our fenced back yard, which fortunately was a relatively flat grassy area. This initial on-site track planning effort gave me a much better feel for exactly how much track and how many turnouts I might actually need. Buddy revised the track plan on paper, and subsequently assisted me with all phases of actual construction.

By April of 1997, I was ready to get started. The railroad, which is shaped like the letter "F" when viewed from the house, would be built in two phases, with the bottom half of the "F" finished first so I could get some trains up and running on Phase 1 while I was

working on Phase 2. I wanted to get started, because I have known too many people who spend so much time planning that they never accomplish anything. Moreover, I'm not afraid of failing or making mistakes! Some things planned well on paper never work out on the actual site, but that's half the fun and challenge of building any model railroad, whether it is located indoors or outdoors.

The perimeter wall for the C&SV was completed first, and some initial dirt fill was added to the site. Landscaping timbers were cut to 18" and 24" lengths, then cut in half and reinforced with fencing wire, to form a circular open space around the large tree.

I wanted my layout to be elevated above ground level, so my husband, Roger, constructed a perimeter retaining wall made of pressure-treated landscaping timbers to contain the dirt I would need for the railroad. He completed the task in two days.

Now I needed dirt, and lots of it! Fortunately, someone in my neighborhood was putting in a swimming pool, and I was able to obtain four dump truck loads of dirt at the best possible price: Free! It took us three days to move the dirt to the back yard by wheelbarrow, but we soon realized that all that dirt wasn't going to be nearly enough. At that point, I also learned that the expression "dirt cheap" doesn't apply in today's world. Dirt is expensive! I shopped around, but had no luck finding what I needed at an affordable price. Fortunately, Roger flagged down a construction truck that was passing through our area, and I was eventually able to secure three huge loads of additional dirt for a grand total of $50. The loads were delivered by a

huge construction dump truck, and I actually ended up with more dirt than I needed. Then it was back to giving the wheelbarrow a workout!

The next step was to provide a stand-off protective border for the large tree that is on the layout site, and which would remain on site. Roger cut landscaping timbers in two lengths (18" and 24") and he then cut each one in half. We laid the timbers on the ground in alternate lengths. Next, we laid heavy gauge fencing wire over the timbers, and used heavy-duty staples to attach the fencing to the backs of the timbers. I dug an 8" deep trench; positioned the retaining wall we had fabricated; poured in dry concrete and dirt; and then added water. The next day, I was able to start filling the surrounding layout area with dirt.

Roger dug holes, eight feet apart, to anchor supporting posts for a back retaining wall, which is separated from the yard's side fence by several feet to provide ready access along the full long length of the "F" shaped layout. The retaining wall is constructed of 4x8 sheets of pressure-treated plywood, which was cut to the appropriate height and then draped with 14 mil black plastic as a moisture barrier. As originally designed, the highest point called for a four-foot high retaining wall, which I knew would be too high. I'm just 5'3" tall, and there was no way I would be able to work on the planned mountain framework if things were that high. So, some modifications were made, and the retaining wall is now three feet tall at its highest point, with the lowest point being two feet.

I had 50 cinder blocks delivered, to be used as dirt retainers in mountain areas and around the proposed tunnels. Although I didn't realize it at the time, this was just the beginning of the cinder block shipments. Ultimately, I ended up using 125 cinder blocks.

I began forming my first mountain by packing the dirt (walking over it, and pounding it repeatedly with a cinder block), and inserting cinder blocks where needed to help hold the dirt in place as the mountain got higher. Every evening, I would give the layout a thorough

A pressure-treated plywood retaining wall was erected along the back portion of the layout—several feet away from the fence to allow access from the rear—to form a visual backdrop for the layout. The plywood was later draped with 14 mil black plastic to serve as an additional moisture barrier.

Cinder blocks were used to keep culvert piping and the soil in place. The cinder blocks and tunnel portals were then mortared in place.

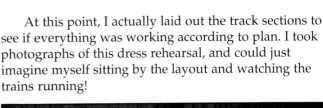

This view shows a finished tunnel portal and its sculpted abutments.

The C&SV's owner and Chief Construction Engineer is seen soldering track jumper wires with a resistance soldering unit. This device, which was borrowed from a member of the Tidewater Big Train Operators club, makes soldering a fast and easy task. A sheet of blue Plexiglas, screwed to plastic stakes planted in the roadbed, was used under each turnout and at track joints.

At this point, I actually laid out the track sections to see if everything was working according to plan. I took photographs of this dress rehearsal, and could just imagine myself sitting by the layout and watching the trains running!

soaking. This helped to compact the dirt more quickly. Roger devoted his time to moving more dirt and applying finishing touches to the perimeter walls. When he had finished, he said his job was done, and "see ya!"

I obtained some rocks—mostly flat ones—from a local rock supplier. I found that they also sold rock screenings that would make good ballast, but that would be purchased later.

The next decision involved what to use for tunnel linings. I decided on black culvert piping, which is sold at home improvement stores in 20' sections that cost about $80. I only needed 11' of piping in a 15" diameter, so this was not a very good deal for me. By shopping around a bit, I was eventually able to buy a five-foot section and a six-foot section for a total of $40. Holes were drilled along the bottom of each section for drainage. I then dug a wide trench about 6" deep, and filled it with rocks to further assist with drainage. The culvert piping was then set in place atop the rocks and leveled. Afterwards, cinder blocks were placed to form a wall that would hold the dirt in place both around, and on top of, the culvert piping. The blocks were mortared together after they were correctly positioned. A rerailer was also installed in the center of each tunnel to prevent a derailed locomotive or car from heading into the tunnel wall.

I borrowed a tunnel portal form from a fellow club member, but found that it was too small for my tunnel entrances. So, I made my own portals out of Quikrete! The wood form I constructed was placed on a board, and then filled about half full with concrete. Strips of fencing wire and small stakes were imbedded for additional reinforcement, and then the form was filled to the top with more concrete. After about thirty minutes, the concrete could be scribed with a nail and straightedge, or freehand, to represent stone, brick, or whatever. I made four portals using this method. Once the tunnel portals are completely dry, they were mortared into position, and then the full length of culvert piping was covered, first with dirt, and then with concrete.

Attention was then turned to contouring the grades. I soon discovered the importance of keeping grades below three percent! As first constructed, the grade near that big tree on the main loop was obviously too steep, since the wheels on my LGB Mogul were slipping, even under a light load. The grade had to be lowered to 3%, because that is the maximum grade I wanted anywhere on the layout. Lowering that previously constructed grade was a major operation! We had to chisel away part of the cinder block over the top of the tunnel, and remove from 5-7" of dirt from the upper elevations. After working on the grade for several days, we were finally able to re-test it—this time with great success.

My trackwork floats on a bed of rock screenings poured in trenchwork. I laid the track out and used chalk to mark the outlines for the trenches. Then the track was removed in small sections so I could dig a trench 6" wide and 4" deep with a hand hoe and spade. The hoe was just the right width for the trenches. Having the right tools made this a simple task. The trenches were filled part way with medium-size rock, then rock screening was added on top to serve as the actual ballast.

The track sections are screwed together at all the rail joiners—a nice feature of Aristo-Craft track is that it comes with pre-drilled holes and the required small screws. Chem-Wik rosin jumper wires were then soldered across the rail joints using a resistance-type soldering unit borrowed from a club member. This type of device makes soldering much faster and easier.

The initial stages of landscaping on Phase 1 of the layout. Tunnel entrances are kept covered when the trains are not operating to prevent small critters from establishing homes in the comfortable interiors.

More dirt and some sizable real rocks form the mountain top. Note how the rocks are embedded in the dirt, rather than simply placed on top of it.

Each section of track is supported at the joints on a 3x5 piece of Plexiglas and a plastic tent stake (plastic stakes won't rot like wood). The stake is pounded into the ground between each connected section. Then the Plexiglas and stake are screwed together with 3/4" brass screws inserted into pre-drilled holes. The stakes hold the track in place, and the Plexiglas supports the joined sections. I also drew outlines of the turnouts on sheets of Plexiglas, extending each track outline about four inches to provide the same kind of support to track sections adjoining the turnouts, and to provide firm and level support for the turnout itself. Turnouts on the layout are all LGB 1600s, equipped with LGB 12030 power supplements for remote operation.

From January until July of 1998, I worked to complete the landscaping on Phase 1 of the layout. I used lots of real rocks where I felt they would be appropriate, and I planted a lot of sedum and several varieties of thyme for groundcover. I also planted dwarf Alberta spruce, still in their containers, so they have grown very little over the past three years. They will eventually be removed; the roots cut back; and then replanted.

Styrofoam was used to form retaining walls, which were then covered with a concrete mixture and sculpted to resemble a sheer rock face.

Four different kinds of wire were used for various types of electrical connections around the layout: 12/2 for AC current, 14/2 for DC current, 18 gauge speaker wire for the Aristo-Craft Train Engineer receiver-to-track and turnout connections, and some telephone wire for the panel indicator lights and signal wiring. Trenches for the wiring were dug along the landscaping timber perimeter, where possible. A hole was drilled through the perimeter around the large tree so DC and AC cables could be passed through and into an electrical junction box at that location.

I decide to keep my monster 20-amp power pack (Regulated Power Supply) in the garage, and we installed a 20-amp breaker to protect the layout from any overload. A 14" deep trench was dug from the layout, under the fence, and to the side of the garage. The heavy duty 12/2 and 14/2 wires were pulled through electrical conduit piping and all fittings were glued. A one-inch hole drilled through the house siding made it possible to feed the wires into the garage. A 20-amp ground fault circuit interrupter (GFCI) was installed at the electric outlet that would supply AC current to the transformer. Also, three outside electrical outlets were installed along the back of the layout.

Mountains. . .

The mountains on my layout are made of a combination of Styrofoam, window screening, and concrete. The foam was cut to shape, and scored with a warm soldering iron before being put into place. This scoring is necessary in order for the concrete mixture to adhere to the foam.

I used both a front and a back section of Styrofoam to form the mountains. One section was nailed to the back of the retaining wall and the other was placed in a trench some distance in front of the retaining wall. Screening was then attached to the front foam sheet

This view shows the space left between the yard fence and the back of the layout. This allows easy access to the rear of the layout for maintenance or other purposes. Teya is working with Styrofoam and screening to form the front slope of the mountain ridge.

with roofing nails, and wadded-up newspaper was shoved underneath to fill the area between the two foam sections. Then the screening was pulled up over the wadded newspapers and attached to the back foam section with more roofing nails.

A thin layer of concrete was then spread over the entire screened area, and basic adjustments to landforms were roughly shaped by either pushing in on the screen while the concrete was still wet, or by shoving more newspapers underneath to budge it out a bit more. The concrete was applied with a three-inch miniature broom with plastic bristles.

Styrofoam support for Clyde's Gorge, which will eventually house the supporting bents for a trestle.

Teya applies the first coat of concrete mix to the Clyde's Gorge area.

Subsequently, two to three thicker layers of concrete were applied in the same way. The same small broom was used to create a rougher texture and to form strata on the mountain. My concrete mixture consisted of two parts Portland concrete, one part mortar, one part sand, and a liquid fortifier. I also used some concrete dyes to add a bit of color to the concrete mix. After the mountains were dry, they were further colored with a diluted solution of dyes mixed with latex paint. Spray paint was also used with some success, but you have to be very careful not to apply it too heavily.

Phrase 2. . .

Phase 2 of the layout was started in August, 1998, and included a ramp made of 2x6 pressure-treated boards with 1x4 side supports, all supported by 4x4 posts. While Buddy and I worked on the ramp, Roger, who had been called back to assist, finished digging an 18" deep by 7' long area for the trestle. I then cut and scored Styrofoam to fit the area Roger had created. The Styrofoam was then covered with four thin layers of concrete mix.

A European-style LGB Mallet, which has been modified to a U.S.-style locomotive, rounds the S-curve on the branch line. Sugkat Valley Yard is behind the train.

The mountains in this section were constructed a bit differently than those in Phase 1, because the retaining wall is only two feet high and is set in about 18 inches from the edge. Nevertheless, the basic construction materials included lots of Styrofoam, wadded-up newspapers, wire screen, wood supports, Liquid Nails adhesive, roofing nails, and concrete.

At this point, I took another look at a couple of "S" curves on the Phase 2 portion of the layout, and decided that they needed to be wider so I would have more room for the town of Capleville, which would be fronted by a long retaining wall. When that realignment was taken care of, it was time to turn attention to the town!

Downtown Capleville. . .

One of our club members had showed me some samples of "stone" that he had carved in Styrofoam with a wood burning tool and soldering iron. He used a dimmer switch to control the temperature. I decided to try this myself, and cut two 18" x 8' Styrofoam boards to serve as the retaining wall for downtown Capleville. I tried both the woodburning tool and soldering iron techniques for carving "stone" in Styrofoam, but prefer the results I got with the soldering iron. I brushed the entire wall with a brass bristle brush before painting it with exterior latex paint. The first two coats were a light gray to represent the mortar. While the second coat of paint was still wet, I began blending-in darker grays, tan, and black paint until I achieved the look I wanted. Creation of this retaining wall marked the beginning of what would eventually be my town.

Because I didn't have a lot of space for a complete downtown area, I knew I would have to resort to three-dimensional flats to represent my city scene. The completed town scene is large, but very lightweight, because it is largely constructed of what is obviously

This is a view of the underside of the Styrofoam "stone" retaining wall which fronts the town of Capleville. Nails and Liquid Nails adhesive was used to hold everything together.

Here's the completed retaining wall, sitting in the driveway of the Caple-Woods home.

one of my preferred materials: Styrofoam. Everything in the town scene is held together with Liquid Nails adhesive and regular nails. In addition to flats that I made myself, I also used parts from a few commercially available structure kits, including some made by Pola and Korber, along with a Mountains-in-Minutes warehouse and storefront to get me started.

Building shapes were cut from 1/2", 3/4", and 1" thick Styrofoam, with styrene strips attached to add depth and to outline some of the buildings. The buildings are painted with exterior latex paint. The only real problem I faced was with the windows: Where to get

An overall view of downtown Capleville. Most of the structures visible here are actually flats, which nevertheless provide a convincing three-dimensional appearance.

This view, from one end of the layout, illustrates how overlapping building flats were used to provide a three-dimensional effect.

lots of them, and cheap. I found a good article about how to make windows with styrene strips, but that was too time consuming. I had lots of clear acetate sheets and a variety of window sizes left over from the kits, so decided to "mass produce" my own windows.

I sprayed the clear sheets whatever color I wanted the final window trim to be. After they dried, I placed several model kit windows on top of the painted sheets; sprayed everything gloss black; and then let everything dry. I then removed the window "templates" and cut out the windows. They are glued in place with Liquid Nails adhesive.

Magazine ads and dry transfer letters were used to make signs for the various buildings. Once glued in place, they were oversprayed with several coats of clear spray to protect them from the elements. I used plastic gutter screening and styrene stripes to make a chain link fence, and I repainted a number of Bachmann telephone poles and glued them into place.

Viaducts and trestle. . .

The viaducts are, of course, also constructed from Styrofoam! Is there anything else? I used 1/2" thick foam because it is more flexible. I cut 18"x 8' lengths, and spliced where needed. The arches were drawn, then cut. To make the inside arches, we cut boards the same measurement as the arch, then Buddy scored the backs half way through so they could be put into place without breaking. I used Liquid Nails and small finishing nails to hold everything together. Also, 4x4 posts were placed between each arch for added support. This

View of the Styrofoam viaduct structure. This form was later filled with dirt and concrete.

section of the layout was then filled with dirt and then concrete, and a foam board was placed on top to seal the area. I used 1" foam for the wall cap. The foam was scored, and then several thin layers of concrete mixture were applied. I had made a foam template the size of the blocks I wanted, and used it and a nail to carve the wall while it was still wet.

The completed viaduct.

T's Textiles was kitbashed by Teya from several Piko kits. The platform for the structure is made of Styrofoam, which was carved with a soldering iron.

Buddy constructed the bents for the trestle. This structure is made of Cedar fencing boards which were planed down to size. Buddy took the pieces home and cut them into the final sizes he needed with a band saw. The bents are held together with wood glue and sequin dressmaker pins. I stained them with a one-step polyurethane. Stringers were fabricated out of several strips of wood that were glued together and screwed in place under each rail. The bents were then set into position; screwed to the stringers; and anchored at the base

with concrete. The last step was to glue the front and back braces in place—a tedious task that I didn't really enjoy very much.

The finale. . .

Early in April, 2000, I finally connected the Phase 1 and Phase 2 mainline. The next eighteen days were spent completing the branch line and installing additional wiring for insulated blocks and sidings. An LGB

An LGB Mallet crosses the now-complete Clyde's Gorge. Teya's friend, Buddy Starks, constructed the impressive trestle.

automatic stop signal was also installed to avoid train wrecks at the railroad's one crossover.

My Golden Spike Ceremony was held on June 10, 2000. Family, friends, club members, neighbors, and a reporter/photographer from the local newspaper were present, and my layout appeared on the cover of the Sunday supplement, along with a two-page story about the layout.

As it now stands, the layout measures 90' x 40' x 30' overall, and includes a 250' mainline and more than 500 feet of total trackwork. The minimum radius of all curves on the C&SV is 8', which serves well enough for the 1940 - 1960 period I have chosen to represent. I didn't really decide on a name for the railroad until just a few months before it was completed, but I always knew that I would somehow incorporate my father's nickname, "Sugkat," into the railroad's name. Jon Miller, another club member, had teasingly named it the "Sink Hole and Money Pit Railroad as his way of needling me about the financial aspects of the project.

They always say that your layout is never really completed, and that is true. I am still working on two control panels. One is inside a General Store mailbox and the other is in a toolbox that will look like a maintenance shed. Now that the major construction is done, I can take my time and add all the small details, such as more people, signs, lights, and more. The joy of building my layout was the construction, and working with Buddy. I do miss that part. We learned a lot from each other. The one person who I could never thank enough is my husband, Roger, for his help and support. He never questioned how much I was spending, or why.

I only wish my father could have seen this layout. I often imagine the two of us together, sitting outside, talking about the hobby, and just watching the trains run. I know it would truly please him that I enjoy this great hobby.

An overall view of just one of many striking scenes along the completed C&SV. Landscaping elements flourish in the relatively mild Virginia climate that is home to the Capleville & Sugkat Valley Railroad.

Nicely illustrating how trains and landscaping can complement each other on a garden railroad, with neither one overpowering the other, this scene on Charles Bednarik's "Triple-R Route" combines a number of attractive elements, including a water feature, rockwork, groundcover and shrubs, a bridge, and properly constructed trackwork.
Photo courtesy of Charles Bednarik

Chapter 10
LANDSCAPING AND ACCESSORIES FOR GARDEN RAILROADS

A garden railroad is, or certainly can and should be, a living thing. Like the real world environment in which it exists, a garden railroad grows, changes, and is continually altered by the forces of nature that act on it. Even the trackwork itself is affected, as are the various accouterments directly associated with the rail line, such as structures, signals, bridges, and the power and control devices that make the railroad run. This real-life interaction between a model railroad and its surroundings is what distinguishes garden railroading from any other form of model railroading. Furthermore, it is the horticultural aspect of garden railroading that often attracts whole families to this fascinating hobby. Some members may simply enjoy the railroading-related activities, while others are drawn to exercising their respective green thumbs with new plantings and the associated creative tasks involved with developing credible scenes for the trains to run through. Truly, garden railroading offers something rewarding for nearly everyone!

It's sometimes the case that garden railroading presents a "chicken-and-egg" situation for the hobbyist. Which came first, the garden or the railroad? If you are planning to build a garden railroad to fit an existing garden, your task will be a bit easier in some ways, and a bit more complex in others. If you're going to build the railroad first, and then complete it with landscaping—the way it is most often done—your track plan can be just about anything you want it to be, consistent with your space limitations, and the landscaped garden becomes the scenery for the stage upon which your iron horses and the supporting cast will perform.

In either case, it is important that the garden landscaping and the railroad itself complement each other, and that neither of these two features compete with or overwhelm the other. Also, in either case you should prepare yourself for the possibility of a bit of back-bending labor, because a railroad through an existing garden won't likely just fall into place without some additional reconfiguring of the terrain, and a garden built after the railroad is constructed is likely going to require even more work, unless you plan to have things look more like a golf course putting green.

• Creating the topography of a garden railroad

Although most real rail lines are constructed as smooth, level, and flat as possible, the topography of the terrain adjacent to these lines is often anything but smooth, flat, and level. In fact, most of us would not even want it to be that way. We enjoy the scenic diversity offered by hills, mountains, rock outcroppings, gullies, steams, lakes, and other such features, just as much as we enjoy the variety and color of the plant life that blankets these features.

Referring back to the layout planning and preparation discussion earlier in this book, the important thing is to plan not only the route your track will follow, but to also consider the major landscaping elements that will truly set the scene for your trains. If you want to have a mountain and a tunnel on your layout, the time to begin planning for that imposing feature is early on, before the first shovel of soil is turned, or the first section of track laid. The same can be said for any proposed water features, such as a waterfall, stream, or pond—all of these somewhat permanent fixtures need to be carefully planned and their locations determined in advance of the railroad's construction. The same sort of advance planning applies to cliffs, ledges, outcroppings, valleys, and the like.

• Soil for the garden railroad

Depending on the extent of your proposed undertaking, and also depending on how ambitious your geological plans may be, it's entirely possible that you'll

It's maintenance time on Ray Jakabcin's Horsebucket & Bryantville Railroad! In this case, the garden—his wife's herb garden—existed before Ray was bitten by the garden railroading bug. As a result, his track plan had to conform to the restrictions imposed by the garden, and it's obvious that he was successful in both his planning and execution.
Photo courtesy of Ray Jakabcin

need to move a whole lot of soil around to achieve the topographic effect you desire. This may be especially true if you plan to elevate your garden railroad above the level of the surrounding terrain (a good idea, by the way). All the soil you need could possibly come from another part of the layout, or from elsewhere on your own property, but there's a good chance that even that won't be nearly enough. In that case, you'll have to obtain some soil—perhaps even a whole lot of soil—from some other source, such as a nearby construction site, if they are seeking a place to dump their excavated soil, or from a garden center, which will gladly sell you the stuff.

If you do end up having to buy fill soil to make up your mountains or to give some logical reason for the existence of retaining walls, tunnels, and the like, buy the least expensive relatively clean soil you can find for the volume of the area to be built up, and then finish everything off with six to eight inches of good topsoil to provide a nutrient-rich footing for future plantings. Do try to find a source for sub-soil that is as clean of rocks, glass, metal shards, and other debris as possible. Otherwise, whatever money you saved in buying the soil will be sacrificed to lost time spent in cleaning it up. Still, there's no need to spend more than absolutely necessary when it comes to buying soil, and money spent on tons of expensive, high-quality topsoil to build a seven-foot high mountain is simply money that could be better used for other purposes. If available in your area, a mix of sand and clay subsoil would be your best bet. This cheap clay- and sand-laden soil will settle and compact more easily, thereby providing a supporting foundation less prone to sinking and sagging during the first few years of your railroad's existence.

Twenty tons of clean soil marks the start of Phase 1 of Bob and Ellen Utley's garden layout construction project. The small flags designate the route that track will eventually follow.
Photo courtesy of Robert Utley

Some three months later, weeds have already begun to intrude on a portion of Bob's layout that was not covered by plastic weed barrier. Bob decided to let the weeds flourish, for the time being, since they helped to prevent erosion while the soil was compacting. Eventually, a dwarf pine forest would be planted in the hilly part of this area.
Photo courtesy of Robert Utley

If at all possible, try to convince your source of free soil to also provide free transport of the soil to your home. Some will gladly do this for you, while others may require that you make other arrangements for hauling the stuff.

Once you have all your soil in place and roughly configured the way you want it to be according to your overall plan, the ideal next step would be to walk away from the area for a year or so and let the soil settle and compact itself as it is exposed to conditions in your area. Some areas may settle as much as eight inches or so in that period, requiring that you go back and add additional soil. But few model railroaders have the patience to wait even a few days, let alone a year, before getting their trains up and running! So, those impatient types may have to resort to "plan B"—a good bit of manual tamping.

The good news is that, for the most part, tamping and tightly compacting the soil is really most important in areas where you plan to place your roadbed. You won't need to worry about tamping and compacting every square inch of your layout area, but you certainly can feel free to do that if you enjoy the exercise. Just be

aware that areas that have not been compacted will, as noted earlier, settle over time—perhaps as much as eight inches or more. Your local home improvement center or hardware store can supply you with a tamping tool, which, essentially, amounts to little more than a hefty piece of metal attached to the end of a pole. You simply stand over the spot to be compacted, and tamp away with as much downward force as your muscles will allow! This procedure is best repeated several times a day over a period of several days—the more often, the better—followed each time by a thorough soaking. After about five or so days of this repetitive muscle-building activity, you should be ready to begin roadbed construction, or even try out for the Olympics.

As if all this talk about soil and compacting wasn't bad enough, it's also appropriate at this point to discuss a really heavy subject: Rocks!

• Rocks for garden railroads

Rocks, ranging in size from those small enough for a single individual to lift, to boulders that require a crane to hoist into position, are a fixture on a great many garden railroads—particularly those that choose to represent more mountainous and rugged areas of the country. You may be one of those individuals fortunate enough (or unlucky enough, depending on your point of view), to already have some significant individual rocks or rock formations in the area to be occupied by your garden railroad. If so, the rocks should be an important element in your early planning efforts, in much the same as any large trees or other not-to-be-moved obstacles would be. If the rocks do already exist on site, you'll have to choose between taking the easy way out—leaving them right where they are and working around them—or finding a way to reposition them so the rocks conform to your overall scheme in the way you want them to.

Rocks being strategically placed on Scott Johnson's garden railroad will provide a logical reason for the use of two bridges along the line. With trackwork already in position, Scott is using smaller rocks to fill gaps and give a finished and solid appearance to the supporting foundation.
Photo courtesy of Scott Johnson

If you don't already have a suitable supply of rocks on your property, you can obtain them from a rock quarry, building supply stores, or search for them "in the wild." If you choose this latter method for obtaining your rocks, do be sure to seek permission and approval from the property owner or appropriate agency before you take any rocks from private or public property. Some state and national parks and forests, for example, do not permit removal of any such geological items.

One important rock-hunting tip: Always make it a point to select and use the same type of rocks in any given location on your railroad. Mixing different rock types within the same scene generally is not a good idea because the result simply doesn't look natural to a viewer, even if that viewer is what you might term "geologically challenged." Keep in mind that a particular rock type may be known by different names, depending on where you live, so if you're buying rocks you are well advised to take a look at what you're getting in advance of the purchase. Also, be sure to vary the size of rocks intended for use in any one location to keep the scene from becoming repetitive, overly structured, and even boring. Using rocks of different sizes will also help you to place them more effectively, and to keep them in place.

Rocks are commonly sold by the pound and measured by "head size," which relates to the size of an average human head. One- or two-head rocks can often be repositioned by hand alone, but anything larger than that will likely require mechanical assistance in some form. This could be a heavy-duty hand truck or dolly with fat rubber wheels, or it may require the use of a tractor or crane. One recollection you don't want to have of your garden railroad construction days is the hernia that was induced by toting rocks around! Once you have selected a final resting place for your rocks, be sure to take the important extra step of "planting" them in their new locations. Don't simply rest them on top of the ground, because then they will look like nothing more than what they are: giant boulders laying atop the ground. Instead, make sure that the base of the

rock is partially buried in the soil, so it appears to have been there for a long time. A good rule of thumb is to bury the bottom third of the rock in the soil.

If you want to learn from the real experts on such matters as rock placement, pick up a couple of rock gardening books the next time you visit your local nursery or home improvement center. There are lots of very good pointers in these publications.

"Big Ben," a 2-8-0 K28 brass locomotive made by LGB, blasts out of Flat Rock Tunnel on Charles Bednarik's Rancocas, Red Hawk, and Rutland garden railroad. The rockwork, as the tunnel's name suggests, is made primarily of large, flat rocks. *Photo courtesy of Charles Bednarik*

• The garden

Once you have contoured the basic landform and have placed any major features such as rocks, retaining walls, bridges, tunnels, and the like, you can temporarily blanket the exposed soil areas of your sculpted terrain with a mulch of some sort—the smaller the size of the mulch material, the better it will conform to the scale of the railroad. The mulch material could be wood chips, bark chips, commercial mulch mix, or even small pebbles. In addition to adding a decorative touch that looks much better than exposed soil, this mulching material will provide a protective layer over your topsoil that will help to prevent erosion and inhibit weed growth until such time as you can get around to planting the area. The mulch can be removed or used elsewhere as you plant small areas of the railroad in stages—the way it really should be done.

That task taken care of, it's now time to turn attention to the plantings themselves. The first and most obvious question is: What should you plant?

What you should plant, and where and when you should plant it, will be largely determined by climate, soil conditions in your region, and the amount of sunlight and/or shade normally available on your garden railroad's site. Availability of water is another consideration, but drip irrigation, sprinklers, or soaker hoses can easily meet that need, in most cases. Regardless of where you live though, and regardless of prevailing conditions at the selected site, you'll have little problem finding sufficient varieties of live miniature plants to

On another part of Scott Johnson's layout, rocks are being placed to frame a scene that includes a nicely weathered mine structure. *Photo courtesy of Scott Johnson*

complement your garden railroad. For example, Miniature Plant Kingdom, a California nursery that specializes in miniature and dwarf plants (see appendix listings for this and other miniature plant specialists), stocks about 1,500 varieties of plants especially well suited to the needs of bonsai, rock garden, and garden railway enthusiasts. Other nurseries around the nation also cater to the needs of bonsai, rock garden, and garden railway enthusiasts.

Your first step in determining what, where, and when to plant should be to identify the U.S. Department of Agriculture (USDA) hardiness zone that you live in. The USDA publishes a detailed "Plant Hardiness Zone Map" of the United States, comprised of eleven zones that are rated for winter hardiness of plants based on "average annual minimum temperature." The zones are designated zone 1 through zone 11, with zone 11 reserved for areas where the average annual minimum temperature is above 40 degrees Fahrenheit (e.g. Honolulu, Hawaii, for example, which is essentially frost free). If you don't know what zone you live in (and be aware that there can be several zones within any given state), you can ask a certified nurseryman in your area, or go directly to the USDA site at **www.USDA.gov** on the Internet. In the gardening section of that web site, you will find the complete zone map. Just click on the map itself or on your state's name, and you'll find all the information you could possibly want or need to know about your specific plant hardiness zone. Lots of other useful information for the home gardener can also be found at that site.

For the most part, you will want to stick with perennials for your garden railroad—plants that last year after year—rather than annuals, which often must be replaced each planting season. But this should certainly not preclude you from using annuals at various spots around the layout, since they provide bursts of color that serve to attract the viewer's eyes and even direct attention to features you want to emphasize.

With literally thousands of varieties of plants available, and in light of the fact that the plant hardiness zones vary widely throughout North America, it would be fruitless to provide specific recommendations relating to plants that are most suitable for your location and needs. Nevertheless, there are some general types and varieties that are commonly used by garden railroaders, and which seem to fare well in terms of overall acceptability in a good number of USDA zones. Basically, as applied to garden railroading, we're dealing with three levels or types of plant life: groundcovers; shrubs and bushy plants; and dwarf and miniature trees.

• Groundcover for garden railroads

The first category is groundcover, which describes the low-growing, ground-hugging, creeping sorts of plants that we might use to represent grass, meadows,

Miniature plants, including aquatic plant life, adorn the garden railroad built by Bill and Linda Fox in Virginia Beach, Virginia. *Photo courtesy of Linda Fox*

or other relatively low, uniform, and widespread foliage. Real grass doesn't qualify for this use simply because it is too far out of scale to represent "grass" on a garden railroad. Instead, varieties of moss-like carpeters, Thyme (*Thymus*), and Sedum (*Sedum*), are most often used to represent what in the real world we know as grass.

Real moss that is already growing elsewhere on your property can, of course, be transplanted to the railroad site to serve as an effective spreading groundcover, as long as the prevailing light conditions are the same in the new area, but you might also consider Irish or Scotch moss (*Sagina subulata* or *Sagina subulata aurea*), or a variety of New Zealand polster (*Scleranthus biflorus* or *Scleranthus uniflorus*). Other mat-like plants that might be used to simulate grass-covered or meadow areas on your layout include Woolly yarrow (*Achillea tomentosa*), Rock cress (*Aubrieta deltoidea*), Coyote brush (*Baccharis pilularis*), and Tiny rubies (*Dianthus*). Creeping veronicas (*Veronica liwanensis, pectinata,* and *rosea*), also serve well for this purpose, as does Corsican mint (*Mentha requienii*), and Snow-in-summer (*Cerastium tomentosum*).

Another view of landscaping techniques employed on the Fox family layout, which adjoins a large deck.
Photo courtesy of Linda Fox

Thymes, which also provide excellent low- or creeping-growth, are available in a great number of varieties. They are a hardy perennial, and will bloom year after year. Most varieties prefer sun to partial shade areas, and they have a blooming period that ranges from a couple of weeks to several months. Some of the more popular varieties of thyme are Golden lemon thyme (*Thymus citriodorus aureus*), Pink chintz thyme (*Thymus serpyllum* 'pink chintz'), Red thyme (*Thymus praecox coccineus*), Mother of thyme (*Thymus Serpyllum* 'mother of'), Minus thyme (*Thymus serpyllum* 'Minus'), Caraway thyme (*Thymus herba-barona*), Wooly thyme (*Thymus pseudolanuginosus*), and Common thyme (*Thymus vulgaris*). Do keep in mind that this list repre-

sents just a very small sampling of what is available.

Sedum is yet another popular groundcover, and this plant fares particularly well in hot, dry conditions. Some sedum varieties produce very colorful blossoms in a myriad of colors ranging from pastels to deeper hues. Among the more commonly seen sedums in garden railroading are Gold moss sedum (*Sedum acre* 'Aureum'), Blue spruce sedum (*Sedum reflexum* 'blue spruce'), Spanish sedum (*Sedum hispanicum*), White stonecrop (*Sedum album micranthum*), Miniature stonecrop (*Sedum album* or *Sedum dasyphyllum*), Dragon's blood (*Sedum Spurium*), and Cape Blanco sedum (*Sedum spathulifolium* 'Cape Blanco').

Again, these are just samplings of what is available and commonly used, and you are well advised to do some asking around to determine what fares best in your particular area. Check with other garden railroaders in your vicinity, if at all possible, because many of them will welcome you to their homes to view their handiwork. This will help to place the plants in proper context with a railroad setting. Seek the advice of a certified nurseryman, too, because they surely will have some experience in regard to plantings that are most apt to do well.

• Shrubs and bushes for garden railroads

The second category includes low-growing shrubs and bushy plants that can be used as scaled-down representations of their full-size counterparts. What you're looking for here are plants that will peak at about six to eight inches in height, give or take an inch or two. As with any living plant, some pruning and trimming may be required to maintain them at the desired shape and height. Included in this category are such plants as:

Lily of the Nile (*Agapanthus*), Miniature boxwood (*Buxus microphylla*), Scotch heather (*Erica canaliculata*), Gardenia (*Gardenia jasminoides*), Lavender (*Lavendula angustifolia munstead*), Box honeysuckle (*Lonicera nitida*), Dwarf myrtle (*Myrtus communis compacta*), Rosemary (*Rosmarinus officinalis*), Fairy lily (*Zephyranthes candida*), Miniature rhododendron (*Rhododendron impeditum*), and Compact lavender cotton (*Santolina chamaecyparissus*).

As noted with the groundcovers category, there are numerous other excellent examples of bushes and shrubs available, and it's best to view any possible selections in person or, at the very least, to spend some time researching them in the various books and catalogs that are available.

• Dwarf and miniature trees for garden railroads

You'll almost certainly want to have some miniature and/or dwarf trees on your layout to provide scaled-down versions of the deciduous and conifer varieties that are so much a part of our full-size world.

Obviously, a true oak, poplar, maple, or other actual tree won't do, because it will quickly grow, both above and below ground, to unmanageable proportions. For that reason, dwarf and miniature trees are most often used in the miniature world of garden railroading.

Miniature conifers on a hillside overlooking the garden railroad of Bill and Linda Fox.
Photo courtesy of Linda Fox

A dwarf tree, plant, or shrub is not the quite same thing as a miniature tree, plant, or shrub, and that's a distinction that should be recognized early-on in your landscape planning. Miniature varieties tend to stay small throughout their life, while some dwarfs, if left relatively unattended, may grow to six feet or more in height in just as few years. Where possible, seek trees that are slow-growing varieties, and which peak at about two feet or so. Both dwarfs and miniatures have their respective uses on a garden railroad, of course, so this is not meant to imply that you should only use miniatures and avoid the dwarfs. It does mean that you'll need to provide some growth space around many dwarfs, and it also means that you'll likely be doing some pruning, and even replanting, with some of these plants.

That said, it just so happens that one of the most popular trees in all of garden railroading is a dwarf. The Dwarf Alberta spruce (*Picea glauca conica*), likely ranks as the hands-down winner when it comes to the most prevalent tree seen on garden railroads throughout North America. With its conical shape and bright green foliage, this small but hearty variety is a popular choice for garden railroad groves and forests. It is also readily available in most areas, and is reasonably priced since it is also a popular form of tabletop Christmas tree sold during the holiday season. It can be purchased and planted on your railroad during that season, since the tree remains dormant during the winter months.

Other excellent finescale trees include Dwarf Japanese garden juniper (*Juniperus procumbens*), Japanese maple (*Acer palmatum*), Japanese red cedar (*Cryptomeria japonica tanzu*), Hokkaido miniature Chinese elm (*Ulmus parviffolia* 'Hokkaido'), Dwarf Irish juniper (*Juniperus communis*), Dwarf birch (*Betula nana*),

Dwarf white birch (*Betula alba* 'Trost's Dwarf'), Miniature birdsnest spruce (*Picea abies*), Blue Star juniper (*Juniperus squamata* 'Blue Star'), Dwarf cedar (*Cryptomeria japonica nana*), Dwarf crape myrtle (*Lagerstroemia indica*), Pomegranate (*Punica granatum nana*), and Miniature elm (*Ulmus parvifolia*).

Some others that might be considered include Mungo pine (*Pinus mungo*), Dwarf balsam fir (*Abies balsamea* 'Nana'), Dwarf bristlecone pine (*Pinus aristata* 'Sherwood Compact'), and Dwarf Serbian spruce (*Picea omorika* 'Nana').

Cypress varieties include such examples as Ellwood cypress (*Chamaecyparis* 'Ellwood'), White cypress (*Chamaecyparis thyoides*), Pygmy cypress (*Cupressus pygmaea*), Italian cypress (*Cupressus glauca*), and Dwarf Hinoki cypress (*Chamaecyparis obtusa*), among numerous others.

Remember that none of the plants in any of these three general categories can really be left unattended. Placing greenery on a garden railroad is not at all like planting a shredded-foam tree or bottle-brush conifer on your indoor layout, where you can stick it in the plaster hillside and then forget it. The living growth on a garden railroad requires regular care and attention involving proper light conditions, adequate watering, proper nutrition, and even trimming , pruning, or an occasional replanting. Even with all of the tender, loving care you can provide, some plants will invariably die and need to be replaced. That's all part of the natural evolution of a garden railroad. Don't hesitate to experiment, and certainly don't view each failure as a setback. Instead, take full advantage of the garden aspect of garden railroading, and view each plant as a new challenge to be met and a new and rewarding learning experience.

• Flowers and common annuals for garden railroads

For those who truly enjoy the gardening segment of garden railroading, and who don't mind the extra effort required in working with seasonal plantings, annuals can provide an excellent way to add vibrant splashes of color to select spots along your railroad. Try to keep the taller flowering annuals away from the track so they don't adversely impact the sense of scale that you are trying to convey, but there's certainly no reason not to enjoy the striking colors that daisies, begonias, impatiens, dwarf petunias, dwarf marigolds, crocuses, pansies, geraniums, and other such flowering plants add to the scene. It is, after all, a *garden* railroad!

• Landscaping tips

• Develop your landscaping and the related garden aspects in small, easy-to-handle steps—one "visual scene" at a time—to avoid becoming overwhelmed by both the work and the weeds.
• If you're new to gardening, take some time to study

some books and magazines on the subject of rock gardening, in particular. Rock-garden plants serve especially well in a garden railroad setting, since they are more properly proportioned, and they tend to grow well in restricted areas, such as between the rocks. The appropriate publications can be found at your local home improvement center, nursery, or at the public library.

• When planting groves of trees, always plant in odd rather than even numbers—three or five trees to a grove, for example. This provides asymmetrical symmetry to the group, which is more pleasing to the eye.

• Keep in mind that top-pruning to inhibit growth of a tree or bush is not enough. The roots must also be pruned if you want to restrict the plant's growth to a suitably small size.

• If possible, select a variety of different types of plants that flower and bloom in various seasons of the year, and which blossom in different colors. This way, you'll nearly always have a splash of vibrant color somewhere on your railroad.

• Try to envision the individual scenes you create on your railroad in terms of that scene's foreground, middle ground, and background. Use small plants in the foreground areas; slightly larger plants in mid-ground areas; and larger plants, trees, and shrubs in the background areas to provide a living backdrop for the entire scene.

• Many woody plants, such as Alberta spruce, can be planted in the ground while still in their pots. Just make sure the pot has a drainage hole. Planting them in their pots will keep them from growing too large. Every few years or so, you can remove the potted plant from the ground, trim the roots, then re-pot and re-plant them. Spread some mulch around the base of the plant and the adjacent area, and they will look as if they are planted directly in the soil.

As you work on the construction of your own garden railroad, you'll come up with other practical tips and shortcuts that will make the experience even more meaningful and enjoyable, especially if you are willing and able to share these hints with others in the hobby. One of the benefits of membership in a local garden railway club, or even of starting one in your own area if such a club doesn't already exist, is the splendid opportunity these shared-interest associations provide for each member to learn something new from the others. It's amazing to behold the number of innovative tips and techniques that can emerge from such a group as they sit around at a fellow member's home, watching the trains run and enjoying a relaxing afternoon.

The living, growing landscape you create and culti-

vate is what really puts the "garden" in garden railroading. In concert with the trains and their related accessories, the garden is what truly gives you railroad a distinctive personality that sets it apart from all others. In fact, because every garden railway must be more or less custom-designed from the ground up, the chances are you'll never see another garden railroad quite like yours. That's something that cannot be said of many indoor model railroads. But what's even more important is the genuihne feeling of satisfaction and pride you'll receive from watching an entire miniature garden railroad take form, and ultimately flourish, under your guiding hand.

• **Water features on garden railroads**

While a water feature—be it a pond, stream, waterfall, or some combination of the three—is certainly not an absolute necessity for any garden railroad, a good many enthusiasts firmly believe that a water attraction of some sort is a "must have" component if the overall scene is to be considered truly complete.

The pond on the Fox garden railroad is stocked with koi and goldfish, and is fitted with a foot bridge for access to other portions of the layout.
Photo courtesy of Linda Fox

Fortunately, if water is what you want, it's not terribly difficult to model realistic, efficient, and leak-proof water features today, thanks to the wealth of pre-formed plastic ponds and waterfalls, and the related pumps and filtering systems, that are available at most major garden centers and home improvement outlets. Actually, a relatively small, molded-plastic pond is a great way for the novice garden railroader to incorporate water on some area of the layout. They are not overly expensive, even considering the additional cost of a recirculating pump, filtering system, and the other required accessories, and they can always be supplemented or replaced with a significantly larger pond or waterfall of some alternative construction later on, after you have gained a bit of first-hand experience in the pros and cons of dealing with a water feature. In fact, it's often the case that garden railroaders become so enamored with their water feature that they quickly outgrow it.

Other commonly used water feature construction techniques include those which use ferrocement liners or commercial vinyl/rubber sheets or pool liners. Each of these methods has its own advantages and disadvantages, but neither of these alternatives are quite as simple and straightforward as the pre-formed plastic pond, so that is a good way to get started.

Perhaps the most important thing to know and remember about water features is that the water must be kept moving, and it must be kept clean. Unless you plan on establishing a mosquito farm as one of the industries along your right-of-way, you'll need to make arrangements to add a sufficiently sized recirculating pump to handle a continual flow and aeration of the water supply. The pond liner dealer will be able to recommend the right pump for the size of pond you're buying, but if you decide to construct a ferrocement, rubber-sheet lined, or other type of custom-made pond, you'll need to do some research to find the type and size of pump that's best suited for the depth and area to be covered.

Two of the four ponds on Ronald Wenger's garden railroad. Ron installed and tested his water features before much of the rail line itself was constructed in order to provide the time needed to achieve the right ecological balance for the aquatic plant life. *Photo courtesy of Ronald Wenger*

A filtering system is also a must. If you've ever had a home aquarium, you already know how quickly algae and other growth can invade a contained water system. There are several types of systems that can be used in a garden railroad setting, including natural (live plant) filtration, skimmer filters, biological filters, and others. The type that's best for your situation should only be selected after consultation with a aqua-farm expert in your area, if available, or discussions with fellow garden railroaders in your general region who have such features on their layouts.

If your pond is deep enough—say a couple of feet or more—it can even become home to some goldfish or koi. You do need some depth to the pond, because a shallow pond is just an open invitation to every cat in the neighborhood to attend a feast at your garden railroad. The fish you stock your pond with won't be to proper scale, of course, but they do add a colorful, active element to what can otherwise be a rather static scene. A side benefit is that they, along with the plant life, help to maintain the quality of the water, and keep it free of insects and mosquito larvae.

There are really only two major problems with koi and some other fish: First, they eat a lot, which causes them to produce a lot of waste, which, in turn, will pollute your beloved pond and eventually kill the fish. Second, some types of fish—koi, for example—aren't cheap! You probably don't want to be spending perfectly good train equipment money on replacing dead fish every couple of weeks or so. For those reasons, among others, a good filtering system is a real necessity if you plan to stock your pond with fish, even though the presence of fish and plant life in the pond will, in itself, certainly help promote a proper ecological balance. Your local aquarium dealer or a fish hatchery will be able to provide recommendations for equipment that will work best in your situation.

If you do have a pond large and deep enough to provide a habitat for fish, you'll also want to include some water plants as part of the scene. Lilies, lotus, water hyacinth, and various floaters are all available to add a bit of seclusion and shelter for the fish, and to enhance the attractiveness of your pond.

You'll also need at least one submersible water pump, either a fountain-type if you're using a pool alone, or a recirculating pump if you need to carry water back to the area at or near the head of a waterfall. Be sure to buy a pump that's adequate to handle the volume of water in your pond(s). Also be certain that the electrical cord of each pump is connected to a household circuit that is equipped with a ground fault circuit interrupter.

Some provision must also be made for drainage and overflow, because heavy rains could flood the pond, and there may also be occasions where you will need to completely drain the pond to repair or replace the pump, clear algae that may have accumulated, or perform some other maintenance.

• Structures and trackside accessories

Structures and various trackside accessories not only bring realism to a model railroad by providing appropriate destinations for the trains, but they also perform a more vital function by imparting some sense of scale to the locomotives and rolling stock operating on the layout. Miniature trees, plants, and groundcover alone—no matter how realistic and convincing—cannot adequately illustrate the proportional relationship that exists between model trains and the environment in which they operate. Trees come in many shapes and sizes, so it's hard to use them as a scale reference. However, most everybody has a good feel for just how large a typical two-story house might be. When a Large Scale locomotive is placed near a properly scaled model of a two-story structure, for example, the viewer is better able to relate the scale of the locomotive or car with the nearby building. From that, the mind is able to infer the model locomotive's true size and proportions in relation to its own prototype because the approximate size of a typical two-story house is already recognized.

Most Large Scale model structures specifically designed for outdoor use, particularly those that are to remain exposed to the elements for an extended period, are made of heavy-duty, weather-resistant plastic that also resists the effects of ultraviolet (UV) radiation resulting from prolonged exposure to sunlight. These invisible UV rays are what cause the siding on your home, among other things, to dry out, fade, crack, and peel over time. Some garden railroaders leave their structures and accessories in place on the railroad throughout the year, while others prefer to remove and store them at the end of a normal running season, particularly if they live in region of the country subject to extremes in weather and climate. Buildings that are not left outdoors year-round will, of course, tend to last longer, and the in-storage period also affords time for touch-up, repainting, and other such maintenance and repairs. Be advised, too, that structures left outdoors for extended periods may also tend to become populated with non-human species of various types. A number of creepy, crawly critters are known to enjoy the sanctity of a Large Scale passenger station, engine house, or other roomy abode.

Structures can be purchased pre-assembled or in kit form. The built-up structures are a bit more costly in most cases, but they can save you time by giving you something that can be quickly positioned on the layout with little preparation or additional effort. Kit-built structures do require a bit of time to assemble, but most go together quite easily, with very few tools required, and they can be a lot of fun to work on during those cold and rainy days when you don't really want to be out in the yard running trains. Another advantage of kit-built structures relates to the opportunity you have to repaint and even reconfigure the structure at an early stage. It's a whole lot easier to paint or repaint

Scott Johnson took the extra effort needed to assure that his trackside structures would be perfectly level from left-to-right, and from front-to-back. A firm supporting foundation was constructed in the area to be occupied by a mine structure. *Photo courtesy of Scott Johnson*

The mine tipple, once in place, sits firmly and squarely on its foundation. *Photo courtesy of Scott Johnson*

the individual components in a kit than it is to repaint the completed building. And if you decide to leave a porch off here or there, or want to change the location of a wall, window, or door, this task is best performed before the component is actually assembled.

Wherever possible, you should try to match your structures, in terms of both architectural style and period, to the overall theme you have chosen for the railroad. You did choose a theme, didn't you? If you're modeling a 1970s mainline railroad in the United States, mid-nineteenth century "Old West" structures trackside are going to look strangely out of place. You also won't need a water tank alongside the rails, unless you want to model a beat-up and dilapidated structure, perhaps overgrown with some vegetation, to represent a slice of the railroad's forgotten past. Likewise, if you're creating a North American railroad, the ornate fittings, tiled roofs, and other obvious characteristics of a typically European building will look somewhat odd and out of place. That also applies to the use of American-type structures on a European-theme line.

Photographs of prototype structures, such as this eight-stall roundhouse, can provide useful construction information for scratchbuilding your own structures, even if you don't plan to build anything quite as imposing. Richard Golding uses photographs to assist him with detailing and weathering the structures that he enjoys building.
Photograph courtesy of Richard Golding

The scale of any structures you select is another very important consideration. The majority of ready-built structures and structure kits in Large Scale are made to around 1:24 scale—a scale that is also conveniently used by many dollhouse enthusiasts, thereby providing the garden railroading community with a ready source of structural supplies and parts. These 1:24 scale buildings, if placed in close proximity to the tracks, will usually look just fine if you're running 1:20.3 scale, 1:22.5 scale, or, quite naturally, 1:24 scale trains, but they may appear too large if you're primarily operating 1:29 scale or 1:32 scale trains. If modern standard gauge operations are what you enjoy most, you will need to do some careful shopping to assure that both the scale and era of the structures conform to your railroad's roster and the layout's overall theme. If you find an out-of-scale structure that you simply can't resist, you can diminish the size discrepancy to a certain extent by placing that structure at some considerable distance from the track, if at all possible.

You can also intentionally use structures of slightly different scales to increase the apparent size of your overall layout, if you approach this with some care. If you place correctly scaled structures in the foreground, then place slightly-smaller-than-scale structures toward the rear areas, you will have invoked what experienced hobbyists (and artists) call "forced perspective," a trick visual effect that makes a given area or scene appear larger and deeper than it really is. The important consideration in creating forced perspective is to have structures that are located adjacent to your trackwork—a passenger or freight station, for example—as close to the correct scale as possible for the type of trains you will normally be running. The smaller middle ground and background buildings then trick the viewer's eyes and mind into believing there is more depth to the scene than there actually is. Try it! It does work!

In many instances, manufacturers don't provide scale information on their packaging, and this situation sometimes leads to confusion and frustration on the part of hobbyists trying to find structures appropriate to the scale of their railroad. For that reason, it's a very good idea to consider purchasing a scale ruler especially designed for Large Scale model railroading. The Scale Card provides a handy pocket-size measuring card for Large Scale, and CTT offers clear plastic rulers in the various Large Scales from 1:22.5 to 1:32 (see Manufacturer/Supplier listings in the appendix). Both devices are quick and easy to use, and either or both would be worthwhile additions to your tool and reference collections.

The Winter Valley Regional Railway displays the structure-building craftsmanship of owner David Winter. David built this imposing grain elevator based on the prototype that exists in Oak Lake, Manitoba. The prototype stands over eighty-two feet high, so David created the structure in 1:29 scale to keep it's actual scale height to less than three feet. All of the other structures on the WV are built to 1:24 scale, for ease of measuring.
Photo courtesy of David Winter

The following are a few select tips worth keeping in mind as you plan for your towns, homes, farms, and industries, and as you undertake the assembly of your first plastic structure kit:

• Keep the total number of structures used on your garden layout to a reasonable minimum. In this regard, too many buildings is worse than too few! The structures you use should be selected carefully. Each should provide a focal point for the area they occupy, and they should not detract from the overall scene, which also includes the terrain, landscaping, and any trains passing by.

• As noted earlier, a good source for structural fittings and accessories for Large Scale models is a dollhouse store or supplier. Many dollhouses are made to 1:24 scale, so accessories used with these building often work well with the Large Scale plastic structures. Some wood dollhouses themselves can be used on a garden railroad, as long as they are properly treated against

Here's the grain elevator in place on the Winter Valley layout. Winter Valley station, in the foreground, was also scratchbuilt. The roof shingles were individually placed, and will withstand exposure to the weather, even though most structures can be easily moved to the indoor portion of David Winter's indoor/outdoor layout.
Photo courtesy of David Winter

exposure to the natural elements. You may even want to store those wood buildings in the garage or elsewhere following each operating session, just as an extra measure of protection.

• Consider repainting all of the components of your new building before you begin assembly. As packaged in the box, most of the structure's smaller components, and even some larger ones, are attached to molded-on armatures, which are known as sprues. Eventually, the parts must be separated from these sprues, but if you plan to repaint the parts, the best time to do so is before you cut them free of their respective sprues. Repainting every part of the structure is a good idea because that is one way to distinguish that structure on your railroad from the thousands of identical structures that may be on garden railroads around the world.

• When you construct a building, consider not gluing the roof to the sides of the building. That will permit you to remove the roof for easy access the structure's interior, if necessary. If the interior space is large

enough, you may even be able to store a few items there, such as a track cleaning block or some other gadget needed along the rail line from time to time. For that matter, the interior space might also be used to conceal a turnout control box, or a similar device.

• When gluing a building's walls together, it's important to keep everything square. You can assure this by using framing clamps to hold two adjoining walls in proper alignment, or you can use heavy-duty rubber bands—one near the top, and one near the bottom—to keep all four walls held tightly together, and aligned, while the glue sets.

• It's a good idea to provide some additional structural support to wall joints and to the underside of the roof, especially if the roof is to be removable. You can use strip styrene, available at most hobby shops, to form cross braces on an angled roof. The roof structures are normally quite rigid if glued according to the kit instructions alone, but this extra reinforcement helps to maintain the proper angle of the roof's major sections

and assure a consistently solid fit atop the building's walls. Wall joints can be similarly reinforced with square styrene strips cemented along the end joints where two walls meet.

• For buildings that are going to remain outdoors for extended periods, apply a bead of outdoor-quality silicone construction sealer along each wall joint. The plastic cement that comes with most structure kits does a good job by itself under normal conditions, but structures that are going to be exposed to the elements for prolonged periods tend to hold up better and longer if they are provided this extra measure of reinforcement.

• When you place structures on your layout, use a carpenter's level to assure that the building is level from front to back and from side to side. Nothing attracts a viewer's attention more rapidly, or looks more unnatural, than a building that is tilted one way or another.

• If you enjoy nighttime running, you'll certainly want to consider adding lights to your structures, both inside and outside. A large variety of appropriate miniature fixtures are available, and they can be easily installed in virtually any building. Just be sure to allow for some secure, hidden, moisture-proof connection to the power supply. Ideally, the lights in all of your structures would operate off a single power source independent of the source used to control the trains. That small power pack that came with your starter set—the one you replaced with a more powerful pack—may be ideal for lighting your buildings. You can even use the variable voltage knob to control the intensity of the lighting and provide a more subdued effect.

• Vehicles and figures

Properly scaled people figures, animal figures, and vehicles of all types are also vital to confirming the proportional relationship of a model train to its surroundings. We all know that most adult human beings are, on average, somewhere between five and six feet tall, so when we see a plastic people figure posed beside a locomotive, it gives us a pretty good sense of how big that locomotive might be in real life. Same goes for automobiles, since most of us are intimately familiar

The figures, vehicles, furniture, barrels, milk cans, and crossing signs on and around the station platform at Winter Valley all work together to create a believable and very realistic scene. Everything in the photo "looks right" because David Winter devoted close attention to the scale of even the smallest details.
Photo courtesy of David Winter

with the size and proportions of our most common form of transportation. It's very easy to relate to the scaled-down size of a typical Ford, GM, Chrysler, or other passenger car, regardless of era.

Remember that figures and vehicles offered by various manufacturers may come in different scales, just as the Large Scale trains are made in at least six common scales. Märklin's 1:32 scale figures, for example, are considerably smaller than Preiser's 1:24 scale figures. By the way, a six-foot-tall figure represented in 1:24 scale would measure about three actual inches tall, while that same fellow in Märklin's 1:32 scale would be nearly a full inch shorter, and smaller in terms of his other proportions, as well.

Large Scale people and animal figures are provided by Aristo-Craft, Bachmann, LGB, Life-Like, Märklin, Merten, Plastruct, Noch, Pola, and Preiser, among others. Many smaller after-market suppliers also are involved in producing figures, some of which are closely related to specific themes. Most of the commercially available figures are made to 1:22.5 or 1:24 scale, but there are exceptions—Märklin's 1:32 scale line of figures provides but one example. By far the most extensive assortment of people and animal figures is made by Preiser, but you should consult current catalogs for photos of what is actually available, particularly if you want to closely match the era of your figures to a chosen theme. Walther's *Big Trains Model Railroad Reference Book* is a good source for locating and comparing much of this information in one convenient place. Advertisements in *Garden Railways* and *Finescale Railroader* magazines also provide good leads to a number of smaller firms that are currently producing figures and other such accessories.

One problem with using miniature figures outdoors is that they often tend to be blown over or knocked over, and you're left with a 1:24 scale Aunt Nellie laying face down in the mud. One way to avoid this problem is to glue the figures down—those that are on the porch or platform of a structure, for example—or to plant them in the ground if they are somewhere else on the landscape. Many plastic figures come equipped with a plastic base, to make them stand upright. Use a razor saw to cut off that base, and apply plastic cement to the bottom of the feet if you're planning to locate the figure on an existing structure. If the figure is to be positioned somewhere on the ground, you can drill a hole in one leg, then glue a finishing nail or long needle in the hole, and plant the figure in the selected location. That same technique can be used for farm animals and other creatures that inhabit your fields and forests.

When it comes to variety, model vehicles greatly outnumber model figures in terms of diversity of scales and variety of offerings. This is largely because toy vehicles constitute a separate and rather large hobby area, independent of model railroading. Some folks collect a certain make of car or truck; others collect only Hess tank trucks; and still others collect farm equipment or emergency vehicles, or some such. The point is, most of the vehicles used on garden railroads were not even produced for that purpose. Most are die-cast models of cars, trucks, farm implements, and construction equipment that were designed by their manufacturers as toys and collectibles on their own merits.

The variety of die-cast vehicles available today is mind boggling, and they are readily available in large numbers at just about any toy store. But as is the case with many Large Scale structures, the vehicle manufacturers often fail to clearly label their packaging with the scale proportion of the enclosed product. This is yet another good reason for carrying a Large Scale ruler with you when you go shopping, or at the very least making a mental note that the vehicles you are seeking should be about x-inches long by y-inches high.

When you are selecting vehicles, people figures or other small accessories and details to place on your layout, be sure to also pay close attention to the period being represented, especially if you have defined a particular era or period for the railroad. Car models become rapidly dated, and a '57 Chevy, although it still could fit in a 2000 setting, certainly won't look right in a early twentieth century scene. The attire worn by human figures also changes over time, and frilly skirted female passengers and males with top hats will look a bit out of place as they're waiting on the platform to board your smooth-sided streamline passenger coaches.

Finally, be sure to consider the myriad of other accessories that might be used on your railroad. Items such as gas pumps, barrels and crates, street lights, telephone poles, and mail boxes all help to bring the railroad setting to live, and to add a sense of purpose to its existence. Many suitable items can be found in catalogs offered by the major manufacturers, but you can also discover them by browsing around toy stores, dollhouse stores, swap meets, and any number of other such establishments and events.

You may have noticed that one category of structures has been omitted from this discussion. That's the category that includes bridges, trestles, and tunnels or tunnel portals. Those topics are covered in the Layout Construction chapter since those specific items are an integral part of the railroad itself, rather than the surrounding landscape.

Getting Started in Garden Railroading

Neglecting maintenance of your Large Scale trains and garden railroad may result in the same fate that has befallen old #12 on Charles Bednarik's "Triple-R Route," as she is hauled off to the scrap yard by Rio Grande 5953. Charles' son, twelve-year-old Ryan, weathered the old steamer to make her look the part of a relic ready for the cutting torch.
Photo courtesy of Charles Bednarik

Chapter 11
MAINTENANCE TIPS FOR GARDEN RAILROADERS

Although most Large Scale model railroad equipment is constructed for rugged and lasting use in all sorts of climates and conditions, this by no means implies that these items should be considered as maintenance free. As with any other object with moving parts, your locomotives, cars, turnout machines, and other such equipment requires regular cleaning and maintenance if you expect these to last a long time and to perform reliably. The little time it takes to clean, lubricate, and properly maintain your equipment will be amply rewarded each time you proudly display your smoothly-operating railroad for family, friends, and visitors.

126

Rule #1 when it comes to maintenance of your equipment is to read, heed, and retain the instruction booklet that is packaged with nearly every set and loco-motive. The initial reading should take place *before* you ever assemble the set or place the item on the track and apply power. We all tend to get a bit "antsy" when it comes to new train purchases, and it's easy to tell our-selves that we'll come back and read the instruction book later after we give everything a test run, but the danger in doing that is that some critical pre-operation procedure may be overlooked or neglected, leading to problems down the road. After you've read and digest-ed the content of these helpful booklets, keep them together in a file of some sort so they'll always be readi-ly available for future reference.

• Maintenance tools and supplies

Most care and maintenance of Large Scale equip-ment can be carried out in the comfort of your home workshop, or even on the kitchen table. As with any well-equipped shop, you'll want to have the proper tools and supplies available nearby when you are ready to perform maintenance procedures on your locomo-tives or rolling stock. The following are the basic items you should plan to have on hand:

• A locomotive and car cradle, which you can either purchase from a commercial supplier (see the appendix section of this book), or construct yourself. The cradle is a sturdy device that's designed to hold your locomotive or car safely and securely in an upside-down position while you're working on the item. The soft foam or fab-ric "cradle" will help to keep any fine detail parts from being damaged. You can make one out of three two-foot long pieces of 2x8 lumber, which you nail or screw together in the shape of a "U". Then, use a number of short nails to attach a piece of heavy fabric or a section of inexpensive bath towel along the long horizontal edges of the two upright legs of the "U"-shaped sup-port. You'll want this material to hang down, in kind of a hammock-like shape, between the two legs. Alternatively, you could fashion a cradle that is lined along the sides and bottom with foam—especially if you can find egg carton-shaped foam pieces of the type often used to protect electronic components in ship-ping. The idea is to be able to take your locomotive or car; turn it upside down; then rest it, top down, in the fabric or foam-lined cradle. The item will be held securely in place, and the soft cushioning will prevent small detail items and/or the item's painted finish from being marred or damaged.

• Screwdriver set or sets, ranging from small jewelers screwdrivers to mid-size screwdrivers, including some equipped with both flat and Phillips-head blades.

• Needle-nose pliers.

• Small, stiff bristle, unused paint brush.

• Cotton swabs and/or pipe cleaners.

• Toothpicks.

• Clean, soft, lint-free rags.

• Electrical contact cleaner.

• "Bright Boy," or other hard rubber eraser, or a track-cleaning block.

• *Plastic-compatible* hobby oil, such as the products offered by LaBelle, Bachmann, Aero Lube, and LGB.

• *Plastic-compatible* lubricating grease (same suppliers as listed for oil).

• Conductive paste (same suppliers as listed for oil, or an auto parts or hardware store).

• LGB Smoke/Cleaning fluid, or other *plastic-compat-ible* electrical contact cleaner fluid.

• Locomotive maintenance tips

Locomotives, of course, have the greatest number of moving and hard-working parts of any item on your railroad. Fortunately, the very nature of their sealed, protected, and weatherproofed construction makes Large Scale locomotives a whole lot easier to service and maintain than comparable models in most other scales. Nevertheless, they still do require periodic atten-tion and care, so it's well worth the time and effort to keep them running smoothly and properly.

• To repeat: Read, heed, and retain all instruction book-lets that come packaged with your locomotives, and be sure to follow the maintenance schedule and proce-dures described therein.

• NEVER use sandpaper or other coarse, gritty abra-sives for cleaning any metal surfaces, including the wheels of locomotives and cars, or the track.

• Use a pipe cleaner or cotton swabs, along with clean, lint-free rags to remove any old oil, grime, or caked-on grease or residue before you apply new lubricants.

• **Use plastic-compatible oil ONLY!** The part you're oiling may be metal, but adjacent components may be made of plastic. And, oil has a way of spreading itself to areas you don't want it to be in, especially if you are too liberal in your application of the oil.

• Apply oil and other lubricants sparingly to any spot where metal contacts metal in the course of normal

operations. Too much oil is often far worse than too little, because excess lubricants can work their way into places that will cause operational problems down the road (literally). A good way to lubricate is to place some oil in a small cup; then dip a toothpick in the cup and use the toothpick to apply a single drop of oil where it is needed. As an alternative, you can use a hypodermic syringe to apply the oil, or purchase hobby oil that already comes fitted with a needle-nose applicator.

• Use gear grease on any exposed toothed gears and in the gearbox, when needed. Do not use oil for lubricating gears.

• Keep oil and grease away from the wheels of your locomotives and rolling stock. Oil on wheel flanges impedes operation, and excess oil also attracts dust, dirt, and other things that you don't want on your wheels. Too much oil on the axle bearings can also work its way down to the track, where it will spread a non-conductive film along the entire length of your railroad.

• Use the conductive lubricant on brushes, brush holders, and the back surfaces of wheels where the brushes contact the wheels. This specially formulated lubricant will conduct electricity, rather than inhibit conductivity as ordinary oil would do. A tiny dab of conductive lubricant can also be applied to the motor's commutator in the event you ever have the motor block—also known as a "brick"—open for any reason.

• After many hours of running, light bulbs, traction tires, and sliding current pickup shoes on locomotives (if they are so equipped) may need to be replaced. Refer to the manufacturer's instructions for procedures to be followed in each of these instances.

• If you have to disassemble any parts of a locomotive to service the item, be sure to make note of which screws, bolts, and other parts went where. It's also a good idea to have a small bowl at hand to contain any removed parts, springs and screws. If you're dismantling the trucks on a diesel locomotive, work on one truck at a time. This will give you a good reference for steps to follow when working on the subsequent truck.

• Create a printed maintenance log for all of your locomotives. Once you have developed a sizable fleet of motive power, it becomes hard to recall which of them was serviced, what service was performed, and when it was done. It's a good idea to inspect and clean the wheels, brushes, and other electrical pickup devices on your locomotives, and to lubricate visible external linkages, after every 20 to 30 hours or so of operation. Plan to give each locomotive on your roster a thorough inspection, cleaning, and complete lubrication, including the gearbox, after every 50 hours or so of running time.

• If a locomotive has been sitting idle for a number of months, even if it was lubricated before being placed in storage, it's a good idea to lubricate it again before placing it back in service.

• Rolling stock maintenance tips

As was noted in the locomotives and rolling stock chapter earlier in this book, many fresh-from-the-factory Large Scale passenger and freight cars come equipped with plastic wheels. Over time, this plastic material tends to wear from the wheels and deposit itself on the track. Once it becomes spread over the rails by passing trains, the combined effects of sun and heat working on this residue can make this baked-in residue difficult to remove. For that reason, it's a good idea to consider investing in metal replacement wheelsets each time you purchase a piece of rolling stock that is factory-equipped with plastic wheels. This may cost a little more up front, but it's well worth the additional expense in the long run. Another real advantage of metal wheels is that they help to lower the center of gravity of the car, resulting in smoother and more reliable operation. Metal wheels also make a nice clickity-clack sound as they pass over rail joints—a pleasant and soothing sound that most railroaders really enjoy.

• You can easily remove or replace the wheelsets on most Large Scale cars by gently spreading the truck sideframe with your hand, thereby freeing one end of the axle. Then slide the other end of the axle out of its corresponding hole in the opposite sideframe.

• Use a pipe cleaner, soaked with contact cleaner, to swab out the bearing holes in on the inside of the journal boxes (the holes where the axles fit), before you replace the wheelsets. A tiny drop of oil or white grease in the axle journals may help to keep cars rolling more freely and quietly. Make sure that no oil remains on the wheel or the sideframe of the truck, though, because this will eventually work its way down to the track.

• While you are cleaning and lubricating your rolling stock, it's a good idea to check for reliable operation of each car's knuckle couplers (unless Kadee couplers are being used). You can do this by closing the coupler; then inserting a finger into the closed knuckle and tugging on it with a moderate amount of force. The coupler should stay closed. It should also open easily and snap closed when you push it into a closed position. Also check each coupler's locking and unlocking action by manually raising the locking lever several times by hand. The coupler knuckle should open and close consistently.

• If your cars are lighted, the current normally comes from brushes making contact with the car's metal wheels (nearly all lighted cars are equipped with metal

wheels). Inspect and/or replace these brushes when they become worn to the point where they are not making solid contact with the inner surface of the wheel. Remember that these brushes are held against the wheel by spring tension. Be careful not to lose the spring when you remove the brush itself—they often have a tendency to jump out at you! Be sure, too, to thoroughly clean that inner wheel surface so it is free of any oil, grease, or grime that might interfere with the brush making uninterrupted contact.

• Maintaining track and turnouts

Track maintenance is as important to a garden railroad as it is to the prototype railroads, where track crews attend to this important maintenance chore on a regular basis. This doesn't mean that you'll be ripping up rails or replacing ties regularly like the real track crews do, but you do need to devote some periodic and careful attention to the overall condition of your trackwork, and you do need to assure that the railheads and flangeways are kept free of any ballast or debris. Most of what's needed to keep your track in good operating condition can be accomplished as part of a regular routine of track inspection and cleaning, which really should occur before each operating session.

In the course of your inspection and cleaning, special attention should be given to the ballast and roadbed that supports your trackwork, because they are most susceptible to damage or displacement caused by wind, rain, frost heaves, or other natural factors. You'll need to promptly replace ballast and/or repair the underlying roadbed wherever there are visible signs of erosion. If you notice a persistent erosion problem in the same location over a period of some months, consider adding retaining walls, ditches, culverts, or similar devices to channel water away from the affected area.

If you're passing electric current through the track to power your railroad, your regular track inspection agenda should also include a check of any jumper wires and rail clamps used at the rail joints. Both wires and clamps can eventually work themselves loose over time, especially if the railroad sees a lot of activity, or is located in a region subject to extreme temperature changes. It takes just a few seconds to check these items to assure solid and dependable connections, and this will save you a lot of time in tracking down a problem later on. Remember, too, that extreme temperature variations can also cause track to expand or contract, resulting in shifted alignment. Most of these misaligned sections should be easy enough to spot by placing your head down to near track level, and sighting along the line. Any improper alignment will be readily visible. Also, be sure to check the electrical connections that run from your power source to the track, to make sure everything in that all-important link is tight and secure.

Unless you're relying exclusively on battery-powered or live steam locomotives to handle the trains on your garden railroad, one necessary and recurring maintenance chore that you'll have to deal with as part of your regular track inspection is track cleaning. Clean track—meaning track that is free of oxidation, leaves, twigs, rocks, dirt, grease, assorted flattened critters, and the residue deposited by the plastic wheels of rolling stock—is absolutely essential for reliable operations. And, since electricity has to flow through the rails to reach the motors inside your locomotives, clean and unobstructed track is perhaps even more essential on a model railroad than it is on the prototype roads.

A particular and persistent problem with model track used outdoors is oxidation—the naturally occurring process that results whenever bare metal is exposed to air, environmental pollutants, and the natural elements for any length of time. Oxidation causes a film to form on the metal surface and, unfortunately, this film is non-conductive on the brass rails most commonly used. It, along with the other impediments noted above, must be removed on a more-or-less regular basis for uninterrupted and reliable operations.

Keep in mind that there's a distinct difference between *cleaning* track with an abrasive device of some sort, and *abrading* the track. What you're really aiming for is a railhead that is rendered clean and shiny with a minimum amount of abrasion (scratching the metal) and wear. Avoid the use of abrasive sandpaper, steel wool, files, metal blades, or any other such materials, since they tend to leave fine scratches in the railheads which, in turn, will simply expedite the buildup of future oxidation and dirt, and provide a ready repository for oily residue.

Yet another important consideration in track cleaning is to use a method that will not disturb the ballast. Dragging out the shop-vac or leaf-blower to suck up or blow away leaves and other debris may be convenient, but it sure won't be very beneficial or practical if it also gobbles up or redistributes a good portion of the ballast you've so carefully laid in place. Things will remain a bit more stable if you mixed some Portland Cement with your ballast before you applied it, but even if that's the case you'll still want to be careful about unduly disturbing the roadbed when you perform routine track cleaning.

Remember, too, that track cleaning may also involve some track clearing—meaning that bushes, plants, shrubs, weeds, and other obstacles adjacent to the track may need to be pruned or trimmed back occasionally to permit unobstructed passage of the trains. This simply amounts to following good gardening practices using the basic tools that you most likely have in your garage or workshop.

Implements for track cleaning abound. The truth be known, there are about as many devices, techniques, and tips for cleaning and maintaining Large Scale track and turnouts as there are types and makes of track itself. However, the most commonly used tools and methods include:

• *Track-cleaning pads and blocks*

Perhaps the least expensive, but most labor-intensive, way to clean your track is with track cleaning pads or blocks, such as the LGB 5004 Track Cleaning Block, or the 3M ScotchBrite pads (the green ones) sold in the housewares or cleaning supply sections of just about any market or home improvement center. These low-abrasive track-cleaning devices are very effective, but they will normally require a bit of back-breaking labor and "elbow grease" on your part because you, in fact, provide the action that makes everything work. One solution is to mount the pads on some sort of pole device, such as a drywall sanding pole (see "Drywall sanders, page 131), so you can perform the cleaning operation from a standing position.

• *Track-cleaning locomotives and cars*

Several of the Large Scale manufacturers, along with a few after-market suppliers, offer special track-cleaning cars that will help make this routine maintenance chore a bit more fun and, in some respects, a bit easier. One manufacturer, LGB, even offers a track-cleaning locomotive and a mount-it-yourself track cleaning device that can be attached to the bottom of most of the firm's two-axle freight or passenger cars.

LGB's track-cleaning locomotive is by no means an inexpensive device to acquire (around $500), but many garden railroaders who have used this self-powered and somewhat novel-appearing locomotive are very satisfied with the results they obtain. The track-cleaning locomotive comes equipped with a powered set of replaceable cleaning wheels that can be adjusted to spin independently of the forward speed of the locomotive. As the locomotive moves forward, the rapidly-spinning cleaning wheels clean and polish the railheads. The locomotive can also be operated without the cleaning apparatus engaged, if desired. It's awfully nice to be able to sit back and let this intriguing unit do the work for you! In most cases, a couple of passes over your trackwork will do the trick.

LGB's car-mounted track-cleaning device is designed to attach to the bottom of many of the firm's two-axle cars. Mounting this device is a simple enough task involving just a couple of screws, and the car can then be pushed along ahead of a locomotive to accomplish the necessary cleaning. Pushing the car, rather than pulling it, is recommended because you want the track area to be cleaned *before* the locomotive makes contact with that portion of rail. The abrasive pads, one over each rail, are kept in contact with the railhead by means of springs, which allow the pads to "float" over rail joints or other irregularities. Some hobbyists prefer to add a bit of extra weight to the track-cleaning car for even better contact between the pads and the track (metal wheels on the track-cleaning car are also recommended). You'll find that you will need to scrape the pad surfaces clean from time to time, since crud will tend to accumulate on them. They're mounted to the spring assembly with adhesive, so they can also be pried loose and easily replaced. These car-mounted pads will not shine the rails as effectively as the aforementioned locomotive, but shiny rails are not really all that important—*clean* rails are!

Aristo-Craft offers a track-cleaning caboose. Similar in function to LGB's car-mounted track-cleaning pad device, the Aristo caboose has a weighted (and replaceable) Brite Boy cleaning pad mounted underneath.

Several after-market suppliers also provide track-cleaning cars especially made for 45mm track. M.O.W. Equipment Co. offers its "Trackman C-2000"—an articulated track-cleaning car that weighs nearly four pounds—which features adjustable pad pressure for light or heavy cleaning tasks. Another firm, Overhead Railways, has a machined aluminum track-cleaning car that uses the LGB 5004 Track Cleaning Block to clean and shine the rails. You'll find these and other suppliers listed in the manufacturers/suppliers appendix at the end of this book.

The track cleaning cars, pushed ahead of a locomotive, may require a number of passes to do a good cleaning job. This isn't a problem if you have a track plan that allows for continuous running, but it can be a bit of a drawback on stub-end spurs and on point-to-point lines.

The LGB Track Cleaning Locomotive has won high praise for Large Scale hobbyists and garden railroaders for its effectiveness and long-term reliability.
Photo courtesy of Ernst Paul Lehmann Patentwerk

Aristo-Craft's Track Cleaning Car has also proven to be an easy and effective means of keeping track clean on a garden railroad. The car is available in a number of popular roadnames.
Photo courtesy of Aristo-Craft

• *Drywall sanders*

Many experienced garden railroaders prefer to use, and highly recommend, an inexpensive drywall sander to clean their track. A drywall sander (also called a pole sander) is essentially a mildly abrasive fabric pad, which resembles a window screen, mounted on the end of a pole, not unlike a long broom handle. The pole attachment helps to make things easier on your back, and it also helps to expedite the cleaning process. Although other types of pads—the green ScotchBrite pads from 3M, for example—can be used to replace the drywall sanding pad, some hobbyists contend that these pads tend to fray faster, and get hung-up on sharp edges such as rail joints and switch points. The drywall pads reportedly hold up better under such conditions. There may be some areas on your railroad that are not easily accessible to the pole-mounted drywall sander—bridges and tunnels, for example—and there you can resort to one of the hand-held track cleaning blocks or pads.

• *Chemical track cleaners*

Any number of different types of track-cleaning fluids, pastes, and other chemical agents have been tried by garden railroaders over time, ranging from products made especially for model track, such as LGB Smoke Fluid/Cleaner and Rail-Zip, to products commonly used for clean-up around the home, such as Simple Green, Goo-Gone, WD-40, Wahl's Clipper Oil, ACF-50, Peek metal polish, and others. The effectiveness of any or all of these products generally depends on who you talk to. Some will swear by a particular liquid cleaner, and others will swear at it. The fact is, liquid cleaners may not be the best way to go when you're dealing with a garden railroad in any event, simply because they require some down-on-you-knees hard labor. They generally require some sort of manual application; followed by some good, hard rubbing; and then a wipe-clean to remove any oily residue. This is fine if you're working on a turnout at your workbench, but it's quite another matter if you have to be down on your hands and knees crawling around several hundred feet of outdoor trackwork.

You may find that one of the tools or methods described above works well enough for you, or you may want to try a combination of, for example, wet-and-dry methods. A lot depends on prevailing conditions in the area of the country where your railroad is located. What will best serve your needs is largely a matter of try-it-and-see experiments, combined with personal experience and preference.

• **Turnout maintenance tips**

Because they are equipped with various moving parts, turnouts require a bit more labor-intensive inspection and maintenance than the rest of the track.

Even turnouts that are protected with temporary covers of some sort during periods of non-operation will require additional cleaning and a light lubrication from time to time to keep everything functioning properly. It's really a good idea to get in the habit of checking every turnout on your layout before each operating session. You can use a small, stiff paintbrush to remove ballast and other foreign material from the area of the points, flangeways, and guard rails. Manually throw the points in both directions to assure that they are operating properly and completely. And, use your track-cleaning tool(s) to keep the tops of the running rails clean and bright, just as you would the regular track sections. This bit of preventive maintenance is apt to save you from ever having to look on helplessly as your new and highly-prized locomotive takes a dive off the turnout and heads onto the ballast en route to an embankment or pond.

If you followed the advice given previously in the "Track and Turnouts" chapter of this book, and have replaced the rail joiners on your turnouts with rail clamps, you'll find that it's MUCH easier to remove the turnouts from your railroad, as necessary, so you can conduct more thorough cleaning, service, and repair work back in the comfort of your home or shop. You may even want to consider establishing a regular "major maintenance" schedule for all of your turnouts, complete with a printed maintenance checklist, so you can approach this task in a regular, systematic, and organized manner. Performing this major maintenance activity on an annual basis is probably adequate for most garden railroads, unless the railroad is subjected to extremes in weather and other conditions.

Begin by giving each turnout a complete visual inspection after you have removed it, followed by disassembly of the operating mechanisms if you suspect or detect a problem. Then, thoroughly wipe-down all surfaces of the turnout and its related components to remove any accumulated grease or grime. Follow this with additional cleaning of the pivots and other moving parts to help keep things operating smoothly and reliably. Check all of the rails, ties, and mechanism housings to make sure that no screws or other parts have worked themselves loose. Some folks recommend applying a drop of Loctite Type 222 (use only Type 222 if you ever hope to remove the screws at some future time) to every screw on each new turnout, before you first install it. The Loctite will hold the screw firmly in place, and prevent vibrations from working the screw loose over extended periods of operation. Also be sure to check the small spaces around the frog, and between the guard rails and stock rails, to assure that these critical areas are properly aligned and free of any obstructions. After you've reassembled the turnout, and before you reinstall it on the layout, clean and shine all of the metal rails with the same materials that you used on the rest of the trackwork. This maintenance procedure, if practiced on a regular basis, will significantly reduce any major turnout-related problems.

The live steam Aster "Big Boy" lives up to its name as it muscles more than 30 freight cars along the elevated right-of-way in Jim Stapleton's large yard. Mike Moore, the locomotive's owner, maintains a careful watch over his consist. The Stapleton's layout is designed primarily for live steam operations, permitting the engineer to follow along with the train.
Photo courtesy of Peter Thornton

Chapter 12

STEAM IN YOUR GARDEN

Want to *really* operate your railroad like the prototype railroads once did? If so, small-scale live steam may be just the thing for you!

"Small-scale live steam" is the term generally applied to steam-powered locomotives that operate, most commonly, on #1 gauge (45mm) track—the same track used by modelers in the battery or track-powered "Large Scale" categories described throughout this book. By extension, the term also covers live steamers in smaller scales, such as O scale and others. Live steam locomotives in all of these scales are correctly called "small-scale" live steam to distinguish them from the significantly more imposing large-scale live steamers, which range in size from ride-aboard locomotives (great fun if you have a *really* big back yard and can afford the equipment), all the way up to full-size prototype steam locomotives.

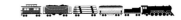

The live steam Aster "Big Boy" lives up to its name as it muscles more than 30 freight cars along the elevated right-of-way in Jim Stapleton's large yard. Mike Moore, the locomotive's owner, maintains a careful watch over his consist. The Stapleton's layout is designed primarily for live steam operations, permitting the engineer to follow along with the train.
Photo courtesy of Peter Thornton

Small-scale live steam locomotives are truly marvels of engineering in miniature! They operate just like the full-size prototypes they represent, aside from the fact that most model locomotive boilers are fired by butane or alcohol instead of the coal, oil, or wood usually burned in life-size steamers. Small-scale live steamers, whether in kit or built-up form, generally come equipped with all of the necessary fittings and accouterments of their big brothers, including water-level sight glass, safety value, reversing lever, throttle, steam-operated whistle, and other features. Many small-scale live steamers can be easily equipped with on-board

Live steam operations on the LaPorte, Bellvue and Western garden railroad built by Gus Sitas. The water, fuel, and various other items needed to keep the live steamers running are visible in the lower right foreground.
Photo courtesy of Gus Sitas

radio control devices that allow for hands-off operation in a realistic manner. Other live steam operators prefer a more hands-on approach, following along on foot as their train navigates its route.

It stands to reason that most small-scale live steam locomotives are intended for operation outdoors, which makes them a natural fit for garden railroads. Although there are no real dangers to indoor operation that cannot be overcome in most situations, the live steamers do tend to drip hot water and oil, and they do involve real flames, so the immediate environment around and under them must be carefully prepared to keep everything safe.

Live steam in any scale is not for the feint of heart. Because these fuel-fired model locomotives operate just like the real thing, they, like their prototypes, require considerable operator attention, care, and maintenance. Fittings need to be adjusted, tightened, and occasionally replaced; care must be given to assure that there is sufficient water in the boiler at all times; and rods, linkages, and bearings need to be properly and regularly lubricated. At the end of an operating session, the locomotive must also be drained, cleaned, lubricated, and made ready for its next run. In other words, the small-scale live steam operator needs to be prepared to actively assume the combined rolls of engineer, fireman, brakeman, hostler, and engine shop foreman—all conveniently rolled into one!

Because they are made primarily of metal, and are fitted with machined parts made to very precise tolerances, live steam locomotives can also be fairly expensive to acquire, with some high-end, full-featured locomotives costing several thousand dollars and up. Still, a number of manufacturers are now producing affordable ($400 or so), high-quality small-scale live steam models that perform very reliably, and that boast many of the features of their more costly counterparts. As with any other product you buy, it pays to do some research first, and seek the advice of someone already experienced in the hobby, before you actually make a purchase. If there's a garden railroad club in your local area, you're almost certain to find one or more members who are legitimate representatives of that "burnt fingers" group noted earlier.

The fraternity of small-scale live steam operators may still be relatively small, even when measured on a worldwide basis, but these hearty souls enjoy exceptionally strong bonds of friendship formed out of a common love of railroading and the desire to learn more about how mechanical objects actually operate. Less concerned with scenic details, structure building, and landscaping than some of their Large Scale garden railroading brethren, live steam fanatics tend to focus more on the fun aspects of actually tinkering with and running their equipment. They often gather at events knows as "steamups" to operate their trains, compare equipment, evaluate new products, swap stories and information, and simply enjoy the camaraderie of their fellow live steam enthusiasts. The largest of these events is held at Diamondhead, Mississippi, in January of each year, and live steam enthusiasts from around the world converge on Diamondhead to see what's new, to demonstrate the running ability of their trains, and to share information in the comfort of a large, fully enclosed steamup hall. In fact, the Mississippi event runs on what amounts to a 24-hour-a-day schedule during the steamup so everyone who cares to has a chance to actively participate.

If you feel that live steam in the garden is an option you may want to explore—either in full measure or in combination with conventional electric-powered trains—you would be well advised to give some special consideration to certain aspects relating to the construction of your railroad, especially if you're still in the planning stages.

For one thing, it would be great idea to consider constructing at least part of your railroad at around waist level. Preparing a live steam locomotive for its daily run takes a bit of time and patience, as does the cleanup procedure that must be followed after the run is completed, and these tasks are more easily and comfortably carried out if the operator is able to work on the equipment while standing, or perhaps sitting on a stool. The pre-operation servicing, for example, involves filling the boiler and/or tender with water, topping-off the fuel tank, starting the fire, and then lubricating the running gear while the steam pressure is building. After five or so minutes, the locomotive is ready for its run. Regular service stops, to take on fuel and water, and to check lubrication, also are as much a part of small-scale live steam operations as they are on the full-size railroads, so operator comfort while performing these tasks is something you should consider.

Another consideration that should be given to a garden railroad intended for live steam operations involves fire prevention. Alcohol is a primary component of the fuel used for many small-scale live steamers, and this stuff burns with a nearly invisible flame. Often, it's not possible to spot the fire until it has begun to damage some other object that *does* burn with a visible flame. Most of the fire potential associated with live steam operations is related to the pre-operation fueling procedure, but fuel spilled as the result of some mishap along the line can also pose a fire hazard. In either instance, this potential hazard is easily prevented by exercising some common sense in planning and construction of your layout. You may, for example, want to avoid using wood ties under your track, and you may want to take special precautions to treat any wood bridges and trestles with a fire-retarding coating of some type. Also, vegetation and various type of mulches placed adjacent to the track should be carefully trimmed back to a safe distance. There's no real danger in operating live steam, so there's really no need to be overly concerned about this matter, but it also never hurts to be prudent, and to implement a few precautionary measures in advance.

Yet another consideration involves planning and constructing your garden rail line so you can easily follow along with your locomotive throughout the full course of its journey, and still be able to see gauges and

A live steam Porter locomotive handles a load of log cars on the Pungo Ridge Railroad constructed by live steam enthusiast Steve Galovics.
Photo courtesy of Steve Galovics

reach the controls in the locomotive's cab in the event that some adjustment is necessary. In most cases, this requires trackwork that is constructed near the outside perimeter of the layout so it is easily accessible. Although many locomotives can be equipped with radio control to regulate speed and direction, not all locomotives are so equipped. For that matter, you may very well be one of those live steam operators who prefers to stay with manual control—kind of like a hands-on engineer walking alongside his locomotive rather than sitting in the cab. In any event, if running live steamers is something you know you'll want to do from the start, you would be wise to assume that you, or one of your visiting live steam colleagues, will need to stay close to a locomotive at all points along its route.

Once the live steam bug bites, prospective entrants into this fascinating phase of the hobby soon develop a list of common-sense questions that need to be addressed before they are willing to take the plunge and invest in a live steam locomotive. Some of the most frequently asked questions include:

• *Are live steam locomotives dangerous?*

Not really, if you pay attention to what you are doing. Small-scale live steamers are mechanical devices and, as such, they do require care and attention to keep them operating smoothly and safely. Every novice to live steam operations soon learns that locomotive boilers become quite hot, and it's usually not long before they become new initiates in the aforementioned "burnt fingers club." After that first incident, a good pair of work gloves quickly becomes part of the live steam engineer's uniform, perhaps along with a protective apron to prevent splatters and spills from damaging or staining clothing.

Always keep in mind that a steamed-up boiler is under considerable pressure, so some attention must be given before each run to assuring that the safety valve is functioning properly. This device regulates the amount of pressure in the boiler, maintaining it at a safe level. When the valve pops, it releases any excess pressure. The safety valve is located atop the boiler, and live steam operators soon learn why you should never position your face or hands over the top of a working boiler.

Also, the fuel used in a live steam locomotive is, of course, flammable, and it needs to be handled with reasonable care. Since alcohol flames, in particular, are very difficult to see on a bright, sunny day, it's important to conduct refueling operations at a spot along your railroad where there is nothing to burn alongside or under the locomotive. A pinch of baking soda added to the alcohol fill bottle will add a bit of orange color to the flame, making it somewhat more visible in sunlit conditions.

Any special safety precautions will be properly emphasized in the owner's manual that comes with your locomotive. If you adhere to these cautionary notices; take the time to gain some understanding of how a steam locomotive actually functions; and faithfully follow all of the prescribed maintenance procedures on a regular basis, you'll have little to worry about. Once you know the basic rules of the game, operating a live steam locomotive is no more dangerous than driving your car or crossing the street—probably less so, depending on where you live!

• *"How long will a small-scale live steam locomotive run before it has to be refueled?"*

Depending on how much fuel and water is carried aboard, either in the locomotive itself or in the locomotive and its tender (if so equipped), actual run times can vary from about 20 minutes to over an hour. For safety reasons, nearly all small-scale live steamers are built so the fuel load will be exhausted well before the locomotive runs out of water. If the reverse of this were to happen, it could, of course, have disastrous consequences for the locomotive and perhaps even for anyone standing in the vicinity.

• *"How will I be able to regulate the speed and direction of my locomotive?"*

Speed can be controlled in one of two ways: manually, by hand, or mechanically, via a radio-controlled throttle linkage. As was previously noted, many small-scale live steam enthusiasts prefer to accompany their locomotives on their journeys. These folks seem to feel that the sensation of actually operating and controlling a live steam locomotive is best achieved by physically adjusting the throttle lever and Johnson bar (reversing lever) by hand, and by closely monitoring the gauges and other functions. That is, after all, how real locomotive engineers attend to their tasks.

Other live steam hobbyists prefer to take advantage of newer technologies that can be used to control a locomotive's speed (and perhaps even blow the whistle), and they elect to use radio control units to run their trains from just about any location along the layout. The radio control (R/C) units used to control live steam locomotives are very much like the R/C units used to control model cars and airplanes—indeed, in many cases they are the exact same units. In the case of radio control, a servo mechanism in the locomotive's cab is linked to the throttle, the reversing lever, and perhaps other devices. The servo responds to—and is activated by—a radio signal transmitted from the control unit held by the operator. With this control unit, the engineer can adjust speed, reverse the locomotive, and even sound the whistle or bell. Best of all, these radio control devices are not overly expensive, especially when one considers the cost of many high-end live steam models. If hands-off control appeals to you, you'll want to see what's required to outfit your locomotive with R/C before you complete the purchase.

The crew of live steamer #27 makes a "comfort stop" during the daily run along the Pungo Ridge Railroad in Southeastern Virginia. *Photo courtesy of Steve Galovics*

• *What kind of fuel is used in a small-scale live steam locomotive?*

The fuel itself is normally either methylated spirits (abbreviated as "meths" in the hobby, and also known as denatured alcohol), or butane, of the type used in cigarette lighters, camping stoves, and gas-powered lanterns. "Meths" is available at your local drugstore, although you'll probably want to ask the pharmacist for denatured alcohol instead of "meths," unless you want to risk drawing a somewhat puzzled look in response. As an alternative, 180-proof alcohol from your local or state liquor store is an acceptable substitute for denatured alcohol. Butane is a gas sold in pressurized containers, such as the type used for refilling some types of cigarette lighters. Since the cost of such small amounts can quickly add up, you'll want to consider buying the larger butane canisters sold for camping equipment. The best source for these larger quantities of butane is a sporting goods or camping outfitters store.

In addition to the fuel, live steam locomotives also require water. However, ordinary tap water, bottled drinking water, or even de-ionized water will not do, because minerals in drinking water, and the reaction of de-ionized water with metal parts inside the boiler, will eventually lead to major problems. What you really need to use is distilled water, which can also be purchased at most drugstores and large grocery stores.

One other substance that is required for all small-scale live steam locomotives is steam oil. This should not be confused with the regular oils that you use to lubricate your locomotive's running gear and linkages. Steam oil is a specially formulated, heavyweight oil (between 200 and 600 weight, as compared with 30-40 weight oil used in your automobile), that is injected into the cylinders to displace moisture and lubricate the moving parts. You'll want to be especially careful to NOT use any other type of oil for this purpose. Steam oil may be difficult to find locally, unless you live near a live steam dealership, but it can be ordered in convenient and long-lasting sizes from most of the live steam distributors found in the appendix section of this book.

• *Can live steam locomotives operate on the same track with electric-powered locomotives?*

Yes, they can if the wheels of the live steam locomotive are properly insulated so they don't short-out the electrical circuit normally provided by the track. If you intend to operate both steam and electrically powered locomotives at the same time, be sure to ask for insulated wheels on the live steamer when you place your order or purchase the locomotive—in most cases, that option is available. If your live steamer doesn't have insulated wheels, you'll need to shut off the track power until you're finished running your live steamer.

A Roundhouse Engineering "Argyle" live steamer pulls a string of Bachmann 1:24 scale cars at one of Jim Stapleton's steamups.
Photo courtesy of Peter Thornton

Another thing to keep in mind: When you run live steam, the track is likely to get a bit dirtier because oil deposits will leave a film on the rails, and this oil will attract dust and dirt. Although this doesn't really harm anything, you will need to clean the track more often if you choose to operate live steam and electric-powered locomotives along the same track.

In the "Power and control systems" chapter earlier in this book, the advantages and limitations of various types of power systems were listed. Since we're actually discussing a completely different form of "power" here, it seems appropriate to follow that same format, and to identify the pro and con considerations that apply to small-scale live steam operations.

ADVANTAGES OF SMALL-SCALE LIVE STEAM OPERATIONS:

• Some recently introduced live steam locomotive models are available at reasonable cost ($400 or so for a small, but safe and reliable, basic unit). The high cost of a live steamer used to be a major obstacle to growth in this segment of the hobby, but this is rapidly changing.

• Live steam provides a true-to-life operating experience that cannot be duplicated with electrically powered model trains. There's a certain vicarious thrill associated with knowing that you are *really* operating like the true-to-life prototype in nearly all respects. Enjoying this sensation in an outdoor setting simply adds to the appeal.

• Track cleaning, aside from removing obvious obstacles, is not required. Although it's still a good idea to clean the railheads periodically to remove any oily film that may build up, you can pretty much operate a live steam locomotive over any trackwork that is properly joined and aligned.

• No track wiring or other electrical connections are required. Turnout motors may be wired independently, if so desired, but many live steam operators prefer to follow along with their train, and this places them in a good position to perform the brakeman's function of manually throwing the turnout points.

• Many live steam locomotives can be equipped with radio control at relatively low cost.

• Multiple live steam locomotives can be operated simultaneously on the same track (assuming that different frequencies are used if the locomotives are equipped with radio control).

• Small-scale live steamers require no additional sound systems or smoke generators. The gentle chuffing from the cylinders and the steam exhaust from the stack are the real thing, and they really help to round out the total live steam experience.

LIMITATIONS OF SMALL-SCALE LIVE STEAM OPERATIONS:

• Live steamers require regular service and maintenance—before, during, and after each run, just like the prototype. In this regard, live steamers are considerably more labor-intensive than their electrically operated counterparts.

• Oil and other deposits deposited on the track by live steam locomotives generally require that the track be thoroughly cleaned before electrically powered locomotives can be operated.

• Small-scale live steam locomotives generally require level track and relatively light loads. Although most live steamers can certainly handle moderate grades, it's necessary to adjust speed on both the upgrade and downgrade portions. This is more easily done if a radio-control system is used. On level track, a small (0-4-0 or 0-6-0) live steamer that has been properly broken-in should be able to handle about eight to ten standard freight cars.

• Certain types of fuel, steam oil, and other live steam supplies may be hard to obtain locally, depending on where the operator lives.

• The operator/engineer/fireman must follow along with the locomotive to control speed and to monitor operation unless the locomotive is equipped with radio control. Even with radio control, the steam-generating system must be monitored frequently.

• Nearly every live steam operator will, at some point, suffer a burned finger or two in the course of learning how to effectively operate a live steam locomotive!

If, after mulling over these advantages and limitations, you still find yourself attracted to this special segment of the hobby, you may very well be ready to begin your adventure into small-scale live steam. Take a garden railroad, and subject it to wind, rain, snow, heat, cold, erosion, and all the other obstacles that nature can throw its way. Then, combine that with a locomotive powered by a functioning steam boiler, and you've come about as close to real railroading action as you're ever apt to get!

Appendix A
Sources of Large Scale, garden railroading, and small-scale live steam equipment and supplies

Manufacturers and major U.S. distributors of locomotives, rolling stock, and sets are listed first, and are presented in alphabetical order by the firm's name.

After-market manufacturers and suppliers—those who provide supporting products and services to the hobby—are listed next, and are presented in alphabetical order by the firm's name. The primary products or service they provide are also specified.

If you wish to inquire about a particular firm's products or services, you should, if possible, first consult the firm's web site on the Internet. Generally, these sites provide current catalogs and product descriptions, technical support information, shipping schedules, dealer lists, and current news and information about the firm. If your question is not answered on the web site, consider sending a brief and succinctly worded e-mail to the firm's e-mail address, if one is listed here or on the web site. If you do not have access to a home computer, or are not connected to the Internet, consider visiting your local library, since most of these facilities have computers available for their patrons. Although web site and e-mail addresses tend to change rather frequently, you'll usually find that keying in an old address will automatically link you to the new address, or provide information so that you may update the address on your own.

If a customer service phone number is listed for the firm, call to request a current catalog. Keep in mind that there may be a charge for these publications.

Finally, if you are writing to one of these firms or businesses, be sure to include a stamped, self-addressed envelope for their response. Again, be aware that there may be a charge for any catalogs they provide.

MANUFACTURERS OF LARGE SCALE, GARDEN RAILWAY, AND SMALL-SCALE LIVE STEAM PRODUCTS:

Accucraft Trains
1785 Timothy Drive, Suite #3
San Leandro, CA 94577-2313
phone: 510-483-6900
fax: 510-483-9100
e-mail: accucraft@worldnet.att.net
www.accucraft.com
(1:20.3 scale electric and live steam locomotives)

Argyle Locomotive Works
241 Belgrave
Gembrook Road
Clematis, VIC 3782
AUSTRALIA
U.S. Distributor:
c/o Sulphur Springs Steam Models Ltd.
P.O. Box 6165, Dept. RB
Chesterfield, MO 63006
phone: 314-527-8326
fax: 314-527-8326
e-mail: sssmodels@aol.com
(Argyle live steam locomotives)

Aristo-Craft Trains
Polk's Model Craft Hobbies
346 Bergen Ave.
Jersey City, NJ 07304
phone: 201-332-8100
fax: 800-310-0521
e-mail: aristo@cnct.com
www.aristocraft.com/aristo
(1:24 scale and 1:29 scale locomotives; rolling stock; track; power packs and radio control units; and accessories)

Aster Hobby
1-13-34 Hakusan
Midori-ku, Yokohama
JAPAN 226
phone: 81-(0) 45-934-5646 (English)
fax: 81-(0) 45-934-9486
e-mail: boss@asterhobby.co.jp
www.asterhobby.co.jp/
U.S. distributor:
c/o Hyde-Out Mountain Live Steam
89060 New Rumley Rd.
Jewett, OH 43986
phone: 740-946-6611
www.steamup.com/aster
(Aster live steam locomotives based on American British, German, and Japanese prototypes)

Bachmann Industries, Inc.
1400 East Erie Ave.
Philadelphia, PA 19124
phone: 213-533-1600
fax: 215-744-4699
e-mail: Bachtrains@aol.com
www.bachmannindustries.com
(Large Scale locomotives and rolling stock)

Backshop Miniatures
10 Swinneyford Road
Towchester
Northants NN12 6HD
ENGLAND
phone: 44-1327-352036
fax: 44-1327-352795
e-mail: backshop@skynet.co.uk
(Small-scale live steam locomotives)

Berlyn Locomotive Works
P.O. Box 9766
Denver, CO 80209
phone: 303-465-2287
fax: 303-465-2287
(1:20.3 scale brass locomotives)

Brandbright Ltd.
The Old School
Cromer Road
Bodham, Holt, Norfolk NR25 6QG
ENGLAND
phone: 44-1263-588-755
fax: 44-1263-588-424
e-mail: brandbright@paston.co.uk
www.steamup.com/brandbright/
U.S. distributor:
c/o Potomac Steam Industries
P.O. Box 2560
Dale City, VA 22193
phone: 703-491-7989
fax: 703-492-8409
e-mail: diesel@erols.com
(Brandbright live steam locomotives)

C&G Products
9577 RR4
Harriston. Ontario N0G IZ0
CANADA
phone: 519-338-2984
fax: 519-338-9999
(1:20. 3 scale and 1:32 scale live steam locomotives)

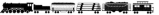

Catatonk Locomotive Works
P.O. Box 335
Newark Valley, NY 13811
phone: 607-642-8119
e-mail: docstream@spectra.net
(live steam Shay and Heisler locomotives—
U.S. distributor)

Cherry Scale Models
The Stables
25 Church St.
Langham, Oakham
Rutland, LE15 7JE
ENGLAND
phone: 01572-757392
fax: 01572-724053
(#1 gauge live steam and electric locomotives)

Cornwall Southern RR Enterprises
c/o Mel Ridley
High Noon, Gorway
Teignmouth, Devon TQ14 8PX
ENGLAND
phone: 01626 779908
e-mail: mel@high-noon.demon.co.uk

Garden Railway Specialists
Station Studio, Princess Risborough
Bucks, HP17 9DT
ENGLAND
phone: 01844-345158
fax: 01844-274352
(customized models based on European-prototype
locomotives)

Geoffbuilt
Box 277
Salisbury
New Brunswick, EOA 3EO
CANADA
phone: 506-372-4364
(custom-built #1 gauge live steam locomotives)

Hartland Locomotive Works
P.O. Box 1743
3022 North State Road 39
LaPorte, IN 46350
phone: 800-362-8411
e-mail: trains@h-l-w.com
www.h-l-w.com
(1:24 scale locomotives and rolling stock)

Legend Steam Locomotives
2408 Grandby Dr.
San Jose, CA 95130
phone: 408-871-0318
e-mail: info@steamup.com
www.steamup.com/legend
(Legend live steam locomotives based on U.S.
prototypes)

LGB of America
6444 Nancy Ridge Dr.
San Diego, CA 92121
phone: 800-669-0607
www.lgb.de/
(1:22.5 scale locomotives and rolling stock; track;
control units. and accessories)

Lionel LLC
50625 Richard W. Blvd.
Chesterfield, MI 48051-2493
phone: 810-940-4100
e-mail: talktous@lionel.com
www.lionel.com
(1:32 scale locomotives and rolling stock)

Longhedge Locomotive Works
Stansted
Essex, CM24 8ST
ENGLAND
phone: 01279-815571
shop phone: 0374 463974 (weekdays,
business hours)
e-mail: longhedge@compuserve.com
(Fine Scale live steam locomotives for #1 gauge)

Mamod Limited
Unit 1A
Summit Crescent Industrial Estate
Smethwick, Warley
Birmingham B66 1BT
ENGLAND
e-mail: mamod@btinternet.com
www.btinternet.com/~mamod/
U.S. distributor:
Diamond Enterprises & Book Publishers
P.O. Box 537
Alexandria Bay, NY 13607
phone: 800-481-1353 (Mon.-Fri., 8-5 EST)
fax: 800-305-5138
e-mail: info@yesteryeartoys.com
www.mamod.com
(Mamod live steam locomotives)

Märklin, Inc.
16988 W. Victor Rd.
P.O. Box 510559
New Berlin, WI 53151-0559
phone: 800-825-0888
www.marklin.com
(1:32 scale, and MAXI line of Large Scale
locomotives, rolling stock, track, and accessories)

Model Die Casting, Inc. (MDC/Roundhouse)
5070 Sigstrom Drive
Carson City, NV 89706
phone: 775-884-4388
www.mdcroundhouse.com
(Large Scale industrial switcher
locomotives and Roundhouse rolling stock)

M.T.H. Electric Trains
7020 Columbia Gateway Dr.
Columbia, MD 21046
phone: 410-381-2580
www.railking1gauge.com
(1:32 scale locomotives, cars, accessories)

Pearse Locomotives
Woodview, Brockhurst, Church Stretton
Shropshire, SY6 7QY
ENGLAND
phone: 01694-723806
fax: 01694-723806
(Pearse live steam locomotives)

Rishon Locomotives
8 Ewandale Cl.
Clunes, NSW 2480
AUSTRALIA
phone: 612-6629-1115
e-mail: rishon@dingoblue.net.au
U.S. distributor:
Sulphur Springs Steam Models, Ltd.
P.O. Box 6165
Chesterfield, MO 63006
phone: 636-527-8326
e-mail: sssmodels@aol.com
(1:20.3 scale live steam locomotives)

Roberts' Lines
P.O. Box 96
East Rochester, NY 14445-0096
fax: 315-986-8529
e-mail: roblines@computer-connection.net
(custom-built metal Large Scale train kits)

Roundhouse Engineering Co., Ltd.
Unit 6, Churchill Business Park
Churchill Road, Wheatley
Doncaster, DN12TF
ENGLAND
phone: 011-44-1302-328035
fax: 011-44-1302-761312
e-mail: sales@roundhouse-eng.com
www.roundhouse-eng.com
(Roundhouse live steam locomotives)

Row & Co.
2341 Fern St.
Eureka, CA 95503
phone: 707-442-1681
fax: 707-442-1681
e-mail: gaugeone@rowco.com
www.rowco.com
(museum quality 1:32 scale brass-construction
locomotives and rolling stock models)

Shawe Steam Services, Ltd.
Howgate, Kimpton Road, Welwyn
Hertfordshire, AL6 9NN
ENGLAND
phone: 01437-814383
(small scale coal-fired locomotives)

St. Charles Station
Rt. 1, Box 225B
Guthrie, MN 56461-9751
phone: 218-224-2598
fax: 218-224-2950
e-mail: stchrls@paulbunyan.net
www.stcharlesstationonline.com
(1:32 scale custom-made brass diesel
locomotives)

USA Trains
P.O. Box 100
Malden, MA 02148
phone: 781-322-6084
www.usatrains.com
(1:29 scale locomotives; various Large Scale rolling
stock items; LGB-compatible track components)

Wada Works, Co., Ltd.
c/o Potomac Steam Industries
P.O. Box 2560
Dale City, VA 22193
phone: 703-491-7989
fax: 703-492-8409
e-mail: diesel@erols.com
(Wada live steam locomotives)

Wrightscale Locomotives
c/o M. D. Wright
Burnside
Aboyne, Aberdeenshire AB34 5ES
ENGLAND
phone: 44-3398-86494
U.S. dealer:
Sulphur Springs Steam Models, Ltd.
P.O. Box 6165
Chesterfield, MO 63006
phone: 636-527-8326
e-mail: sssmodels@aol.com
(1:20.3 scale live steam locomotives)

**AFTER-MARKET SUPPLIERS OF
LARGE SCALE, GARDEN RAILWAY,
AND SMALL-SCALE LIVE STEAM
PRODUCTS:**

Abracadata
e-mail: abracadata@POBoxes.com
www.abracadata.com
(track planning software)

Above All Railways
7861 Alabama Ave., #5
Canoga Park, CA 91304
phone: 818-348-3684
fax: 818-348-6426
www.aboveallrailways.com
(overhead track systems for Large Scale trains)

American Craft Products, Inc.
1530 N. Old Rand Rd.
Waucona, IL 60084
(1:24 scale dollhouse miniatures)

Appalachian Gardens
P.O. Box 82
Waynesboro, PA 17268
phone: 717-762-4312
fax: 717-762-7532
(scale-size plants for garden railroads)

Arnold Digital
GERMANY
e-mail: info@arnold-digital.de
www.arnold-digital.de
(DCC components for Large Scale)

Aztec Mfg. Company
2701 Conestoga Dr., #113
Carson City, NV 89706
phone: 775-883-3327
fax: 775-883-3357
e-mail: aztecmfg@usa.net
www.aztectrains.com
(track cleaning cars in all scales)

Barrett Railways
991 6th St.
Hermosa Beach, CA 90254
phone: 310-379-4929
(#1 gauge rolling stock)

Barry's Big Trains
P.O. Box 93934
Las Vegas, NV 89139-3934
702-260-9111
fax: 702-260-9111
(drive units for re-powering Bachmann 4-6-0
locomotives)

Battery Backshop
18030 SW Lower Boones Ferry Road, #2
Tigard, OR 97224
phone: 503-624-7491
e-mail: backshop@pacifier.com
www.batterybackshop.com
(battery powered radio control units)

Big River Lines
3466 Aveley Place
San Diego, CA 92111
(scale galvanized steel and corrugated sheet metal)

Big Train Backshop
P.O. Box 991
San Luis Obispo, CA 93406
phone: 805-541-0546
fax: 805-541-0546
(cast plastic structures for 1:20 and 1:24 scale
trains)

BK Enterprises
12874 County Road 314B
Buena Vista, CO 81211-9102
phone: 719-395-8076
(precision-built turnouts)

Bill Gagne's Railroad Accessories
8 N. Munroe Terrace
Dorchester, MA 02122
(wood bridges, ties, and tunnel portals)

Bluestone Perennials
7211 Middle Ridge Rd.
Madison, OH 44057
phone: 800-852-5243
(plants for garden railroads)

Bridgemasters
1077 Promenade Ave.
Placentia, CA 92870
phone: 714-985-9007
fax: 714-985-1976
www.bridge-masters.com
(bridges, trestles, and other accessories for
Large Scale trains)

Bridgewerks
27068 La Paz Rd., #453
Laguna Hills, CA 92656
phone: 949-831-9351
fax: 949-362-9751
www.bridgewerks.com
(electrical control systems and metal bridges for
Large Scale railroads)

By Grant
1709 Geneva St.
Aurora, CO 80010
(bridge kits, locomotives, and custom
garden railway construction)

California & Oregon Coast Ry (C&OC)/Llagas Creek
P.O. Box 57
Rogue River, OR 97537
phone: 541-582-4104
fax: 800-866-8635
dmanley@cdsnet.net
(1:20.3 scale switchstand kits; Llagas Creek
track components)

Caboose Industries
1861 Ridge Road
Freeport, IL 61032-3637
(turnout operating levers)

Campbell/Fortney Corp.
2217 W. State Street
Alliance, OH 44601
(sound systems)

Cargo-to-Go
P.O. Box 100
So. Weymouth, MA 02190
fax: 781-331-9350
e-mail: barobr@mediaone.net
www.cargo-to-go.com
(cargo loads for Large Scale trains)

CDS Lettering Limited
P.O. Box 2003, Station "D"
Ottawa, Ontario K1P 5W3
CANADA
(dry transfer lettering)

Centerline Products, Inc.
18409 Harmony Road
Marengo, IL 60152
phone: 815-923-1105
fax: 815-923-1106
e-mail: info@centerline-products.com
www.centerline-products.com
(rail and wheel cleaning products)

Chicago Model International (CMI)
P.O. Box 170
Deerfield, IL 60015
(Star-Tec power supplies, throttles, and
sound systems)

Classic Case Company
P.O. Box 395
Rolling Prairie, IN 46371
phone: 800-897-3374
e-mail: Classic@ccase.com
www.ccase.com
(display cases for Large Scale models)

C.M. Models
20 Terry Lane E.
Wareham, MA 02571
www.llareggub.com
(custom-built freight and passenger cars)

Columbine Hobby Company
P.O. Box 309
Pine, CO 80470
(1:24 scale building kits)

CTT Incorporated
109 Medallion Center
Dallas, TX 75214
(track planning template for LGB track, and scale
rulers for 1:20.3, 1:22.5, 1:24, and 1:32 scales)

Dallee Electronics, Inc.
246 W. Main St.
Leola, PA 17540
phone: 717-661-7041
www.dallee.com
(electronic components for Large Scale trains)

Del-Aire Products
321 N. 40th St.
Allentown, PA 18104
phone: 610-391-0412
e-mail: delaire@fast.net
www.delaire.com
(air-powered turnout control systems)

Digitrax
450 Cemetery Street, #206
Norcross, GA 30071
phone: 770-441-7992
e-mail: sales@digitrax.com
www.digitrax.com
(DCC controllers and decoders for Large Scale)

Douglas Brooks Creative Models
307 MacKay Ave.
Ventura, CA 93004
http://swiftsite.com/dbcreativemodels
(model palm trees—all scales)

Downtown Deco
4319 Rainbow Drive
Missoula, MT 59803
phone: 406-251-8005
(structure kits in 1:32 and 1:24 scale)

Robert Dustin
P.O. Box 77
Thompson, CT 06277
phone: 860-923-0174
(decals and plates for Large Scale)

Eaglewings Iron Craft
1522 E. Victory, Suite 1
Phoenix, AZ 85040
www.eaglewingsironcraft.com
(overhead train systems for Large Scale trains)

East Cary Car Co.
3828 St. Joseph Ct.
Lake Station, IN 46405
(loads, wheelsets, and accessories
for Large Scale rolling stock)

Eldorado Railways
28 Encantado Loop
Santa Fe, NM 87505
phone: 817-548-5656
(assembled trestle bents and bridges
for Large Scale railroads)

E-R Model Importers
1000 South Main St.
Newark, NY 14513-2141
(Preiser figures for Large Scale)

Ertl Company
P.O. Box 500
Dyersville, IA 52040-0050
(figures, vehicles, and trees)

ESU/LokSound
GERMANY
www.loksound.com
(DCC components for Large Scale)

Evergreen Scale Models
18620-F 141st Ave., NE
Woodinville, WA 98072
(styrene plastic in strip and sheet form)

F&SC R.R.
P.O. Box 1628
Sutter Creek, CA 95685
(western storefronts and complete buildings)

Fall Creek Railroad Structures
P.O. Box 191636
Sacramento, CA 95819
phone: 916-383-6001
e-mail: fcwrr@aol.com
(Large Scale engine display and test stand;
1:20.3 turntable)

Fall River Productions
4916 Duffer Pl.
Albuquerque, NM 87114
phone: 505-792-9279
e-mail: jdclark1@uswest.net
(custom laser-cutting services)

Father Nature
P.O. Box 161
Hershey, PA 17033
www.fathernaturetrees.com
(hand-made trees for indoor use)

Finescale Locomotive Company
c/o IE&W Railway Supply
38200 Charles Town Pike
Purcellville, VA 20132-2927
phone: 540-882-3886
fax: 540-882-9670
(#1 gauge rolling stock)

G Action Models
11920 SW 35 Terrace
Miami, FL 33175
305-221-4872
www.anglefire.com/biz/gaction
(custom-built operating lift bridge;
passenger cars; other rolling stock)

Garden Texture
P.O. Box 690444
Charlotte, NC 28227
phone: 704-847-7169
fax: 704-814-6993
http://home.earthlink.net/~gardentextur
(plans and kits for custom-built Large Scale buildings
and bridges)

Gary Raymond
P.O. Box 1722-G
Thousand Oaks, CA 91358
phone: 805-492-5858
(metal wheel sets for Large Scale rolling stock in various scales)

Glenn Snyder Display Systems
260 Oak Street
Buffalo, NY 14203
phone: 716-852-4676/716-648-5817
fax: 716-852-4677
e-mail: glenn@gsds.com
www.gsds.com
(wall-mounted train display shelves)

G.P. Ramsden
1602 South 4th Street
Wilmington, NC 28401
phone: 910-762-2916
(coal, log, and oil loads for Bachmann's Shay and Climax locomotives)

Grandt Line Products, Inc.
1040-B Shary Court
Concord, CA 94518
(plastic windows and doors)

H&R Trains
6901 U.S. Hwy. 19 North
Pinellas Park, FL 33781
phone: 727-526-4682
e-mail: hrtrains@hrtrains.com
www.hrtrains.com
(stainless steel track)

Harper Model Railways
3057 Lander Rd.
Pepper Pike, OH 44124
216-464-8126
(British prototype rolling stock kits and parts)

Hartford Products, Inc.
18 Ranch Road
Cedar Crest, NM 87008
phone: 505-286-2200
fax: 505-286-2141
e-mail: HartfordPr@aol.com
www.hartfordpr.com
(custom 1:20.3 scale, #1 gauge rolling stock kits, ready-to-run, and parts)

Hi-Lights
c/o Ralph Williams Landscaping Design
P.O., Box 758
Harvard, MA 01451
phone: 978-456-8455
e-mail: gdnrails@aol.com
www.trainsandtrees.com
(outdoor lighting systems)

Hillcraft Model Builders
4195 Chino Hills Parkway, #225
Chino Hills, CA 91709
phone: 909-393-0645
www.hillcraftgmodels.com
(handcrafted Large Scale wood structures)

Hillman's Railclamps
P.O. Box 1253
Lodi, CA 95241
phone: 209-389-1868
fax: 209-369-1868
e-mail: hillman-rc@softcom.net
www.hillmansrailclamps.com
(rail clamping devices for Large Scale track)

Hillside Railway
25746 Po Ave.
Mission Viejo, CA 92691-3924
phone: 949-951-8578
e-mail: hillsidery@aol.com
(brass wheel contact kits)

Hobby Innovations
1789 Campbell Rd.
Mountain City, TN 37683
phone: 423-727-8000
(Vinylbed roadbed for indoor/outdoor use)

Industrial Miniatures
Route 1, Box 169-B
Milbank, SD 57252
(1:24 scale structures)

Innovative TrainTechnology
P.O. Box 5042
West Hills, CA 91308
phone: 818-992-6124
www.ittcsoundeffects.com
(digital sound modules for enhancement of Large Scale scenes)

Isabel Central Enterprises
P.O. Box 771407
Wichita, KS 67277-1407
(handmade 1:25 scale wood structures; modular roadbed)

I.S.L.E. Laboratories
P.O. Box 636
Sylvania, OH 43560
(Mountains-in-Minutes foam scenic supplies)

Istra Metalcraft
6089 Lee Ann Lane
Naples, FL 34109
phone: 941-597-6445
(7 a.m.-3:30 p.m., EST)
fax: 941-597-6230
(rail-bending device for Large Scale track rails; locomotive carriers; other accessories)

ITTC
P.O. Box 5042
West Hills, CA 91308
phone: 818-992-6124
www.ittcsoundeffects.com
(digital sound modules)

Jig Stones
c/o Sticks & Stones
P.O. Box 211
Elbridge, NY 13060
phone: 315-689-3402
www.jigstones.com
(silicon rubber molds for garden railroad structures)

J.S. Woodcrafts
P.O. Box 5161
Palos Verde, CA 90274
phone: 310-539-4246
e-mail: jswoodcrafts@cs.com
(custom structures)

Jules Toy Trains
3500 Winding Creek Road
Sacramento, CA 95864
phone: 916-489-2966
e-mail: julestoys@aol.com
www.julestoytrains.com
(ceiling-mounted track systems)

Just Plain Folk
111 West Broad Street
Palmyra, NJ 08065
phone: 856-786-0080
fax: 856-786-1481
e-mail: trackntrains@erols.com
www.trackntrains.com
(figures for Large Scale railroads)

Kadee Quality Products Co.
673 Avenue C
White City, OR 97503
phone: 541-826-3883
fax: 541-826-4013
www.kadee.com
(couplers for Large Scale locomotives and rolling stock)

Keith Seeber
(formerly Olde Mountain Miniatures)
366 Starksville Rd.
Fort Plain, NY 13339
(custom built structures, bridges, trestles, and rolling stock)

Keithco, Inc.
P.O. Box 1806
Lake Oswego, OR 97035
phone: 503-635-7604
fax: 503-699-0434
www.locolinc.com
(Locolinc R/C and sound systems for Large Scale locomotives)

Korber Models
2 Tidwell Ave.
Medford, NJ 08055
(cast resin structure kits)

Large Scale Sound Works
P.O. Box 153
Kingston, NJ 08528-0153
phone: 609-924-5089
(sound system plans and kits for Large Scale trains)

Larry Larson Graphics
104 Conejo Place
Durango, CO 81301
phone: 970-259-3863
e-mail: larryrgs@frontier.net
(dry transfer lettering)

LED Light (The)
37-9 Canoga Ave.
North Las Vegas, NV 89030-5734
phone: 702-657-6913
e-mail: help@theledlight.com
www.theledlight.com
(LED lights for Large Scale trains and accessories)

LENZ Agency of North America
P.O. Box 143
Chelmsford, MA 01824
phone: 978-250-1494
fax: 978-445-LENZ
e-mail: support@lenz.com
www.lenz.com
(DCC components for Large Scale)

Life-Like Products, Inc.
1600 Union Avenue
Baltimore, MD 21211
www.lifelikeproducts.com
(figures, signs, trees, and other accessories
for Large Scale)

Lindsay Machine Works
1004 S. Washington St.
Denver, CO 80209
(Railbender rail-bending tool)

Little Railways
1621 Cherry St.
Williamsport, PA 17701
(1:20 scale narrow gauge rolling stock)

Llagas Creek Railways
c/o C&OC Railways
P.O. Box 57
Rogue River, OR 97537
phone: 800-866-8635
www.llagastrack.com
(Large Scale track components and rail benders)

Loco-Boose Hobbies
P.O. Box 6905
Huntsville, AL 35824
phone: 256-828-7500
e-mail: Lbh@bellsouth.net
www.locoboose.com
(suspended railway systems for home
or business)

Lone Star Bridge & Abutment
1218 A-8 Colorado Lane
Arlington, TX 76015
phone: 817-548-5656
(custom designed wood bridges)

Loy's Toys
P.O. Box 88
Wesley, AR 72773
phone: 501-456-2888
e-mail: LoysToys@compuserve.com
www.loystoys.com
(installation of Digitrax Digital Command
Control components)

Mainline Enterprises
26502 Golden Valley Rd., Ste. 112
Santa Clara, CA 91351
phone: 661-424-1771
e-mail: mainlineenter@aol.com
(roadbed system for Large Scale)

Meg's Dirty Toys
4 Chickadee Lane
Laguna Beach, CA 92656
(operating western lanterns for Large Scale use)

Mesa Railway
8139 E. Main St., Ste. 9
Mesa, AZ 85207
phone: 480-986-4815
www.mesarailway.com
(design, construction, and supplies for garden and
overhead railways)

Micro Engineering Company, Inc.
1120 Eagle Road
Fenton, MO 63026
phone: 636-349-1112
(Large Scale turnout kits)

Micro Fasteners
110 Hillcrest Road
Flemington, NJ 08822
phone: 800-892-6917
fax: 908-788-2607
e-mail: info@microfasteners.com
http://microfasteners.com
(scale screws and other devices for Large Scale)

Microscale Industries
18435 Bandilier Circle
Fountain Valley, CA 92708
(decals)

Micro-Mark
340-2826 Snyder Avenue
Berkeley Heights, NJ 07922-1538
www.micromark.com
(tools for garden railroaders)

Midwest Products Company, Inc.
P.O. Box 564
Hobart, IN 46342
(pre-cut wood strips and sheets)

Miniature Plant Kingdom
4125 Harrison Grade Road
Sebastapol, CA 95472
phone: 707-874-2233
e-mail: mpk@neteze.com
www.miniplantkingdom.com
(live miniature plants via mail order)

Mini Forest by Sky
P.O. Box 1156
Mulino, OR 97042
phone: 503-632-3555
fax: 503-632-5575
www.miniforest.com
(dwarf plants and groundcover for garden railroads)

Model Builders Supply (MBS)
40 Engelhard Drive, Unit 11
Aurora, Ontario L4G 6X6
CANADA
phone: 905-841-8392
fax: 905-841-8399
e-mail: service@modelbuilderssupply.com
www.modelbuilderssupply.com
(scale building materials, structural details, casting
and scenic materials)

Model Power
180 Smith Street
Farmingdale, NY 11735
(Lage Scale building kits and accessories)

Model Rectifier Corporation (MRC)
80 Newfield Ave.
Edison, NJ 08837
phone: 732-225-6360
www.modelrec.com
(Power packs and DCC components for Large Scale)

M.O.W. Equipment Co.
107 Greenwood Drive
Temple, PA 19560
phone: 610-929-8373
e-mail: trackmanc2000@aol.com
(track-cleaning car for Large Scale)

New England Hobby Supply
71 Hillard St.
Manchester, CT 06040
(1:24 scale structure kits)

Nitro-Electric Locomotives Limited
e-mail: NitroElectric@excite.com
www.geocities.com/wahoo_001/index2.html
(Custom-made nitro-methane gas-powered diesel
locomotives)

North Coast Engineering
1900 Empire Blvd., Suite 303
Webster, NY 14580
phone: 716-671-0370
fax: 716-671-9337
e-mail: jscorse@aol.com
www.tttrains.com/northcoast
(DCC components for Large Scale)

Northeast Narrow Gauge
P.O. Box 191
Wiscasset, ME 04578
phone: 207-882-7154
fax: 207-882-9884
www.nemodel.com
(wood and metal bridge kits)

Northeastern Scale Models, Inc.
P.O. Box 727
Methuen, MA 01844
(basswood strips and sheets; windows and doors)

NorthWest Short Line
Box 423
Seattle, WA 98111-0423
phone: 206-932-1087
fax: 206-935-7106
e-mail: info@nwsl.com
www.nwsl.com
(wheelsets and other items for Large Scale
locomotives and rolling stock)

Northwest Remote Control Systems
8026 NE 124th Street
Kirkland, WA 98034
phone: 425-823-3507
e-mail: trainsnwrcs@halcyon.com
www.halcyon.com/dnkgoods
(remote control systems and parts)

Oakridge Corporation
P.O. Box 247
Lemont, IL 60436
(1:24 scale structures; dollhouse miniatures)

Old and Weary Car Shop
104 Oak Street
Orangeburg, NY 10962
(decals)

Old Pullman Model Railroads, Inc.
P.O. Box 690128
Vero Beach, FL 32969-0128
(Large Scale Standards Gauge for checking track
gauge and wheel spacing)

Overhead Railways
25672 -A Taladro Circle
Mission Viejo, CA 92691
phone: 800-297-6410
www.overheadrailways.com
(track cleaning car and on-board camera mount for
#1 gauge track)

Ozark Miniatures
P.O. Box 107
DeSoto, MO 63020
fax: 636-586-2480
e-mail: ozmin@jcn1.com
www.ozarkminiatures.com
(white metal castings for Large Scale and live steam
detailing)

Pacific Coast Garden Railway Supply
12081 Pradera Rd.
Camarillo, CA 93012
phone: 805-491-2025
(structures for Large Scale layouts)

Parker Co. (The)
P.O. Box 1546
Camarillo, CA 93011
fax: 805-987-6432
e-mail: coparker@msn.com
www.coparker.com
(wide-radius turnouts compatible with most
Large Scale track)

Parker's Nursery
17 N. Fretz
Edmond, OK 73003
phone: 877-839-3367
www.parkersrailroad.com
(Redwood Western Building Kits for Large Scale)

PBL
P.O. Box 769
Ukiah, CA 95482
(resistance soldering equipment)

People You Know You Need
10772 63rd Avenue North
Seminole, FL 33772
www.peopleyouneed.com
(people figures for Large Scale)

P.H. Hobbies, Inc.
6861 T. Drive South
Athens, MI 49011
phone: 517-741-4221
e-mail: phousey@phhobbies.com
(power suppies, sound systems, reversing systems)

Phoenix Sound Systems
3502 West Liberty Road
Ann Arbor, MI 48103-9013
phone: 800-651-2444
fax: 734-662-0809
www.phoenixsound.com
(sound systems for Large Scale steam
and diesel locomotives, and for railcars)

Pine Valley Scenic Railway Productions
336 Wendell Terrace
Syracuse, NY 13203
phone: 315-479-9515
e-mail: ThomRe1App@aol.com
(custom-crafted 1:24 scale Large Scale structures)

PML Products
201 West Beach Ave.
Inglewood, CA 90302
phone: 310-671-4345
fax: 310-671-0858
www.pmli.com/products-site/train.html
(track connecting devices and switching magnets)

Power Systems, Inc. (PSI)
56 Bellis Circle
Cambridge, MA 02140
(Dynatrol command-control system)

Precision Products
763 Cayuga St., Unit #2
Lewistown, NY 14092
phone: 716-754-2997
www.appliedimaginationinc.com
(various structure-building materials)

Precision Scale
3961 Highway 93 North
Stevensville, MT 59870
(metal detail parts and rail)

PSI/Dynatrol
56 Bellis Circle
Cambridge, MA 02140
phone: 617-661-0660
www.tttrains.com/psidynatrol
(DCC components for Large Scale)

Railbed Systems
1147 W. Lowell Ave.
Havelhill, MA 01832
phone: 978-372-6503
fax: 978-372-6503
www.railbed.com
(#1 gauge track support bed)

RailDreams, Inc.
P.O. Box 125
Lake Linden, MI 49945
phone: 906-296-0462
fax: 906-296-0862
e-mail: raildrms@up.net
www.raildreams.com
(custom designed and constructed garden railways)

Rail Plaque
1022 Wesley
Oak Park, IL 60304
phone: 708-386-4350
(roadbed for Large Scale)

RailRoadAve. Model Works, LTD
Box 550
Willits, CA 95490
phone: 707-459-2770
www.railroadavenu.com
(Urethane cast structure kits)

Railway Design Associates
P.O. Box 96
Monson, MA 01057
(1:24 scale structure kits)

Ralph Williams Landscape Design
P.O. Box K
Harvard, MA 01451
phone: 978-456-8455
fax: 978-456-8455
(lighting systems for garden railways;
on-track speed measuring device for Large Scale)

Ramtraxx (Wangrow Electronics, Inc.)
P.O. Box 98
Park Ridge, IL 60068-0098
e-mail: systemone@wangrow.com
www.wangrow.com

Reed's Train Store
8039 La Mesa Blvd.
La Mesa, CA 91941
phone: 619-464-1672
e-mail: reeds@abac.com
(Instant R/C radio control power packs)

Remote Control Systems
P.O. Box 1118
Bayswater, Victoria 3153
AUSTRALIA
distributor:
c/o Sulphur Springs Steam Models Ltd.
P.O. Box 6165, Dept. RB
Chesterfield, MO 63006
phone: 314-527-8326
fax: 314-527-8326
e-mail: rcs@alphalink.com.au
www.alphalink.com.au/~rcs/
(radio control systems for live steam)

Republic Model Works, Inc.
P.O. Box 4846
Apache Junction, AZ 85220
phone: 480-354-0670
e-mail: repmw@yahoo.com
(structure kits)

R&G Railroad Co.
15314 Black Shadow Drive
Moreno Valley, CA 92551
phone: 909-242-4258
fax: 909-247-8395
www.randgrailroad.com
(overhead/around-the-wall track
mounting system for Large Scale trains)

R&S Enterprises
P.O. Box 643
Jonestown, PA 17038
phone: 717-865-3444
www.rrtrack.com/rrtrack
(sectional track planning software—all scales)

Rite-O-Way Rail Plaque
1022 Wesley
Oak Park, IL 60304
phone: 708-386-4350
(roadbed for LGB track)

RJJR Inc.
Littleton, CO
fax: 720-489-0826
e-mail: rjjrinc@aol.com
www.rjjrinc.com
(work station/locomotive cradle and paint station)

RR-Track
c/o R&S Enterprises
P.O. Box 643
Jonestown, PA 17038
phone: 717-865-3444
www.rrtrack.com
(sectional track layout software)

Russ Simpson
1968 Cemetery Rd.
Placerville, CA 95667
(Large Scale switch stands and detail parts)

Ryan Equipment Company, Inc.
749 Creel Drive
Wood Dale, IL 60191
phone: 630-595-5711
fax: 630-595-5794
(D&RGW 1:24 scale freight car trucks)

Sandy Mush Herb Nursery
316 Surrett Cove Rd.
Leicester, NC 28748-5517
(plants for garden railroads)

San-Val Trains
7444 Valjean Ave.
Van Nuys, CA 91406
phone: 800-423-3281
(Large Scale wheels, track locking devices, track
cleaners, and smoke fluid)

Santa Clarita Railroad Co.
15151 Lotusgarden Drive
Canyon Country, CA 91351
fax: 661-252-3461
e-mail: gregtomey@marfred.com
(locomotive cradles and track leveling devices)

Scale Card (The)
P.O. Box 1078
Highland, CA 92346-1078
www.thescalecard.com
(scale proportion cards)

Shawmut Car Shops
307 North Michael St.
St. Mary's, PA 15857-1149
phone: 814-834-9455
http://users.penn.com/~nana47/index.html
(custom-built Large Scale cars; locomotive conver-
sions; custom-built motorcars; custom decals)

Shiloh Signals
145 East Blvd.
Gloversville, NY 12078
phone: 518-773-3078
(trackside signals for Large Scale trains)

Shortline Car and Foundry
14918 Lake Forest
Dallas, TX 75240
phone: 972-233-6108
fax: 972-233-3172
www.largescale.com/shortline/index.htm
(1:24 scale freight cars, trucks, and detail parts)

Sierra Sound Systems/SoundTraxx
463 Turner Drive, Suite 104A
Durango, CO 81301
phone: 970-259-0690
e-mail: sales@soundtraxx.com
www.soundtraxx.com

Sierra Valley Enterprises
2755 Saratoga Ave.
Merced, CA 95340
(custom-built 1:20.3 and 7/8-inch scale rolling
stock and wheel sets)

Skid-Do Industries
90 Mosier Parkway
Brookville, OH 45309
phone: 937-833-5677
www.skid-do.com
(fiberglass tunnel sections)

SLM
P.O. Box 28047
Baltimore, MD 21239
www.slmonline.com
(Large Scale model figures)

Sodders Enterprises
609 Edgelawn St.
Parkersburg, WV 26101
http://home.wirefire.com/tes
(scale corrugated metal roofing, siding, fencing
materials)

SoundTraxx
463 Turner Drive, Suite 104A
Durango, CO 81301
phone: 970-259-0690
fax: 970-259-0691
(digital sound systems for Large Scale steam locomotives)

Split Jaw Rail Clamps
12705 SE Schiller
Portland, OR 97236
phone: 503-762-4822
e-mail: Splitjaw@railclamp.com
www.railclamp.com
(rail clamping devices for Large Scale track)

Stainless Unlimited
P.O. Box 224
Augusta, MO 63332
phone: 314-228-4767/314-742-5880
www.stainlessunlimited.com
(stainless steel bridges)

Sticks & Stones
P.O. Box 211
Elbridge, NY 13060
phone: 315-689-3402
(silicon rubber molds for Large Scale structures)

Stoneworks
16935 Main St.
P.O. Box 186
Galesville, WI 54630
phone: 608-582-2082
fax: 888-511-4258
www.RRStoneworks.com
(stone structures and parts for Large Scale)

Sunset Valley Railroad
(formerly Garich Light Transport)
13428 209th SE
Issaquah, WA 98027
phone: 425-255-2453
fax: 425-255-2453
e-mail: svrrted@sprynet.com
(track, turnouts, and tools, including rail benders)

Tender Case (The)
812 Aloha Street
Camarillo, CA 93010-2302
phone: 800-851-5994
(display cases for Large Scale items)

Testor Corporation
620 Buckbee St.
Rockford, IL 61104
(Floquil, Polly S, and Polly Scale paint products)

Timothy I. Miller Co.
P.O. Box 86757
San Diego, CA 92138
(Economy R/C radio control throttles)

Tomar Industries
9520 E. Napier Ave.
Benton Harbor, MI 49022
phone: 616-944-5129
fax: 616-944-5129
(marker lights for Large Scale rolling stock)

Tony's Train Exchange
57 River Rd.
Box 1023
Essex Jct., VT 05452
phone: 800-978-3472
e-mail: info@ttx-dcc.com
(DCC sales/service/installation)

Trackside Details
1331 Avalon St.
San Luis Obispo, CA 93405
(Gn3 gauge and 1/2-inch scale parts)

T-Tracker
3735 N.E. Shaver Street
Portland, OR 97212
e-mail: ttracker2@aol.com
(track assembly devices and other trackside accessories)

VCS Realroad
8866 Summerhill Point
Alpine, CA 91901-2779
phone: 619-445-5145
fax: 619-445-5305
e-mail: realroad@flash.net
(various Large Scale accessories, including automatic station stop devices, etc.)

Venango Valley Models
Box 2847
Las Vegas, NM 87701
www.kaysingstudios.pair.com
(Large Scale cast Hydrostone structure kits and accessories)

Woodland Scenics
P.O. Box 98
Linn Creek, MO 65052
phone: 573-346-5555
e-mail: webmaster@woodlandscenics.com
www.woodlandscenics.com
(variety of scenery materials for all scales)

Woodlanders, Inc.
1128 Colleton Ave.
Aiken, SC 29801
phone: 803-648-7522
(plants for garden railroads)

Thomas A. Yorke
P.O. Box 677188
Orlando, FL 32867
(1.20.3 scale boiler kit and accessories)

ZIMO Elektronik
Schonbrunner Strasse 188
A-1120 Vienna
AUSTRIA
www56.pair.com/zimo
(DCC components for Large Scale)

ZTT Controls
75 Portway
Wells
Somerset BA5 2BJ
ENGLAND
e-mail: sales@ztccontrols.co.uk
www.ztccontrols.co.uk/
(DCC components for Large Scale)

3rd PlanIt (El Dorado Software)
2222 Francisco #510, PMB 196
El Dorado Hills, CA 95762
phone: 916-939-3452
fax: 916-939-3452
e-mail: 3pi@trackplanning.com
www.eldoradosoft.com
(track planning and layout design software)

7/8n2 Railway Equipment Co.
54 Claybrook Rd.
Rocky Mount, VA 24151
e-mail: seven8n2@aol.com
(7/8-inch scale freight trucks and parts)

Appendix B
Clubs and associations for garden railroad enthusiasts

Some garden railroaders prefer to pursue their hobby alone—a kind of "escape" from the real world, if you will. Others enjoy the fellowship and creative learning experience that group membership provides. And, of course, some folks simply don't have space in their home or yard to enjoy the type of Large Scale railroading activity that interests them most. If you fall into either or both of these latter two categories, a garden railroading or Large Scale club may be just the thing for you.

Following is a list of known local, regional, national, and international clubs and associations for the garden railroader and Large Scale model railroad enthusiast. Nearly all of these organizations welcome new members with open arms, so don't hesitate to contact

them if the social aspects of club membership and sharing the hobby with others appeals to you.

Note that national and international groups are listed alphabetically by country, then alphabetically by the organization's name.

Local and regional groups are presented alphabetically by state, then alphabetically by the organization's name.

Contact names and mailing addresses listed here are those of the individuals responsible for membership information. Because area codes seem to change so often, phone numbers are not provided. Contact Directory Assistance for the phone number if you wish to speak with the contact person. Web site and/or e-mail addresses are also listed, where known.

NATIONAL/INTERNATIONAL ASSOCIATIONS

Australia

LGB & G Scale Model Railway Club of Australia
c/o Colin Everitt
54 Sommerville Road
Hornsby Heights
New South Wales 2077

Great Britain

Gauge One Model Railway Association
c/o Laura Foster
112 Clarendon Rd.
Broadstone, Dorset BH18 QHY

16mm Narrow Gauge Modelers Association
c/o Bruce Flaxman
40 Grain Rd., Wigmore
Gillingham, Kent ME8 OND
www.16mmngmodellers.org.uk/

G-Scale Society
c/o Bob Perrat
18 Petts Hill
Northolt, Middlesex UB5 4NL
www.g-scale-society.co.uk

New Zealand

Christchurch Garden Railway Society
c/o Derek Parker
1 Wetlands Grove
Pacific Park
Christchurch 03 388 6429

Switzerland

US G-Scale Friends
c/o Heinz Daeppen
Pappelweg 10
CH-4500 Solothum

United States

AW NUTS (Always Whimsical, Not Usually to Scale) GRS
Greg & Susan Robinson
P.O. Box 8523
Red Bluff, CA 96080

LGB Model Railroad Club
1854 Erin Drive
Altoona, PA 16602
www.lgbmrrc.com

National Model Railroad Association
4121 Cromwell Road
Chattanooga, TN 37421-2119
www.nmra.org

Diamondhead International Steamup
c/o Jerry Reshew
5411 Diamondhead Drive East
Diamondhead, MS 39525
e-mail: JReshew@mindspring.com
www.diamondhead.org

Garden Hi-Railers Association
(2 & 3 rail, O & Std. Gauge)
c/o Douglas L. Gray
9353 Forest Ct., SW
Seattle, WA 98136-2828

LOCAL & REGIONAL GARDEN RAILWAY CLUBS

ARIZONA

Arizona Big Train Operators
c/o Tony Vacek
20860 N. 110th Dr.
Sun City, AZ 85373

Arizona Garden Railway Society
c/o Glen Lynch
6845 W. Canterbury Dr.
Peoria, AZ 85345-8711

Tucson Garden Railway Society
c/o Nick Buchholz
3401 W. Blacksill Dr.
Tucson, AZ 85741

ARKANSAS

Arkansas Western Garden Railway Society
c/o Dan Tursky
54 Estremedura Dr.
Hot Springs Village, AR 71909

Central Arkansas Garden Railway Society
c/o Bruce Stockbridge
#7 Chaparral Lane
Little Rock, AR 72212-3619

CALIFORNIA

Bay Area Garden Railway Society
c/o Jack Verducci
205 De Anza Blvd., Suite 40
San Mateo, CA 94402
www.bagrs.org

Blossom Valley Garden Railroad
c/o Gregory F. Lange
5956 Cabral Ave.
San Jose, CA 95123
http://members.aol.com/
_ht_a/glanlg/club2/

Central California Coast Garden Railway Society
c/o Roise Marian
263 Vista Court
Los Osos, CA 93402

Fairplex Garden RR Volunteers
c/o Bob Toohey
P.O. Box 2250
Pomona, CA 91769-2250

Fullerton Railway Plaza G-Gaugers Assn.
c/o Stan Swanson
P.O. Box 3987
Fullerton, CA 92834
www.trainweb.com/frpa

Greater Humboldt Bay Garden Railway Society
c/o Richard Heisler
4265 Excelsior Rd.
Eureka, CA 95503

Lake Tahoe, Truckee, and Northwestern Historical Modeling Society
c/o Nelson Van Gundy
15695 Donner Pass Rd.
Truckee, CA 96161

Lancaster & Northwestern RR
c/o Revell Walker
616 W. Lancaster Blvd.
Lancaster, CA 93534

Orange County Garden Railway Society
c/o Orlyn Clover
1013 N. Elaine Dr.
Santa Ana, CA 92703-1612

Redwood Empire Garden Railway Society
c/o Don Herzog
4125 Harrison Grade Rd.
Sebastopol, CA 94572

Sacramento Valley Garden Railway Society
c/o Bob Dean
7701 Ziebell Ct.
Citrus Heights, CA 95610

San Diego Garden Railway Society
c/o Larry Rose
4924 Wood St.
La Mesa, CA 91941
http://sdgrs.com/

San Joaquin Valley Garden Railway Society
c/o Monte Scott
208 Alameda Ave.
Chowchilla, CA 93610
www.scottfalls.com/sjvgrs1.html

Shasta Garden Railway Society
c/o Duane Wainright
15738 Horseless Carriage Dr.
Redding, CA 96001

South Coast Garden Railroad Club
c/o Bill Orluske
51 N. Linden Drive
Ventura, CA 93004-1236

Southern California Garden Railway Society
c/o Ted Greeno
8164 Sewell Ave.
Fontana, CA 92335

Temecula Valley Garden Railway Society
c/o John Robinson
2353 Mimosa Ave.
Hemet, CA 92545-5301

COLORADO

Del Oro Pacific, Rocky Mtn. Division
c/o Rusty Allen
44239 City Road 42
Del Norte, CO 81132

Denver Garden Railway Society
c/o Mike Harris
P.O. Box 9256
Denver, CO 80209

Mile High Garden Railway Society
c/o Byron Fenton
2783 S. Meade St.
Denver, CO 80236

Northern Colorado Garden Railroaders
c/o Del Tapparo
4118 Clayton Ct.
Fort Collins, CO 80525
www.//members.home.com/glampke/NCGR/

Rocky Mountain G-Scalers
c/o Chuck Holding
2245 Havenridge Dr.
Colorado Springs, CO 80920
San Juan Large Scalers
c/o Lynn Daugherty
602 The Eagle Pass
Durango, CO 81301

CONNECTICUT

Central Connecticut "G" Gauger Modular Group
c/o David E. Snow
68 Hacienda Circle
Plantsville, CT 06479-1912
e-mail: david.e.snow@snet.net
Connecticut "G" Scalers
c/o George Edgerton
111 Fan Hill Rd.
Monroe, CT 06468

DELAWARE

NorDel Large Scalers
c/o Keith Heck
213 S. Dillwyn Rd.
Windy Hills
Newark, DE 19711

FLORIDA

Florida Garden Railway Society
c/o George Sheldon
1194 Trotwood Blvd.
Winter Springs, FL 32708

Florida Garden Railway Society--Tampa Bay Div.
c/o Pete Hartes
1124 Shadow Run Dr.
Lakeland, FL 33813
www.trainweb.org/fgrs/

GEORGIA

Central Georgia Garden Railroad Society
c/o Frances & Charlie Tidd
phone: 1-770-889-2474
www.geocities.com/RodeoDrive/
4497/CentralGAGRS.htm

Georgia Garden Railway Society
c/o Frances Tidd
3540 Cove Creek Ct.
Cumming, GA 30040

ILLINOIS

Chicago Area Garden Railway Society
c/o Helmut Zehnpfennig
P.O. Box 1534
Arlington Heights, IL 60005

Chicago Big Train Operators
c/o Jim Rusch
P.O. Box 448
Lake Bluff, IL 60044
http://members.home.net/blattan/

Southern Illinois Train Club, G Div.
c/o Scott Fowler
18194 Highway 14
Benton, IL 62812

INDIANA

G-Trac Modular Model RR Club
c/o Joel Tuscan
7011 Hazelett Rd.
Fort Wayne, IN 46835
Indiana Big Train Engineers Club
c/o Dave Lynn
8332 Mockingbird Lane
Indianapolis, IN 46256
http://members.iquest.net/~oseidler/ibtec.html

IOWA

Cedar Valley Garden Railway Society
c/o Joe Hall
620 33 St. NE
Cedar Rapids, IA 52402

Central Iowa Garden Railway Society
c/o George Hagele
4705 Liberty Ave.
Newton, IA 50208

KANSAS

Northeast Kansas Garden Railway Society
c/o Jerry Eaton
1308 SW Caledon
Topeka, KS 66611-2412
http://home.sprintmail.com/
~dkrice/nekan.htm

Wichita Garden Railway Society
c/o Claudia Rollstin
606 S. Green
Wichita, KS 67211

LOUISIANNA

Baton Rouge Model Railroad Clubs—G Scale Section
125 South Donmoor
Baton Rouge, LA
contact: Peter Oelschlaeger
phone: 225-664-1146
www.dovetailstudio.com/trains

MARYLAND

Mason-Dixon Large Scale RR Society
c/o Alan K. Harbold
P.O. Box 148
Bel Air, MD 21014

MASSACHUSETTS

Cape Cod Garden Railway Society
P.O. Box 2111
Orleans, MA 02653-2111

MICHIGAN

Lakeshore Garden Railway Club
c/o Robert Greening, Jr.
693 Pear Tree Lane
Grosse Point Woods, MI 48236

Southwestern Michigan Garden Railway Society
c/o John Piehl
6450 E. Becht Rd.
Columa, MI 49038

MINNESOTA

Minnesota Garden Railway Society
c/o Jim Thiewes
12004 Red Oak Ct. N
Burnsville, MN 55337

MISSOURI

Gateway Garden Railway Club
c/o Jack Flach
6233 Nottingham
St. Louis, MO 63109

Ozark Garden Railway Society
c/o Robert Newquist
P.O. Box 516
Mt. Vernon, MO 75712

MONTANA

Big Sky Garden RR Society
c/o John Millard
P.O. Box 1576
Noxon, MT 59853

NEBRASKA

Nebraska Garden Railway Society
c/o Don Hofsheier
13804 Josephine St.
Omaha, NE 68138

Prairie Garden Railway Society
c/o Jim & Lee Johnson
808 Carlos Drive
Lincoln, NE 68505

NEVADA

Garden Railroaders of Las Vegas
c/o Terry Handy
6544 Hill View Ave.
Las Vegas, NV 89107-1210

Las Vegas Garden Railway Society
c/o Jim Hayes
6912 Cortez Ct.
Las Vegas, NV 89145-5315
e-mail: jhayes4u2c@aol.com
www.communitylink.koz.com/lvrj/lvgrs

NEW HAMPSHIRE

New Hampshire Garden Railway Society
c/o David Miller
P.O. Box 381
Brookline, NH 03033
www.amesburysoccer.org/NHGRS.html

NEW JERSEY

Central Jersey G Scalers
c/o John Vastano
14 N. Martine Ave.
Fanwood, NJ 07023-1310

South Jersey Garden Railway Society
c/o Anita Brown
1103 Seaside Ave.
Absecon, NJ 08201-1440

NEW MEXICO

New Mexico Garden Railroaders
c/o Ed Fagyal
4400 Glencroft Ave. NW
Albuquerque, NM 87114

NEW YORK

Central New York Large Scale Railway Society
c/o Gordon H. Davis
315 Viking Place
Liverpool, NY 13008

Genessee "G" Garden Railway Society
c/o Kevin Strong
242 Wadsworth Ave.
Avon, NY 14414

Southern Tier Garden Railway Society
c/o John Gordon, Sr.
159 Lewis St.
Endicott, NY 13760-6255
www.geocities.com/stgrs/index.html

Westchester Garden Railway Society
c/o H. B. Leeds
14 Maple Ave.
Tarrytown, NY 10591

NORTH CAROLINA

North Carolina Garden Railway Society
c/o J. D. Long
2116 Mariner Circle
Raleigh, NC 27603
www.ncneighbors.com/1292/

Piedmont Garden Railroaders
c/o Jim Arnold
34 Mountain Lake Drive
Hendersonville, NC 28739

OHIO

Columbus Garden Railway Society
c/o William R. Logan
1421 Norma Road
Columbus, OH 43229
www.dj-inabox.com/cgrs/cgrs1.htm

Greater Cincinnati Garden Railway Society
c/o Larry Koehl
405 Werner Drive
Ft. Wright, KY 41011-3639
www.w-v.K12.ky.us/gcgrs/
gcgrshome.htm

Miami Valley Garden Railway Society
c/o Frank P. Klatt
3145 Kerry Drive
Beavercreek, OH 45434-6372
www.dj-inabox.com/Mvgrs/
MVGRS1.htm

Northern Ohio Garden Railway Society
c/o Robert Rowell
3661 Leafland St. NW
Uniontown, OH 44685

OKLAHOMA

Oklahoma Garden Railway Society
c/o Ron Hall
1429 NE 26th
Moore, OK 73160

Tulsa Garden Rail Road Club
c/o Ron Salach
3302 S. Peoria
Tulsa, OK 74105

OREGON

Emerald Empire Garden Railway Society
c/o Gary Lane
3323 Fillmore St.
Eugene, OR 97405-1923

Northwest "G" Railroad Club
c/o Doug Wilken
P.O. Box 91
Salem, OR 97308-0091

Rose City Garden Railway Society
c/o David Linn
2000 N.E. 42nd Ave., #366
Portland, OR 97213

Southwest Oregon Large Scale Trains
c/o Joseph Zajac
424 Girard Drive
Medford, OR 97504-6314

PENNSYLVANIA

Pennsylvania Garden Railway Society
c/o Clem O'Jevich
32 S. Market St.
Nantichoke, PA 18634

Pittsburgh Garden Railway Society
c/o Lee Brandes
7228 Baptist Rd., #200
Bethel Park, PA 15102

South Eastern Pennsylvania Garden Railway Society
c/o A. D. Dabney
18 Ardmoor Lane
Chadds Ford, PA 19317
www.geocities.com/RodeoDrive/
4497/SEPGRS.htm

Susquehanna Valley Garden Railway Society
c/o H. Eugene Boll
3925 Ridgewood Rd.
York, PA 17402

TENNESSEE

Nashville Garden Railway Society
c/o Ross Evans, Jr.
Box 50419
Nashville, TN 37205
http://nashvillegardenrailway.org/
index.htm

State Line All Scales Model Railroad Club
c/o Mark Bentley
243 Ramey Road
Bristol, TN 37620

TEXAS

Heart of Texas G-Gaugers
c/o Charles Kusser
599 Mahalo Court
Bastrop, TX 78602

Houston Area "G" Gaugers Model RR Club
c/o Chuck Blumentritt
18210 Forest Town Dr.
Houston, TX 77084
www.donaldburger.com/hagg.htm

Lubbock Model Railroad Association
P.O. Box 54674
Lubbock, TX 79453
http://home.earthlink.net/~jackseay/index.html

Midland-Odessa Large Scale Engineers
c/o Bill Luxford
3904 Elderica Court
Odessa, TX 79765-8522

North Texas Garden Railroad Consortium
c/o Dennis Cherry
11565 Cromwell Circle
Dallas, TX 75229
e-mail: dbcherry@flash.net
http://www.ntgrc.org

San Antonio Garden Railway Society
c/o Mark Burns
142 Kimberly Drive
San Antonio, TX 78227-4458
e-mail: swrwy@yahoo.com (Towne Comee)

UTAH

Hostler Model Railroad Club
c/o Paul Karczewski
1125 N. Main, Apt. 1G
Layton, UT 84041
http://members.xoom.com/hostler/

Utah Garden Railway Society
c/o Jon Groneman
391 E. 200 S.
Springville, UT 84663
www.ugrs.org

VERMONT

Vermont Garden Railway Society
c/o Douglas R. Johnson
P.O. Box 250
E. Montpellier, VT 05651

VIRGINIA

Big Lick Big Train Operators
c/o Dave Meashey
3666 Bond St., SW
Roanoake, VA 24018
e-mail: kndmeashey@dellnet.com

Tidewater Big Train Operators
c/o Jon D. Miller
302 Laurel Path Rd.
Yorktown, VA 23692
e-mail: JLSRails@aol.com

WASHINGTON (state)

Inland Northwest Garden Railway Society
c/o Steve Hughes
3410 N. Garry Rd.
Otis Orchards, WA 99027

Puget Sound Garden Railway Society
c/o John Bigelow
8240 N.E. 25th St.
Medina, WA 98039
www.psgrs.com

WASHINGTON D.C.

Washington, Virginia, Maryland Garden Railway Society
c/o Ron Eisenbarth
1544 Red Oak Drive
Silver Spring, MD 20910

WEST VIRGINIA

Mountaineer Garden Railroad Club
c/o Frank Blake
24 Beaver Drive
Hurricane, WV 25526

Ohio River Valley Garden Railroad Club
c/o Thomas L. Nibert
3 Riverview Lane
Huntington, OH 25702

Potomac River Highlands Garden Railway Society
c/o Johnnie Schwartz
Rt. 1, Box 122-A14
Keyser, WV 26726

WISCONSIN

Glacial Garden Railway Society
c/o George MacDonald
P.O. Box 206
Pewaukee, WI 53072

Wisconsin Garden Railway Society
c/o Tom Smith
2410 Stuart Ct.
Madison, WI 53704
http://hometown.aol.com/TSTEMRICH/WGRS.html

CANADA

TBA & PHO Garden Railway Society
c/o Ricky Lcc
63 Montrose Crescent NE
Calgary, ALBERTA
T2E 5P3

Rocky Mountain Garden Railroaders
c/o Mr. Sandy Alexander
248 Queensland Drive SE
Calgary, ALBERTA
T2J 3R8
www.trainweb.org/rmgr/intro.html

Greater Vancouver Garden Railway Club
c/o Bob McDiarmid
Box 683
Port Coquitlam, BRITISH COLUMBIA
V3B 6H9

Vancouver Island Garden Railway Club
c/o Grant Stephens
4759 Spirit Place
Nanaimo, BRITISH COLUMBIA
V9V 1N8

London Garden Railway Society
c/o Terry Morton
39 Cherish Court
London, ONTARIO
N6K 4H2

Central Ontario Garden Railway Association
c/o Ross Webster
RR #3
Georgetown, ONTARIO
L7G 4S6
www.geocities.com/Heartland/Bluffs/3020/cogra.html

Ottawa Valley Garden Railway Society
c/o Fred Mills
36 Starwood Rd.
Neapean, ONTARIO
K2G 1Z1
www.ovar.org/ovgrs/index.html

Appendix C
Garden railroading in cyberspace

The Internet, and its associated World Wide Web (WWW or simply "web"), offers an ever-expanding source of valuable information for the Large Scale and garden railroading enthusiast. You'll find just about everything you could possibly imagine on the web, ranging from a manufacturer's current catalog and dealers who will take on-line product orders to garden railroading club sites and inspirational photos of individual home layouts.

The listings presented here provide known web site addresses for manufacturers and suppliers; publishers of books, magazines, and videos; on-line forums and chats groups for exchanging information with your fellow hobbyists; general reference sites for technical and prototype railroading information; and sites hosted by garden railroading clubs and associations.

Many of these sites also provide direct "links" to other related sites that may interest you, including the home pages of sites hosted by infividual garden railroaders and their families. All of these sites, regardless of where they may be in the world, are as close as a simple click of your mouse button.

Keep in mind that web site addresses do change from time to time as businesses expand or as groups and individuals move from one location to another. In most cases, keying in the old address will bring up a screen that will automatically link you to the new site, or inform you how to locate the new address.

MANUFACTURERS/SUPPLIERS:

Name (refer to Manufacturers & Suppliers section for complete mailing addresses)	Internet address	Product/Service
Abracadata	www.abracadata.com	track planning software
Above All Railways	www.aboveallrailways.com	overhead track systems
Accucraft Trains	www.accucraft.com	locomotives and rolling stock
Argyle Locomotive Works	www.argylloco.com.au/	#1 gauge live steam locomotives
Aristo-Craft Trains	www.aristocraft.com	locomotives, rolling stock, track, power units, accessories
Arnold Digital	www.arnold-digital.de	DCC components
Aster Hobby	www.steamup.com/aster/steamframe.html	#1 gauge live steam locomotives
Bachmann Trains	www.bachmannindustries.com	locomotives, rolling stock, track, accessories
Battery Backshop	www.batterybackshop.com	radio control and battery power conversions
Barry's Big Trains	www.tttrains.com	Digital Command Control systems and accessories
Bragdon Enterprises	www.bragdonent.com/gfguide.htm	Geodesic Foam Scenery materials/instructions
Bollinger Edgerly Scale Trains	www.besttrains.com/pro_99.html	custom rolling stock, scenery supplies, structure kits
BridgeMasters	www.bridge-masters.com	trestles, bridges, culverts, retaining walls, portals, signs
Bridgewerks	www.bridgewerks.com	bridges, power controllers and wire
Bullyland Figures	www.bullyland.com	Large Scale figures
BUSCH	www.busch-model.com/English.htm	scenic items and accessories
Cargo-to-Go	www.cargo-to-go.com	cargo accessories and details for Large Scale trains
Chooch Enterprises	www.choochenterprises.com/homeframe.html	tunnel portals, retaining walls, scenic accessories
Classic Case Company	www.ccase.com	display cases
C.M. Models	www.llareggub.com	custom-built rolling stock
Dallee Electronics	www.dallee.com	sound and control systems, signal /automation equip., strobes, light systems
Del-Aire Product	www.delaire.com	air-powered switch machines
Digitrax	www.digitrax.com	Digitrax Digital Command Control systems
Edge Distributing	www.edgedistributing.com	MiniBlox Building System
ESU	www.loksound.de	DCC components
G Action Models	www.angelfire.com/biz/gaction/index2/html	custom models, operating rolling stock and structures

Garden Craft	www.gardencraft.com	garden supplies for garden railroads
Garden Texture	www.gardentexture.com	custom structures and bridges
Glenn Snyder Display Systems	www.gsds.com	wall-mounted display systems
Guts, Gravel & Glory Scenic RR Supplies	www.chaffee.net/ggg/	structure kits
H&R Trains	www.hrtrains.com	stainless steel track
Hartford Products, Inc.	www.hartfordpr.com	quality kits and parts for #1 gauge trains
Hartland Locomotive Works	www.h-l-w.com	locomotives and rolling stock
Hillcraft Model Builders	www.hillcraftgmodels.com	handcrafted structures
Hillman's Railclamps	www.hillmansrailclamps.com	rail-joining clamps
Isabel Central Enterprises	www2.southwind.net/%7Eice/	fiberglass modular roadbed, structures
ITTC Sound Modules	www.ittcsoundeffects.com	sound modules and components
JigStones	www.jigstones.com	buildings and bridges
Jules Toy Trains	www.julestoytrains.com	ceiling-mounted track systems
Just Plain Folk	www.trackntrains.com	Large Scale figures
Kadee Quality Products, Inc.	www.kadee.com	couplers for Large Scale trains
Kaysing Studios	www.kaysingstudios.pair.com	garden railway structures
Keithco, Inc.	www.locolinc.com	Locolinc radio control systems
LED Light (The)	www.ledlight.com	LED lights and related items for Large Scale trains and accessories
Legend Steam Locomotives	www.steamup.com/legend	#1 gauge live steam locomotives
Lenz	www.lenz.com	DCC components
LGB Trains/LGB of America	www.lgb.de	locomotives, rolling stock, track, power units. accessories
Llagas Creek Railways	www.llagastrack.com	Gauge 1 track supplies
Loco-Boose Hobbies	www.locoboose.com	suspended railway systems for Large Scale trains
Lone Star Bridge and Abutment	www.tttrains.com/lonestar/	wooden and cast-stone bridges and abutments
Loy's Toys	www.loystoys.com;	Digital Command Control systems
Mamod/Wilesco Steam Locomotives	www.mamod.com	#1 gauge live steam locomotives
Märklin Trains	www.marklin.com	locomotives, rolling stock, track, power units, accessories
McMaster-Carr	www.mcmaster.com	small detail parts for Large Scale
MDC Roundhouse	www.mdcroundhouse.com	Large Scale locomotives and rolling stock
Mesa Railway	www.mesarailway.com	overhead railway systems
Micro Fasteners	http://microfasteners.com	small detail parts for Large Scale
Micro-Mark	www.micromark.com	small tools, supplies, and detail parts for modelers
Miniature Lumber	www.customcuts.com	scale-size lumber items
Miniature Plant Kingdom	www.miniplantkingdom.com	miniature plant specialists for garden railroads
Miniatronics	www.miniatronics.com	electronic components for model railroads
Mini Forest by Sky	www.miniforest.com	live plants and shrubs for garden railroads
Model Rectifier Corp. (MRC)	www.modelrec.com	power units for all scales
MTH Electric Trains	222.railking1gauge.com	One-Gauge line
North Coast Engineering	www.tttrains.com/northcoast	DCC components
Northeast Narrow Gauge	www.nemodel.com	Large Scale wood and metal locomotive and rolling stock kits
Northwest Remote Control Systems	www.halcyon.com/dnkgoods	remote control equipment and accessories
NorthWest Short Line (NWSL)	www.nwsl.com	specialty parts for modeling
Overhead Railways	www.overheadrailways.com	overhead railway systems and track cleaning cars
Ozark Miniatures	www.ozarkminiatures.com	"G" and 1:20.3 scale kits and detail castings
The Parker Co.	www.coparker.com	turnouts for Gauge 1 garden railways
Parker's Nursery	www.parkersrailroad.com	structures, figures, die-casts
P&M and NC Bridges and Bents	www.pmncbridges.com	bridges, bents, log cars
PCN Radio Control	www.alphalink.com.au/%7Ercs/	remote control systems
People You Know You Need	www.peopleyouneed.com	scale people figures
Phoenix Sound Systems	www.phoenixsound.com	sound modules and components
PICO	www.piko.de/	structures and accessories (distributed by LGB)

POLA	www.pola.de/POLAindex.html	structures and accessories
Precision Products	www.appliedimaginationinc.com	model building supplies; Plastic Veneer materials
PSI/Dynatrol	www.tttrains.com/psidynatrol	DCC components
QSI Industries (Maxx Traxx)	www.qsindustries.com/maxx_traxx.pdf	sound boards and related components
Railroad Ave. Model Wroks, Ltd.	www.railroadavenue.com	Urethane structure kits
Ramtraxx	www.wangrow.com	DCC components
R & G Railroad Co.	www.randgrailroad.com	wall- and ceiling-mount train systems
R & S Enterprises	www.rrtrack.com/	sectional track layout planning software
Remote Control Systems of New England	www.mv.com/ipusers/rcs/	radio control units
Railbed Systems	www.railbed.com	track foundation system for LGB track (outdoors and indoors)
Raildreams, Inc.	www.raildreams.com	design and construction of custom-built model railroads
Remote Control Systems	www.rcs-rc.com	in-cab radio control systems
Ram Track Electronic Devices	www.ramrcandramtrack.com	lighting systems, sound devices, lights, control and power devices
Ro & Co.	www.rowco.com	custom Large Scale locomotives and rolling stock
Roundhouse Engineering Co., Ltd.	www.roundhouse-eng.com	#1 gauge live steam locomotives
RR-Track	www.rrtrack.com	sectional track layout planning software
Scale Card (The)	www.thescalecard.com	scale cards for all scales
Shawmut Car Shops	http://users.penn.com/~nana47/index.html	custom-built cars, motorcars, and self-propelled cars; custom painting and decals
Sheridan Products	www.sheridanproducts.com	#1 gauge narrow gauge caboose kits
Showcase Miniatures	www.showcaseminiatures.com	character figures
Skid-Do Industries	www.skid-do.com	fiberglass tunnel sections
Small Parts, Inc.	www.smallparts.com	detail parts for Large Scale model making
Soundtraxx	www.soundtraxx.com	DCC components
Split Jaw Rail Clamps	www.railclamp.com	rail-joining devices
Stainless Unlimited	www.stainlessunlimited.com	custom-built bridges
Stoneworks	www.rrstoneworks.com	natural rocks/stones, ballast, structures, misc. parts
Sunset Valley RR (formerly Garich Light Transport)	www.largescale.com/svrr/	Code 250 track components, railbenders, etc.
Supply Line Model Railroad Kits and Figures	www.slmonline.co;	miniature figures
Track N' Trains	www.trackntrains.com/tnt.htm	"Just Plain Folk" figures for Large Scale model railroads
Umelec	www.netwings.ch/umelec	DCC components
USA Trains;	www.usatrains.com;	locomotives, rolling stock, track
Venango Valley Models	www.kaysingstudios.pair.com	garden railway structures
Vollmer	www.vollmer-kit.com	structure kits
Wada Works Co., Ltd.	http://users.erols.com/diesel/gas.html	#1 gauge live steam and diesel locomotives
Wangrow	www.wangrow.com	DCC components
Wm. K. Walthers	www.walthers.com	distributor of Large Scale products
Woodland Scencis	www.woodlandscenics.com	scenery accessories
Zimo	www56.pair.com/zimo	DCC components
ZTC Systems	http://ourworld.compuserve.com/homepages/ztc	DCC components
7/8n2 Railway Equipment Company	www.largescale.com/seven8n2/index.html	7/8n2 equipment

PUBLISHERS OF GARDEN RAILROADING AND LARGE SCALE PERIODICALS:

Name;	Internet address;	Description of editorial content
(Refer to References section for complete mailing addresses)		
AW NUTS Magazine	www.awnuts.com	Promotes and features whimsical modeling in Large Scale
FineScale Railroader Magazine	www.finescalerr.com	Features detailed large scale modeling techniques
Garden Railways Magazine	www2.gardenrailways.com/gr	Exclusively garden railroading and Large Scale modeling
LGB Telegram Magazine	www.lgbtelegram.com	Exclusive publication sponsored by (and for) LGB trains
Narrow Gauge and Shortline Gazette Magazine	www.ngslgazette.com	Premier publication for the Narrow Gauge enthusiast
Steam in the Garden Magazine	www.steamup.com	Premier U.S. publication for the live steam hobbyist

Appendices

ON-LINE DISCUSSION FORUMS AND CHATS (open to all interested parties):

Aristo-Craft Trains Forum	www.aristocraft.com	Forum devoted exclusively to Large Scale trains
16mm Narrow Gauge Modelers e-group	www.egroups.com/group/16mmngm/	E-mail list service for the 16mm narrow gauge enthusiast
FineScale Railroader Forum	www.finescalerr.com	Has forum and chat site devoted to Large Scale trains
Large Scale Central	www.largescalecentral.com	Exclusively Large Scale topics/ forums
Large Trains On-Line	www.largetrainsonline	Forums devoted to Large Scale trains
My Largescale.com	www.mylargescale.com	Exclusively Large Scale topics/forums
Narrow Gauge Online	www.finescalerr.com/ngol	Narrow Gauge site created by FineScale Railroader Magazine
RailForum.com	www.reilforum.com	Includes Large Scale/Garden RR forum
Yahoo Clubs: Garden Railroading	http://clubs.yahoo.com/clubs/gardenrailroading	Chats/messages/photos/news/links/etc.
Yahoo Clubs: G Scale Group	http://clubs.yahoo.com/clubs/gscalegroup	Discussion groups/messages/chat/etc.
7/8-inch scale enthusuasts	www.7eights.com	Site for 7/8-inch scale enthusiasts

ON-LINE REFERENCE SITES FOR GARDEN RAILROADERS:

Name;	Internet address;	description of content
Bonsaiweb.com	www.bonsaiweb.com	Tips for the gardener in garden railroading
Da Trains	www.urbaneagle.com/datrains/index.html	Reference charts for scale, grades, track, etc.
Digital Command Control/Large Scale	www.trainweb.org/largescaledcc/	Technical information relating to DCC in Large Scale
DG&RR Railroad Tips & Tricks page	http://home.flash.net/~dbcherry/kinks.htm	Dennis Cherry's Large Scale tips page
Family Garden Trains	www.btcomm.com/trains/articles/index.htm	Various articles of interest to garden railroaders
George Schreyer's Large Scale Trains Page	http://trainweb.org/girr	THE premier site for Large Scale technical tips and information
G-Scale-Links.com	www.g-scale-links.com	Links to manufacturers, organizations, private sites, etc.
Hobby Retailers (locator)	www.hobbyretailer.com	Hobby shop locator/search site
JJ&C RailRoad Technical Tips	http://home.att.net/~therealms/technica.htm	Technical tips for garden railroaders
Live Steam magazine	www.livesteam.net/	Devoted to live steam locomotives, marine, traction, and autos
Live Steaming	www.livesteaming.com	Information and links for all live steam enthusiasts (including small scale)
Living Steam Railways Home Page	www.roundhouse-eng.com/	Live steam resource sponsored by Roundhouse Engineering
Locomotive Gyrating Warning Lights	www.trainweb.com/gyra	Everything about locomotive lighting
Metzbahn	http://hometown.aol.com/metzbahn	LGB prototypes, LGB locomotive ID numbers, links
Model Railroad Magic Web Site	www.fantasonics.com	A philosophical—and fun—approach to model railroading sound effects
Narrow Escape Online	www.narrowescape.com/3ft/	A Large Scale industrial and light railway modeling resource
National Steam Tram Home Page	www.mousby.freeserve.co.uk/	Devoted to steam tram transport history and modeling
RailServe.com	www.railserve.com	Lists web site links for all train-related topics, including prototype railroads
Saskatoon Railroad Modellers Construction Tips	http://members.home.net/sask.rail/construction/index.html	Large Scale construction articles of all types
Shay Locomotives Reference Site	www.ShayLocomotives.com	2800 pages of Shay information
Small Scale Live Steam	www.nmia.com/~vrbass/steam	Small scale live steam resources site
Steam in the Garden magazine	www.steamup.com	Reference site, forums, and links
TrainBoard.com	www.trainboard.com	Railroad and model railroad (all scales) forums
U.S. Dept. of Agriculture	www.USDA.gov	Gardening and plant hardiness zone information
www.RailFonts.com	www.railfonts.com	Railroad-related type fonts offered for sale

GARDEN RAILROAD CLUBS AND ASSOCIATIONS:

Name (refer to Clubs & Associations section for complete mailing addresses)	Internet address	Location/comments
Arizona Model Railroad Club	www.azmodelrr.com	Arizona
Baton Rouge Model Railroad Clubs	www.dovetailstudio.com/trains	Louisiana
Bay Area Garden Railway Society	www.bagrs.org/	California
Big Train Engineers Model RR Club of Indiana	http://members.iquest.net/%7Eoseidler/ibtec.html	Indiana
Blossom Valley Garden Railroad	http://members.aol.com/_ht_a/glanlg/club2/	California
Chicago Big Train Operators	http://members.home.net/blattan/	Illinois
Central Georgia Garden Railroad Society	www.geocities.com/RodeoDrive/4497/CentralGAGRS.htm	Georgia
Central Ontario Garden Railway Association	www.geocities.com/Heartland/Bluffs/3020/cogra.html	Ontario, Canada
Columbus Garden Railway Society	www.dj-inabox.com/cgrs/cgrs1.htm	Ohio
Diamondhead International Steamup	www.diamondhead.org	Mississippi
Florida Garden Railway Society--Tampa Bay	www.trainweb.org/fgrs/	Florida
Fullerton Railway Plaza Association	www.trainweb.com/frpa	California
G-Scale Society (UK)	www.g-scale-society.co.uk	United Kingdom (national)
Greater Cincinnati Chapter/Garden Railway Soc.	www.w-v.K12.ky.us/gcgrs/gcgrshome.htm	Ohio
Hostler Model Railroad Club	http://members.xoom.com/hostler/	Utah
Houston Area "G" Gaugers Model RR Club	www.donaldburger.com/hagg.htm	Texas
Indiana Big Train Engineers Club	http://members.iquest.net/~oseidler/ibtec.html	Indiana
JLS Railroad	www.trainweb.org/jlsrr/	New York
LGB Model Railroad Club	www.lgbmrrc.com	(national)
Long Island Garden Railway Society	www.trainweb.org/jlsrr/ligrs/	New York
Lubbock Model Railroad Association	http://home.earthlink.net/~jackseay/index.html	Texas
Miami Valley Garden Railway Society	www.dj-inabox.com/Mvgrs/MVGRS1.htm	Ohio
Nashville Garden Railway Society	http://nashvillegardenrailway.org/index.htm	Tennessee
National Model Railroad Association	www.nmra.org	(national)
New Hampshire Garden Railway Society	www.amesburysoccer.org/NHGRS.html	New Hampshire
Nihon Teien Tetsudo (Japan)	www.steamup.com/sitgonline/forum/articles/teientetsudo/nihonteientetsudo.html	Japan (national);
North Carolina Garden Railway Society	www.ncneighbors.com/1292/	North Carolina
North Texas Garden Railroad Consortium	http://web.ntgrc.org/usr/ntgrc/	Texas
Northeast Kansas Garden Railway Society	http://home.sprintmail.com/~dkrice/nekan.htm	Kansas
Northern Colorado Garden Railroaders	www://members.home.com/glampke/NCGR/	Colorado
Ottawa Valley Garden Railway Society	www.ovar.org/ovgrs/index.html	Canada
Pittsburgh Garden Railway Society	http://trfn.clpgh.org/pgrs/	Pennsylvania
Puget Sound Garden Railway Society	www.psgrs.com	Washington
Rocky Mountain Garden Railroaders	www.trainweb.org/rmgr/intro.html	Canada (Calgary)
San Diego Garden Railway Society	http://sdgrs.com/	California
San Joaquin Valley Garden Railway Society	www.scottfalls.com/sjvgrs1.html	California
Saskatoon Railroad Modelers	http://members.home.net/sask.rail/	Canada
South Eastern Pennsylvania Garden Railroad Soc.	www.geocities.com/RodeoDrive/4497/SEPGRS.htm	Pennsylvania
Southern Tier Garden RR Society	www.geocities.com/stgrs/index.html	New York
St. James Model Railroad Club	www.geocities.com/TheTropics/Shores/4683/index.html	Minnesota
Utah Garden Railway Society	www.ugrs.org	Utah
Wisconsin Garden Railway Society	http://hometown.aol.com/TSTEMRICH/WGRS.html	Wisconsin

Appendix D
Garden railroad references

Large Scale and garden railroad reference books and price guides:

An Introduction to Alcohol Firing
by Roger Loxley
Sidestreet Bannerworks
Box 460222
Denver, CO 80246
phone: 303-377-7785
fax: 303-377-7785
e-mail: sidestreet@americanisp.net
www.sidestreetbannerworks.com

Beginner's Guide to Large Scale Model Railroading
by Mark Horowitz and Russ Larson
Greenberg/Kalmbach Books
Kalmbach Publishing Co.
21027 Crossroads Circle
P.O. Box 1612
Waukesha, WI 53187-1612
catalog/orders: 800-533-6644
http://books.kalmbach.com

Greenberg's Pocket Price Guide: LGB, 1968-1996
Greenberg/Kalmbach Books
Kalmbach Publishing Co.
21027 Crossroads Circle
P.O. Box 1612
Waukesha, WI 53187-1612
catalog/orders: 800-533-6644
http://books.kalmbach.com

Large-Scale Model Railroading Handbook, 2nd Edition
by Robert Schleicher
Krause Publications
700 E. State St.
Iola, WI 54990-0001
catalog/orders: 800-258-0929
www.krause.com/Books

LGB Explore Guide Book (English)
LGB of America
6444 Nancy Ridge Drive
San Diego, CA 92121
phone: 858-535-9387
fax: 858-535-1091
www.lgb.de/index.htm

Model Railroading with LGB
Greenberg/Kalmbach Books
Kalmbach Publishing Co.
21027 Crossroads Circle
P.O. Box 1612
Waukesha, WI 53187-1612
catalog/orders: 800-533-6644
http://books.kalmbach.com

Official Guide to LGB
Greenberg/Kalmbach Books
Kalmbach Publishing Co.
21027 Crossroads Circle
P.O. Box 1612
Waukesha, WI 53187-1612
catalog/orders: 800-533-6644
http://books.kalmbach.com

Success in Working our Model Steam Locomotives
reprint of Bassett-Lowke publication, circa 1937
Sidestreet Bannerworks
Box 460222
Denver, CO 80246
phone: 303-377-7785
fax: 303-377-7785
e-mail: sidestreet@americanisp.net
www.sidestreetbannerworks.com

Walthers Big Trains Model Railroad Reference Book—2000 (product catalog)
Wm. K. Walthers, Inc.
5601 W. Florist Avenue
Milwaukee, WI 53218
phone: 1-800-4TRAINS (customer service)
e-mail: custserv@walthers.com
www.walthers.com
Large Scale and garden railroad magazines:

Large Scale and garden railroad magazines:

A.W. N.U.T.S. Magazine
P.O. Box 8523
Red Bluff, CA 96080
phone: 800-830-2234
www.awnuts.com
• Explores the whimsical, fun-filled approach to garden railroading. The magazine's name stands for "Always Whimsical, Not Usually To Scale."

Big Train Operator Magazine
c/o Ralph Wilcox
1854 Erin Drive
Altoona, PA 16602
www.lgbmrrc.com
• Official publication of the LGB Model Railroad Club. Contents include feature articles, collector information, manufacturer product announcements, and club news.

Classic Toy Trains Magazine
Kalmbach Publishing Co.
21027 Crossroads Circle
P.O. Box 1612
Waukesha, WI 53187-1612
phone: 800-446-5489
www.classtrain.com
• Some coverage, from time-to-time, of Large Scale railroading products and layouts.

Finescale Railroader Magazine
1574 Kerryglen St.
Westlake Village, CA 91361
phone: 805-379-0904
www.finescalerr.com
(complete current issue of magazine is available on-line at web site)
• Focuses on finescale modeling in all scales, with emphasis on large scale trains and garden railroading, including some coverage of small scale live steam.)

Garden Rail Magazine
c/o Catherine Ambler
P.O. Box 9, Skipton
North Yorks, BD23 4UX England
phone: 01729-830552
fax: 01729-830552
e-mail: GardenRail@cdsc.softnet.co.uk
www.soft.net.uk/cdsc
• British publication that extensively covers the garden railroading scene in Great Britain. Contains advertising from manufacturers, suppliers, and retailers.

Garden Railways Magazine
P.O. Box 1612
21027 Crossroads Circle
Waukesha, WI 53187-1612
phone: 800-533-6644
fax: 414-796-1615
e-mail: customerservice@kalmbach.com
www.gardenrailways.com
• Largest circulation U.S. magazine devoted exclusively to garden railroading, including regular coverage of small scale live steam. Provides feature articles, product announcements and reviews, and garden layout construction and maintenance tips.

G1MRA Journal
C/O Ms. L. Prior
121 Moorside Rd.
Kinson, Bournemouth
Dorset BH11 8DQ England
• Quarterly journal of the Gauge One Model Railway Assn. in England.

LGB Telegram Magazine
P.O. Box 332
Hershey, PA 17033-0332
phone: 717-312-0617
fax: 717-312-0817
e-mail: LGB Telegram@mindspring.com
• Official publication of LGB. Presents feature articles, how-to construction articles, and product announcements from the manufacturer.

Live Steam Magazine
Village Press, Inc.
2779 Aero Park Drive
Traverse City, MI 49686
phone: 231-946-3712
fax: 231-946-9588
www.villagepress.com/livesteam
• Focus is on large scale live steam of all types, including large scale live steam and prototype steam locomotives, but regularly includes some small scale live steam coverage.

Märklin *Insider* Magazine
Märklin Club North America
P.O. Box 510851
New Berlin, WI 53151-0851
phone: 414-784-0717
www.marklin.com
• Official publication of the Märklin Club. Covers Märklin's Z, HO, and #1 Gauge (including MAXI) product lines. Content includes feature articles, how-to construction articles, technical tips, historical articles, and manufacturer product announcements.

Narrow Gauge and Short Line Gazette Magazine
4966 El Camino Real, #101
Los Altos, CA 94022
phone: 650-941-3823
fax: 650-941-3845
e-mail: gazette@worldnet.att.net
www.ngslgazette.com
• Publishes articles of interest to narrow gauge enthusiasts in all scales.

Small Scale Steam Hobbyist
791 County Farm Road
Monticello, IL 61856
subscribe through Sulphur Springs Steam Models:
P.O. Box 6165
Chesterfield, MO 63006-6165
phone: 636-527-8326
e-mail: sssmodels@aol.com
www.steamup.com/sulphur/
• New quarterly publication for live steam enthusiasts scheduled to debut early in 2001.

Steam in the Garden Magazine
P.O. Box 335
Newark Valley, NY 13811
phone: 607-642-8119 (Mon.-Thurs., before 9 p.m. EST)
fax: 303-975-6211
e-mail: rbrown5@stny.rr.com
www.steamup.com
• The premier U.S. publication for the small scale live steam enthusiast. Focuses exclusively on small scale live steam railroading, including some coverage of live steam boats.

Large Scale and garden railroad videos:

"Day Trip to Duck End" and
"Return Ticket to Duck End"
(layout tours videos)
Sidestreet Bannerworks
Box 460222
Denver, CO 80246
phone: 303-377-7785
fax: 303-377-7785
e-mail: sidestreet@americanisp.net
www.sidestreetbannerworks.com

"How to Build Your Garden Railway" (how-to video)
Sidestreet Bannerworks
Box 460222
Denver, CO 80246
phone: 303-377-7785
fax: 303-377-7785
e-mail: sidestreet@americanisp.net
www.sidestreetbannerworks.com

"Garden Railways: A Video Album"
(layout tours video)
Sidestreet Bannerworks
Box 460222
Denver, CO 80246
phone: 303-377-7785
fax: 303-377-7785
e-mail: sidestreet@americanisp.net
www.sidestreetbannerworks.com

"An Introduction to Small Scale Live Steam"
(how-to video)
Sidestreet Bannerworks
Box 460222
Denver, CO 80246
phone: 303-377-7785
fax: 303-377-7785
e-mail: sidestreet@americanisp.net
www.sidestreetbannerworks.com

"Building a Basic Garden Railroad" (how-to video)
Large Scale Model Railroad Association
phone: 877-LGSCALE (547-2253)
www.largescale.org

"Building a Garden Railroad" (how-to video)
Robinsong Productions
910 Paloverde Drive
Loveland, CO 80538

"Video Rides the Rails" (layout tours video)
Robinsong Productions
910 Paloverde Drive
Loveland, CO 80538

"Live Steamers in Action" (layout tours video)
Valhalla Video
1100 Irvine Blvd., #325G
Tuslin, CA 92780-3534
phone: 888-843-3698
fax: 714-544-3290
www.valhallavideo.com

"Garden Railway Dreamin'" (layout tours video series, Volumes 1-6)
Valhalla Video
1100 Irvine Blvd., #325G
Tuslin, CA 92780-3534
phone: 888-843-3698
fax: 714-544-3290
www.valhallavideo.com

"National Garden Railway Convention 2000"
(layout tours video)
Broadcast Images
9340 Hazard Way, Ste. B
San Diego, CA 92123
phone: 888-869-9277
e-mail: rrvideos@broadcastimages.net

"Garden Railways of San Diego" (layout tours video)
Broadcast Images
9340 Hazard Way, Ste. B
San Diego, CA 92123
phone: 888-869-9277
e-mail: rrvideos@broadcastimages.net

"Garden Railways of Durango" (layout tours video)
Broadcast Images
9340 Hazard Way, Ste. B
San Diego, CA 92123
phone: 888-869-9277
e-mail: rrvideos@broadcastimages.net

"Detailing Large Plastic Rolling Stock"
(how-to video)
Digital Video Images, Inc.
P.O. Box 2584
Littleton, CO 80161-2584
phone: 303-220-8998
fax: 303-220-8933
www.sni.net/~tpspeer/

"Modifying and Scratch-Building Large Scale Figures" (how-to video)
Digital Video Images, Inc.
P.O. Box 2584
Littleton, CO 80161-2584
phone: 303-220-8998
fax: 303-220-8933
www.sni.net/~tpspeer/

"Modifying the Bachmann Shay" (how-to video)
Digital Video Images, Inc.
P.O. Box 2584
Littleton, CO 80161-2584
phone: 303-220-8998
fax: 303-220-8933
www.sni.net/~tpspeer/

"How to Build Wooden Rolling Stock Kits"
(how-to video)
Digital Video Images, Inc.
P.O. Box 2584
Littleton, CO 80161-2584
phone: 303-220-8998
fax: 303-220-8933
www.sni.nct/- tpspeer/

"Weathering With Joe Crea" (how-to video)
Digital Video Images, Inc.
P.O. Box 2584
Littleton, CO 80161-2584
phone: 303-220-8998
fax: 303-220-8933
www.sni.net/~tpspeer/

"Large Scale Triple Header" (layout tours video)
Digital Video Images, Inc.
P.O. Box 2584
Littleton, CO 80161-2584
phone: 303-220-8998
fax: 303-220-8933
www.sni.net/~tpspeer/

"Love That Shay" (layout tours video)
Digital Video Images, Inc.
P.O. Box 2584
Littleton, CO 80161-2584
phone: 303-220-8998
fax: 303-220-8933
www.sni.net/~tpspeer/

Resources
for Model Railroad Enthusiasts

Model Railroad Resources
A Where-To-Find-It Guide for the Hobbyist

Compiled and Edited by Allan W. Miller

This new book will lead you to more than two thousand sources of information and supplies. Covering all of the popular model railroading scales, this book includes manufacturers, distributors, and suppliers; clubs and organizations; publishers and periodicals; key Web sites; leading retailers and dealers (listed by product specialty and state); sources for parts and repairs; appraisers; and museums and public displays.
Softcover • 6 x 9 • 192 pages
25+ b&w photos
Item# MRRRG • $16.95

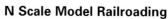

N Scale Model Railroading
by Robert Schleicher

Includes step-by-step instructions on how to use the smallest-size model railroad locomotives, cars, and accessories to build tabletop empires. Model railroading is easier than ever, thanks to a host of new techniques, materials, and products and they are all available to you. This book will show you how to use them.
Softcover • 8-1/2 x 11 • 224 pages
200+ b&w photos • 16-page color section
35 color photos
Item# NMRR • $23.95

The HO Model Railroading Handbook
3rd Edition
by Robert Schleicher

Learn to build exciting model railroad layouts with hot ideas, trends and products presented in an easy-to-follow, how-to style. The most well-respected and knowledgeable author in the field supplies all modelers, from beginners to experts, with the latest tips, tricks and techniques for building a new layout or refreshing an existing setup.
Softcover • 8-1/2 x 11 • 224 pages
250 b&w photos • 50 color photos
Item# HOMR3 • $19.95

Scenery for Model Railroads, Dioramas & Miniatures
3rd Edition
by Robert Schleicher

Transform setups from miniature to magnificent with these expert-proven techniques. You'll learn the easiest and most effective methods for recreating the splendor of nature-but in miniature! Foolproof techniques are explained with easy-to-follow directions, step-by-step photographs and handy Reference Cards.
Softcover • 8-1/2 x 11 • 160 pages
120 b&w photos • 16-page color section
Item# MRDM3 • $22.95

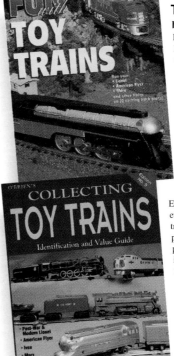

Fun With Toy Trains
by Robert Schleicher

In addition to 24 exciting track plans, you will learn many facts on topics such as multiple train operation and how to use operating accessories to move logs, barrels, coal, and other commodities.
Softcover • 8-1/2 x 11 • 224 pages
160 b&w photos • 8-page color section
Item# CMTH • $23.95

O' Brien's Collecting Toy Trains
5th Edition
edited by Elizabeth A. Stephan

Experts and collectors provide insight into the ever-popular and always expanding world of train collecting. With more than 2,200 photographs, 6,000 items, 18,000 prices and 16 pages of color, collectors are sure to find the item they're looking for. The new alphabetized format will make this edition easy to use.
Softcover • 8-1/2 x 11 • 448 pages
2,200 b&w photos • 16-page color section
Item# CTT5 • $24.95

Standard Guide to Athearn Model Trains
by Tim Blaisdell and Ed Urmston Sr.

This book features more than 4,000 different models and a handy checklist format that will help you catalog your collection. Designed for both novices and professional collectors/dealers, this reliable guide will help you on your journey into this hot collectible field.
Softcover • 8-1/2 x 11 • 288 pages
420 b&w photos • 80 color photos
Item# ACB1 • $24.95

Railroadiana
by Bill & Sue Knous

Climb aboard for a memorable ride on the rails of yesteryear. Interest in train collectibles is booming and the experts at one of America's top railroad auction houses have compiled the ultimate guide to identifying and valuing items from more than 30 popular categories, including dining car china, lanterns, locks, timetables, and much more. Packed with thousands of detailed listings, current pricing and nearly 1,000 photos; an essential reference for all antique dealers and collectors.
Softcover • 8-1/2 x 11 • 368 pages
900+ b&w photos
Item# RRDI • $30.00

Shipping & Handling: $4.00 first book, $2.00 each additional. Non-US addresses $20.95 first book, $5.95 each additional.
Sales Tax: CA, IA, IL, PA, TN, VA, WA, WI residents please add appropriate sales tax.
Satisfaction Guarantee: If for any reason you are not completely satisfied with your purchase, simply return it within 14 days of receipt and receive a full refund, less shipping charges.

To place a credit card order or for a FREE all-product catalog
Call 800-258-0929 Offer RRB1
M-F 7am - 8pm • Sat 8am - 2pm, CST

ATB Antique Trader Books

kp **krause publications**
since 1952
P.O. Box 5009, Iola WI 54945-5009 **Offer RRB1**
www.krausebooks.com